The Responsibility to Understand

The Responsibility to Understand

Hermeneutical Contours of Ethical Life

Theodore George

EDINBURGH
University Press

Edinburgh University Press is one of the leading university presses in the UK. We publish academic books and journals in our selected subject areas across the humanities and social sciences, combining cutting-edge scholarship with high editorial and production values to produce academic works of lasting importance. For more information visit our website: edinburghuniversitypress.com

First published in hardback by Edinburgh University Press 2020

Edinburgh University Press Ltd
The Tun – Holyrood Road
12(2f) Jackson's Entry
Edinburgh EH8 8PJ

Typeset in 10/13 Meridien by
IDSUK (DataConnection) Ltd, and
printed and bound by CPI Group (UK) Ltd, Croydon, CR0 4YY

A CIP record for this book is available from the British Library

ISBN 978 1 4744 6763 6 (hardback)
ISBN 978 1 4744 6764 3 (paperback)
ISBN 978 1 4744 6765 0 (webready PDF)
ISBN 978 1 4744 6766 7 (epub)

Contents

Acknowledgements

This book would not have been possible without a number of opportunities and the help of many colleagues. These opportunities include support from the Freiburg Institute for Advanced Studies at the University of Freiburg for a research stay in the summer of 2014, the invitation from the Simon Silverman Phenomenology Centre at Duquesne University to deliver the André Schuwer Lecture at the annual meeting of the Society for Phenomenology and Existential Philosophy in 2016, and the opportunities to present and develop ideas with the extraordinary scholars who comprise the College of Fellows at Western Sydney University over the past few years. I am especially grateful to John Sallis, Dennis Schmidt, Günter Figal, James Risser, Gert-Jan van der Heiden and Nancy Moules, whose work and encouragement have been indispensable and an inspiration. I continue to mourn the loss of my friend and colleague at Texas A&M, John McDermott, and miss our conversations about hermeneutics and pragmatism.

Several chapters of this book are derived, in part, from previous publications. These include 'The Responsibility to Understand', in Gert-Jan van der Heiden (ed.), *Phenomenological Perspectives on Plurality* (Leiden: Brill Publishing, 2014), pp. 103–20; 'Are We a Conversation? Hermeneutics, Exteriority, and Transmittability', *Research in Phenomenology*, vol. 47, no. 1, 2017, pp. 331–50; 'De la invisibilidad a la intimidad: Honneth, Gadamer y el reconocimiento del otro', trans. Juanita Maldonado Colmenares, in María del Rosario Acosta López (ed.), *Reconocimiento y diferencia* (Bogotá: Siglo del Hombre Editores, 2010), pp. 295–318; 'Thing, Object, Life', *Research in Phenomenology*, vol. 42, no. 1, 2012, pp. 18–34; 'From Work to

Play: Gadamer on the Affinity of Art, Truth, and Beauty', *Internationales Jahrbuch für Hermeneutik*, vol. 10, 2011, pp. 107–22; 'The Promise of World Literature', *Internationales Jahrbuch für Hermeneutik*, vol. 13, 2014, pp. 128–43; and 'Art as Testimony of Tradition and as Testimony of Ordering', *Internationales Jahrbuch für Hermeneutik*, vol. 16, no. 1, 2017, 107–20.

Preface: The Unbearable Lightness of Ethics

The present enquiry is oriented first of all by a provocation, or, perhaps really, by a *cri de coeur*: a *cri* to restore the validity of a certain weightiness of our factical concerns for the study of philosophical ethics. This weight concerns the urgency of our factical questions about who we are, about who we believe we need to be in response to the demands of individual situations, and about how to develop our abilities to live and to act well. The present enquiry can therefore be grasped with Gadamer as a 'rehabilitation'. By 'rehabilitation', Gadamer has in mind the restoration of the validity of questions (as well as the concepts used to address such questions) that have fallen into forgetfulness, whether because they have succumbed to the conflagration of history or because they remain so effective that they have become lost in a familiar obviousness. Gadamer does not himself carry out an extended rehabilitation of the validity of the weight of our factical concerns for ethical life *per se*. In *Truth and Method*, he introduces the notion of rehabilitation principally in order to restore the validity of authority and tradition against attempts made in the Enlightenment era to discredit the notion of prejudice.[1] Still, as Gadamer develops the notion of rehabilitation, it may be used to describe any attempt to restore the validity of questions (and concepts) passed down from tradition whose effectiveness has fallen out of focus. And, as I wish to implore in this 'Preface', even a cursory survey of the current milieu of philosophical ethics suggests the need for a rehabilitation of the weight I mention.

Thus, my *cri* begins: The more that professional philosophers adhere to the orientation of current debate – that is, the more they attempt to contribute to the edifice of abstract ethical systems and to define, justify and refine abstract ethical problems and principles – the more they at the same time confront us with what the novelist and essayist Milan Kundera describes as 'the unbearable lightness of being'.

Kundera's turn of phrase not only serves as the title of one of his most celebrated novels but also names a *leitmotif* of several of his writings. Kundera invokes this phrase to describe a sudden reversal we experience when we attempt to escape from the burden of our factical concerns about our being. His approach to the topic of being therefore differs from, say, a metaphysician's interest in the first cause of beings or the nature of substance. While Kundera does not align his question about our factical concern for our being with the topic of responsibility, or, for that matter, hermeneutical consider- ations of understanding and interpretation, it should be no surprise that his approach is consanguine. This is because his approach to the unbearable lightness of being, like Gadamer's hermeneutics, suggests the influence of Martin Heidegger. Kundera, like Gadamer, finds an important point of departure in Heidegger's early claim that, in our existence, we are distinguished in our being by our concern for our own being.[2] Gadamer's relation to Heidegger's analysis of existence will become an important consideration in the present enquiry. For now, however, Kundera's description of the unbearable lightness of being helps us to identify the character of the feeling we have when we encounter the predominant orientation of current debate in philosophical ethics. This orientation feels unbearably light.

Kundera clarifies his notion of the unbearable lightness of being by means of a distinction between our concerns for our *being* and those that guide our will to survive or to *live*. While Kundera's claim is reminiscent of Heidegger's differentiation of questions about the being and life of Dasein in *Being and Time*,[3] Kundera treats the issue with reference to a number of figures of modern literature. He explains his idea of the difference most succinctly in a brief gloss of the 'To be or not to be' soliloquy in Shakespeare's *Hamlet*. Kundera asserts, 'it's precisely in that famous soliloquy that the difference between living and being is made clear'.[4]

Kundera argues that Hamlet's contemplation of suicide coalesces around his insight into the inexorability of his responsibility to decide whether and how to be – and not simply about whether he wills to survive. Hamlet's contemplation leads him to hesitate, as

Kundera reminds us, because his conscience speaks against suicide. Hamlet is only concerned about the call of his conscience, however, because of his dread that there may be an afterlife, in which he will remain answerable if he does violate his conscience through suicide. In light of this, Kundera argues, we see that Hamlet's hesitation derives from his responsibility for his being and not from a will to continue to survive. As Kundera interprets Hamlet, 'if after death we go on dreaming, if after death there still *is* something, then death (nonlife) does not free us from the horror of being'.[5] For Kundera, Hamlet's concern is about what it means to be, about whether and how to be and not about whether he wills to continue to survive.

Kundera suggests that Hamlet's question epitomises the responsibility each of us has for our being. Thus, each of us comes to experience this concern regardless of whether we, like Hamlet, entertain the possibility of an afterlife. For each of us, and for so long as each of us continues to be, our concerns about what it means to be, about who we are, and about whether it is proper to be so, abide. No doubt dread, such as Hamlet's about the possibility of eternal consequences for our transgressions, can put the difference between concerns for being and those for life into rather stark relief! But, our factical concern for our being does not depend on our belief in this possibility. No wonder Kundera thus believes that the notion of being 'makes everyone uncomfortable', even more so than questions of 'existence', of our 'condition', or even of 'life'.[6] And, no wonder, too, that this question of being harbours the potential to undo us completely, as it did Hamlet, to the edge of torpor and despair.

Kundera describes the unbearable lightness of being as a reversal we experience whenever we attempt to escape from responsibility for our being. At issue here is the idea that our experience from time to time confronts us with our own unique versions of Hamlet's question. Given the burden of the question of whether or not to be, it is understandable that we sometimes wish either to ignore it altogether or to find refuge in religious dogmas, metaphysical systems, political ideologies or elsewhere. In this, we think of Nietzsche's suspicion of the solace many have taken in the dogmas of Christianity or for that matter of science.[7] In relation to the United States (or, more widely, the West), we may think especially of Foucault's observation of the ideological significance of classical and neo-liberalism that lead many to imagine they are 'entrepreneurs of themselves', defined by professional status, success and wealth.[8] Of course, refuge from the burden of concern about our being may be sought not only in religion, science or liberalism; if these three mainstays of escape are as prevalent as they are familiar to us, there may nevertheless be as many attempted escape routes as there are individuals and situations.

Kundera suggests that we may be overcome by the unbearable lightness of being whenever our efforts to escape get the better of us. The more we attempt to escape the burden of our concerns for our being, he suggests, the more we risk being crushed by the very absence of weight we initially sought. This, he believes, is because it is precisely the burden of our concern about our being that sustains us and gives orientation to our lives. He writes, in a celebrated passage from *The Unbearable Lightness of Being*:

The heavier the burden, the closer our lives come to the earth, the more real and truthful they become.

Conversely, the absolute absence of burden causes man to be lighter than air, to soar into heights, take leave of the earth and his earthly being, and become only half real, his movements as free as they are insignificant.

What then shall we choose? Weight or lightness?[9]

For Kundera, our attempts to escape into the heights, whether through refuge in religion, science, liberalism or elsewhere, do not so much unburden as unmoor us. In consequence, he suggests, our attempts at escape cannot succeed but rather always threaten to lead us full circle into the oppressiveness of a superficial, gratuitous and banal existence. Kundera provides one of his most memorable descriptions of this reversal through his portrait of the character Tamina in *The Book of Laughter and Forgetting*. In a surreal sequence, he imagines Tamina exiled to an island populated by children, which he describes as all but an allegory for what he sees as the fatuousness and juvenility of modern life. It is in this context that he describes Tamina's experience of reversal:

she feels the nausea that emanates from weightless things. That hollowness in her stomach is exactly that unbearable absence of weight. And just as an extreme can at any moment turn into its opposite, so lightness brought to its maximum becomes the terrifying *weight of lightness*, and Tamina knows she cannot bear it for another moment.[10]

Kundera's lesson, it seems, is that once we are confronted by Hamlet's question, weight is inevitable for as long as we continue to be. We can either refuse or accept such a weight of responsibility for our being; yet, the more we attempt to refuse it, the more we prepare the way for our arrival in an even more intolerable condition than the one we had tried to flee.

The burden of factical concern for our being has consequences for our all of our relations. In what follows, we shall consider relations as diverse as those with things, animals, other persons and our shared lives in common. But, for now, something of the weight of our relations can be discerned in reference to our relations with others in particular. In this, Kundera's approach to the unbearable lightness of being can be supplemented by consideration of an oft-cited passage from a 1903 letter from Kafka to Oskar Pollak. It makes sense that Kundera's ideas are supported by Kafka's since Kundera in fact takes himself to be a literary heir of his predecessor from Prague. Although Kafka does not mention factical concern for our being directly, he may nevertheless be said to evoke it through his statement that human beings are 'as forlorn as children lost in the woods'. For Kafka, as we may surmise, we are forlorn in that we are left without any pre-ordained or pre-given understanding of what it means to be. Yet, the absence of this understanding by no means absolves us of our concern for our being. Quite to the contrary, this absence only intensifies all demands to become properly responsive. Kafka writes,

We are as forlorn as children lost in the woods. When you stand in front of me and look at me, what do you know of the griefs that are in me and what do I know of yours? And if I were to cast myself down before you and weep and tell you, what more would you know about me than you know about hell when someone tells you it is hot and dreadful? For that reason alone we human beings ought to stand before one another as reverently, as reflectively, as lovingly, as we would before the entrance to hell.[11]

We are called by our encounters with one another to reverence, reflection and love because such encounters mutually remind us of the forlornness that attends our respective existence, and, therefore also, our respective vulnerability, as we each struggle with and suffer the burden of being.

Kundera's considerations help us to identify the feeling that some of us, at least, too often have in our encounters with current debate in

philosophical ethics. In view of Kundera's approach, our participation
in such debate may be said to result in an experience of the unbearable lightness of being. Surely, for many of us, and even for many
professional ethicists among us, it is the weight of our factical concern
for our being, for whether and how to be, that first urges us to take up
the study of ethical life. Yet, it strikes us that, in current debate in the
discipline of ethics, the weight of our factical concern is more often
than not pressed to the margins, if it is mentioned at all, in favour of
the definition of terms of art or abstract thought experiments. On the
strength of Kundera's insights, we may wonder whether the marginalisation of this weight is itself tinged with escapism.

It is, in any case, not difficult to show that the weight of factical
concern for our being gets pressed to the margins within professional philosophy. As a first example, we can consider the tendency,
typical within the discipline of ethics – no less, really, in main-
stream scholarship than in the classroom – to frame debate from
the outset as an attempt to adjudicate various theoretical 'options':
usually, the big three – utilitarianism, deontology, virtue ethics –
and specific derivations of each. Certainly, the employment of this
frame appears at first to be innocent enough and, in the classroom
in particular, pedagogically expedient. Yet, the employment of this
frame too often marginalises Hamlet's question about responsibility
for whether and how to be, in favour of more abstract and often
arcane analyses of the comparative advantages and disadvantages
of purportedly opposing viewpoints. Here, discussion, whether in
scholarship or in the classroom, seems as if inevitably to pass over
our respective questions about what it means to be, about who we
are and how, in view of this, we are properly to be, turning instead
directly to the clarification of the merits and difficulties of more or
less already worked out theories or positions.

We may also consider, as a second example, the trend of interest
in so-called 'metaethics'. The idea of metaethics, as the neologism
suggests, is to position ourselves above or outside of debates within
ethics in order critically to examine metaphysical, epistemological and other un- or, in any case, under-scrutinised presumptions.
Given this purported orientation of metaethics, it may appear ironic
that scholarship in metaethics continues to neglect factical concerns
about our being. Metaethics, to my knowledge, has not drawn significant attention to the ethical stakes of Hamlet's question. So much

so, that we might be left to wonder whether metaethical debate, too, is tinged with a will to escape the weight of these concerns.

If the practice of philosophical ethics presses factical concern for our being to the margins, as these examples suggest, then it is no wonder that participation in this discipline leads many of us, at least, to experience a reversal of the kind Kundera describes. I confess that, for my part, the more I bring the weight of my factical concern for my being to bear on current debate in philosophical ethics, the more I experience the unbearable burden of this marginalisation. For me, the weight of my factical concerns has led me to experience much of current debate in philosophical ethics as ethereal and only half real. All at once, an argument appears to be barely more relevant to me than the old scholastic debates about the number of angels that fit on the head of a pin. And, like Kundera's protagonist Tamina, I am left with a hollow pit in my stomach that I can barely abide.

One of the hopes that guides the present enquiry is to contribute to philosophical ethics by rehabilitating the validity of the weight of factical concerns for current debate. No doubt, this rehabilitation project can and should be approached from a diversity of philosophical angles. In what follows, I shall seek to contribute my part to this project in reference to what I call 'the responsibility to understand', a term I develop from out of post-Gadamerian hermeneutics. To the extent that this rehabilitation project is guided by a concern for the worrisome condition of current debate in philosophical ethics, it is at the same time an attempt to contribute to what Vattimo, following Heidegger, refers to as recovery, or, perhaps, convalescence (*Verwindung*) – in this case, the convalescence of the field of philosophical ethics. Such convalescence will, no doubt, take quite some time and effort. In this, the present enquiry is not meant as a definitive argument for current debate within philosophical ethics to begin from the weight of our factical concerns for our being. Rather, it is meant as an outline, a *Grundriss*, of the contours of this weight; with this, my wish is to provide a touchstone that invites further contributions to the convalescence of philosophical ethics.

Theodore George

Introduction: Contemporary Hermeneutics and the Question of Responsibility

Few topics have received broader attention within contemporary philosophy than that of responsibility. In current debate, philosophers take up questions of responsibility not only in the context of more traditional moral and ethical problems but, increasingly, in the context of multiple political concerns, concerns for non-human others, historical memory, and a host of other matters. Moreover, current interest in such questions of responsibility draw on a similarly broad range of approaches and methods, from those customarily associated with analytic philosophy to those associated with phenomenology and existentialism, deconstruction, critical theory, feminist theory, race theory and post-colonial theory. Yet, despite the expanse of current interest, philosophers have failed fully to appreciate the contributions that can be made to questions of responsibility by the tradition of hermeneutics. It is the *raison d'être* of the present enquiry to examine the sense of responsibility at issue in the hermeneutical experiences of understanding and interpretation, as well as their significance for several current debates within philosophy. Hence, the topic of the enquiry may be summed up as: *the responsibility to understand*.

The claim that hermeneutics offers a distinctive and persuasive contribution to philosophical discussions of responsibility may, initially at least, appear to be idiosyncratic. Within the broader world of professional philosophy, hermeneutics is typically thought to concern not responsibility but rather first and foremost the study of the understanding and interpretation of texts and persons. In this, hermeneutics is usually thought to include considerations of the art, techniques, methods and epistemological foundations of research in the humanities and related disciplines. To be sure, scholars have long recognised that hermeneutics contributes to practical philosophy; that it has important practical applications, such as legal hermeneutics; and, too, that philosophers associated with hermeneutics, such as Hans-Georg Gadamer, draw on important traditions of practical philosophy in humanism and ancient Greek philosophy. Yet, the question of responsibility is much more crucial to hermeneutics than is usually appreciated. This, at least, appears to be the suggestion made by Gadamer, one of the most influential proponents of hermeneutics in the post-war era. In a revealing interview with Carsten Dutt, Gadamer indicates that hermeneutics, in focusing on understanding and interpretation, is in fact focused on the most pivotal matter of ethical life.[1] He states:

Determining what is rational in the specific, concrete situation in which you find yourself – which certainly can have many parallels to other situations yet remains the specific situation in which you stand – is something you must do for yourself. What is rational in the sense of the right thing to do in this situation is not prescribed to you in the general orientations you have been given about good and evil in the same way that instructions for use that come with a tool tell you how to use it. Rather, you have to determine for yourself what you are going to do. And to do this you have to arrive at a comprehension of your situation, reach an understanding with yourself about it. In other words, you have to *interpret* it![2]

Ethical life, as Gadamer argues, requires that we make reasonable decisions about what to do – that we try to do the right thing – in each of the specific situations we find ourselves in. Yet, as he has it, 'general orientations' about good and evil do not of themselves offer enough to prescribe actions. It is not enough simply to determine in advance and then adhere to generalities about good and evil. Rather, in order really to make good on our responsibility, what counts is to understand and interpret what is good – what the good means – right here and now.

As a hermeneutical consideration of responsibility, then, the present enquiry is less presumptuous but promises more than typical philosophical accounts in which the concern is to establish a theory of responsibility, or, in any case, to clarify and justify some aspect of a theory. The presumption is that such theory offers a fundament to distinguish in advance of practice between right and wrong, or what is praiseworthy and blameworthy. The present enquiry is less presumptuous because it argues that theory does not provide a basis for practice, but, on the contrary, is at best secondary in comparison to the demand to understand and interpret that is placed on us through our concrete involvement in specific situations.

The present enquiry, however, thereby promises more than is typical of philosophical accounts of responsibility. This is because it brings into focus an important, yet underappreciated, hermeneutical contour of responsibility itself. This contour of responsibility is prior to theory as the demand to understand and interpret that first grants us access to the ethical stakes of a situation and allows us to determine what counts as the good within that situation. The responsibility to understand may thus be grasped as a responsiveness to the possibilities of the situations we find ourselves in. This responsiveness is directed toward what, initially at least, and often irresolutely, we cannot comprehend about a situation and, accordingly, what we cannot easily calculate about, predict, control or master. In this, the responsibility to understand names an original element or 'moment' of ethical life. In every situation of our practical endeavours, we cannot avoid the fact that we always first have to begin by trying to understand and interpret what is best to do; and, as a situation unfolds, or when one situation ends and another begins, we find ourselves once again in the same position, ineluctably.

*   *   *

It should perhaps be no surprise that current discussions of responsibility largely have left hermeneutics out of account. After all, it is hardly incorrect to describe hermeneutics as the study of understanding and interpretation and, on this basis, to associate it with the art, techniques, methods and foundations of interpretive enquiry. The chief claim of the present enquiry, however, is that things come to look radically otherwise after the contributions to hermeneutics made by Gadamer. In this, the present enquiry comprises a contribution to what may be called post-Gadamerian hermeneutics. Specifically, the responsibility to understand comes into focus through a reconsideration of Gadamer's attempt to advance what he calls the 'ontological turn' in hermeneutics initiated by Heidegger's discovery of the 'hermeneutics of facticity'. This, to be sure, is a provocative claim. For, even if a cursory survey of Gadamer's magnum opus *Truth and Method* does suggest that he wishes to advance Heidegger's ontological turn in hermeneutics, his attempt appears to focus more on the role of tradition and language in understanding than on that of responsibility.

As Gadamer describes this philosophical hermeneutics in the 'Introduction' to *Truth and Method*: 'the hermeneutics developed here is not . . . a methodology of the human sciences, but an attempt to understand what the human sciences truly are, beyond their methodological self-consciousness, and what connects them with the totality of our experience of the world'.[3] For Gadamer, a philosophical hermeneutics of this kind results from consideration of what he calls the 'hermeneutic phenomenon',[4] or, more to the point, 'the phenomenon of understanding'.[5] Later, however, in the vital chapter of *Truth and Method* called 'Overcoming the epistemological problem through phenomenological research', Gadamer specifies that such consideration is based on Heidegger's discovery of the hermeneutics of facticity. As Gadamer observes, with his hermeneutics of facticity, Heidegger describes the phenomenon of understanding in an ontological register, in terms of the being of Dasein, or existence. Gadamer writes:

Understanding is not a resigned ideal of human experience adopted in the old age of the spirit, as with Dilthey; nor is it, as with Husserl, a last methodological ideal of philosophy in contrast to the naivete of unreflecting life; it is, on the contrary, the *original form of the realization of Dasein*, which is being-in-the-world. Before any differentiation of understanding into the various directions of pragmatic or theoretical interest, understanding is Dasein's mode of being, insofar as it is potentiality-for-being and 'possibility'.[6]

For Heidegger, as Gadamer observes, philosophical consideration of the phenomenon of understanding runs deeper than the context of the human sciences; it concerns the being of existence as such.

Gadamer suggests that his philosophical hermeneutics is an attempt to advance the ontological turn, first of all by calling for a 'historical hermeneutics' that is already recognisable in Heidegger's hermeneutics of facticity.[7] By a 'historical hermeneutics', Gadamer does not have in mind a hermeneutics that examines the role of understanding within human sciences such as history. Rather, he has in mind a hermeneutics clarifying that and how the human sciences are based originally in a sense of understanding that is itself conditioned historically. Understanding, for Gadamer, is always already what he calls 'historically effected'[8] because already a matter of 'belonging to traditions'.[9] He indicates that he 'will try to determine whether Heidegger's ontological radicalization', that is, his hermeneutics of facticity, 'can contribute to the construction of a historical hermeneutics'.[10] Gadamer acknowledges that 'Heidegger's intention was undoubtedly a different one', but nevertheless thinks that a 'historical hermeneutics' is already discernible in Heidegger's hermeneutics of facticity because Heidegger's existential analysis of understanding reveals that understanding itself is bound up with thrownness. For Heidegger, all understanding concerns our own future possibilities to be; it takes shape as what he calls projection. But, such projection is never unconditional – for Heidegger, all of our efforts to understand are themselves both made possible and limited by those possibilities for understanding available to us within the situations we already find ourselves 'thrown' into. For Gadamer, the basis of a 'historical hermeneutics' follows from this. He writes:

the general structure of understanding is concretized in historical understanding, in that the concrete bonds of custom and tradition and the corresponding possibilities of one's own future become effective in understanding itself. Dasein that projects itself on its own potentiality-for-being has already 'been'. This is the meaning of the existential of 'thrownness'.[11]

Gadamer affirms Heidegger's analysis that understanding is bound up with thrownness. But, he believes that Heidegger's analysis calls for a 'historical hermeneutics' because the sense of understanding Heidegger outlines only ever finds real expression when historically effected, when unfolding within the context of customary practices and the historical transmission of meaning.

Gadamer's attempt to advance the ontological turn, though, culminates in a consideration of the role of language in hermeneutical experience. Certainly, as much may be surmised by Gadamer's title for Part III of *Truth and Method*, 'The ontological turn [*Wendung*] in hermeneutics guided by language'.[12] As this title suggests, Gadamer's attempt to advance the ontological turn takes shape as a further turn toward language. Crucial, however, is that Gadamer believes this further turn to language is required in order to deepen his analysis of 'historical

hermeneutics'. In this, he maintains that the achievement of understanding in an encounter with tradition '*is actually an achievement of
language*'.[13] Gadamer believes his claim is based in a typical phenomenon. He has in mind the common experience of coming to understand
something through conversation with another person and, based on
the example of this common experience, the experience of coming
to understand something in an encounter with the past through the
interpretation of a text. In light of this typical phenomenon, Gadamer
thus argues that his 'historical hermeneutics' requires a further hermeneutical consideration of language. This is because the achievement
of understanding in our encounters with the past only ever finds real
expression linguistically, as in conversation and text interpretation.
He writes: 'The linguisticality of understanding is *the concretion of historically effected consciousness*.'[14] Gadamer's attempt to advance the ontological turn in hermeneutics leads him, first, to develop a 'historical
hermeneutics' of 'historically effected' belonging to tradition that he
believes concretises Heidegger's hermeneutics of facticity. But, next, as
Gadamer believes, this 'historical hermeneutics' must itself be further
concretised through a hermeneutical consideration of language.

Gadamer's hermeneutical consideration of language in *Truth and
Method* is difficult. It is no coincidence that many of his subsequent
writings and the important debates that he engaged in coalesced
around questions about his notion of language and its role in hermeneutical experience.[15] Essentially, though, Gadamer's consideration
of language intends to clarify what is meant in his 'historical hermeneutics' by 'belonging' to traditions. He writes: 'Above we spoke of
the way the interpreter *belongs* to his text [encountered from tradi-
tion] . . . we can now define more exactly the idea of belonging on
the basis of the linguistically constituted experience of the world.'[16]
Gadamer defines the notion of hermeneutical belonging to traditions through a friendly contrast with a notion of belonging that is
typical of metaphysics in the classical world and in medieval European philosophy. In metaphysics so conceived, 'belonging' concerns
the relation of being and truth. As Gadamer writes, 'In metaphysics *belonging* refers to the transcendental relationship between being
and truth, and it conceives of knowledge as an element of being
itself and not primarily as an activity of the subject.'[17] In this metaphysical notion of belonging, two things stand out. First, the relation of truth and being is grasped as intrinsic to being itself; and,

second, this relation is grasped as an infinite foundation of the finite pursuit of knowledge. Accordingly, the achievement of knowledge is grasped as nothing else than a realisation of being *in* its truth, and not primarily as the result of some extrinsic activity, such as that of a subject-enquirer.

On the one hand, Gadamer is friendly toward this metaphysical notion, in that he, too, believes that the relation of being and truth is intrinsic to being itself. Yet, on the other hand, Gadamer's consideration of language brings out a contrast between hermeneutical and metaphysical belonging. For him, the hermeneutical belonging of being and truth is not an infinite foundation of our finite pursuit of knowledge. Quite to the contrary, as Gadamer believes, the hermeneutical belonging of being and truth is itself a finite 'occurrence',[18] one that only ever transpires in specific, concrete pursuits of understanding. These pursuits of understanding take place in individual experiences of language, that is, individual conversations, text interpretations, and so on. It is therefore precisely Gadamer's notion of hermeneutical belonging that finds voice in the *motto* of his philosophical hermeneutics: *'being that can be understood is language'*.[19] Gadamer, with his 'historical hermeneutics', has claimed that our pursuit of understanding something from tradition always involves 'belonging' to tradition. In such a pursuit, we experience a relation of being and truth. It is not, however, that our pursuit of understanding something from tradition finds an infinite foundation in this relation. Rather, our pursuit of understanding is *itself* the finite occurrence of this relation: in the pursuit of understanding something from tradition, what we pursue is the being of that thing in its truth, as the being of that thing is brought out in an individual experience of language such as in conversation about or interpretation of that thing.

Gadamer's philosophical hermeneutics can, then, be grasped as an attempt to advance the ontological turn in hermeneutics achieved by Heidegger's discovery of the hermeneutics of facticity. But, as this cursory survey of *Truth and Method* suggests, Gadamer's attempt appears to coalesce in considerations of tradition and language, and to develop these themes as 'concretisations' of Heidegger's existential analysis of understanding. He does not develop the theme of responsibility in any detail.

It is true that Gadamer develops his philosophical hermeneutics in reference to themes from practical philosophy. Most notably, he argues that Aristotle's *Nicomachean Ethics* provides an important '*model of the problem of hermeneutics*'.[20] Gadamer acknowledges that Aristotle 'is not concerned with the hermeneutic problem and certainly not with its historical dimension . . .'.[21] Still, he finds in Aristotle's treatment of the problem of *phronēsis*, or practical judgement, a lodestone for his examination of understanding, which is a comparably a 'special case' of 'applying something universal to something particular'.[22] But here, Gadamer's turn to this practical 'model' of hermeneutical experience does not focus on the theme of responsibility, and he develops this 'model' in reference to Aristotle's ethics, not Heidegger.[23]

Yet, as I shall argue in the present enquiry, Gadamer's attempt to advance the ontological turn does, indeed, concern responsibility, and this concern takes shape as a further 'concretion' of Heidegger's hermeneutics of facticity. However, whereas Gadamer develops the themes of tradition and language as 'concretions' of mainline ideas from Heidegger's existential analysis of understanding, his concern for responsibility addresses a related, but distinct and subtle, Heideggerian source. This source is Heidegger's claim from the 'Letter on Humanism' that although it would be anathema to pursue a general ethical theory on the basis of his analysis of existence, that analysis nevertheless suggests the possibility of what he calls an 'original ethics'. Heidegger's suggestion of this possibility is, of course, difficult to interpret. It is not obvious what, precisely, he means by the possibility of an 'original ethics' or the idea that existence is itself originally ethical. My claim here, however, is that Gadamer's attempt to advance the ontological turn in hermeneutics extends beyond themes of tradition and language. His attempt also focuses on responsibility, and this precisely as a further 'concretion' of Heidegger's analysis of existence, this time, of Heidegger's suggestion that existence is originally ethical. If this claim is correct, then Gadamer's philosophical hermeneutics can itself, at least in part, be described as an original ethics, and, likewise, his notion of understanding can, at least in part, be described as originally ethical.

It should be noted that Gadamer's attempt to advance the ontological turn along ethical lines is more consistent with Heidegger's thought than it might initially appear. It is true that Heidegger registers hesitation, even suspicion, about the desire to establish an ethics on the basis of his thought.[24] Some scholars have concluded from Heidegger's aversion to ethics that he intends for his thought to be absent of implications for ethical life, as if his concerns for existence were supposed to be indifferent toward or neutral about matters of ethical concern. This conclusion is understandable, given Heidegger's disavowal of the field of ethics, but it misses the point of Heidegger's disavowal.

Heidegger disassociates his path of thinking from the discipline of ethics not because he thinks that the hermeneutics of facticity is devoid of ethical implication; rather, he disavows the field of ethics because he believes the presuppositions that characterise much of this field are derivative of his analysis of existence. These presuppositions thus distort the actual ethical stakes of existence. In this, Heidegger calls for a return from the derivative distortions of the field of ethics to 'original ethics', that is, an understanding of ethical life that is more original because it remains part and parcel of an analysis of existence itself. Heidegger's critique of the field of ethics, like other aspects of his path of thought, is freighted with claims of a breath-taking sweep that concern the history of being, the history of metaphysics and, importantly in this context, the tradition of humanism.[25] As we shall see, however, his critique of the field of ethics focuses on the fact that debate is about the establishment, justification and adjudication of ethical theories, standards and principles – what Gadamer calls 'general orientations' – that are in turn purported to be legitimate regardless of the specifics of factically given situations. Heidegger, as will become clear, believes by contrast that more original ethical insight can be discerned from attention to the hermeneutics of facticity because this hermeneutics brings into relief the contingency and thus incalculable singularity and difference of every respective factically given situation. Accordingly, Heidegger's point is not to abandon all concern for ethical life, but, on the contrary, to disavow ethical theory in favour of a concern for ethical life that focuses on the openness, the attunement, the imagination and the decisiveness that are required of us whenever we are called to discern and address the peculiar ethical demands that are made on us in every respective situation we find ourselves in.

*   *   *

The present enquiry, then, is a post-Gadamerian examination of the responsibility to understand. This project unfolds from a reconsideration of Gadamer's attempt to advance the ontological turn in hermeneutics achieved through Heidegger's discovery of the hermeneutics of facticity. For the most part, this will take shape as a fresh look at familiar motifs in Gadamer's thought, and, in this, at some of his relevant debts to Heidegger.

The present enquiry thereby stakes out an original approach within post-Gadamerian hermeneutics. Research in contemporary hermeneutics could hardly be more diverse: the term has been evoked in the context of everything from research on analytic philosophers such as Robert Brandom or John McDowell to research on teaching literature in secondary schools.[26] This diversity is no doubt a testament to the significance of hermeneutics across the academy. Some of the most influential contributions in post-Gadamerian hermeneutics, however, stem from the same point of departure as that of the present enquiry: the reconsideration of Gadamer's attempt to advance the ontological turn in hermeneutics. Within post-Gadamerian hermeneutics, these reconsiderations have led to different positions. On the one hand, post-Gadamerian philosophers such as Gianni Vattimo have forwarded a 'postmodern' position on Gadamer's attempt. More recently, on the other hand, post-Gadamerian philosophers such as Günter Figal forward a 'realistic' position on Gadamer's attempt. Figal's 'realistic' approach suggests that Gadamer's attempt to advance the ontological turn hews closely to the early Heidegger's emphasis on concrete, factical life. The present enquiry builds specifically on these more recent 'realistic' approaches, arguing that hermeneutical experience, as a feature of factical life, always also entails the experience of responsibility.

These post-Gadamerian reconsiderations, as I am calling them, are thus distinguished as attempts to advance Gadamer's attempt to advance Heidegger's achievement of the ontological turn in hermeneutics. Really, they are attempts to advance the advance of an advance, insofar as Heidegger's achievement of the ontological turn in hermeneutics can itself be described as an advance of his predecessors. Accordingly, these post-Gadamerian reconsiderations follow one of the most primogenital presuppositions of modern hermeneutics: namely, that research in philosophy (as in other human sciences) advances not first on the basis of methods analogous to those found in the natural sciences, but rather through the interpretive reconsideration of predecessors. Here,

research is advanced by interpretive encounters with predecessors that make explicit questions, problems and novel insights that
are recognisable but that have not yet been recognised through
such encounters. Thus, post-Gadamerian reconsiderations are
distinguished as attempts to advance hermeneutics itself by making explicit questions, problems and insights that are recognisable
but that have not yet been recognised in Gadamer. The present
enquiry is post-Gadamerian in just this sense: it is an attempt to
advance hermeneutics by making explicit questions, problems
and insights about a sense of responsibility that is recognisable,
but that has not yet been recognised, or, in any case, not fully
enough recognised, in Gadamer.

The larger context of postmodern reconsiderations of Gadamerian
hermeneutics can be discerned in what Jean-François Lyotard referred
to in his *The Postmodern Condition: A Report on Knowledge* as the 'culture',
or broader milieu, of postmodernism in our times.[27] For Lyotard, this
broader milieu is characterised by a crisis in the credibility of what
he calls the 'grand narratives' typical of modern science.[28] By 'grand
narrative', Lyotard has in mind a second-order discourse or 'metadis-
course' that functions to legitimate discourses of the sciences.[29] For
example, in the European Enlightenment, metadiscourses about historical progress function to legitimate capitalist economic theory. For
Lyotard, the crisis in the credibility of grand narratives leads, on the
one hand, to the danger that the vacuum created by this loss of credibility will be filled by the reduction of knowledge to 'an informational
commodity' produced and exchanged for the sake of increasing wealth
and power.[30] On the other hand, this crisis also leads to a new possibility, namely, that of the creation of narratives whose meanings promise novelty in virtue of the fact that they have been freed from the
function they had in the modern discourse of legitimating science.[31]
Lyotard, for his part, sought to clarify the scope, limits and character of this postmodern possibility of the creation of such narratives in
a number of manners, but perhaps most famously by developing a
novel 'game' theory of language in *The Differend* and other writings. In
the same broader postmodern milieu, however, a number of philosophers have sought to clarify this (and other) postmodern possibilities
for the creation of new meaning through the advancement of research
in hermeneutics. In the Anglophone world, for example, Richard
Rorty endorsed such an approach, and the postmodern possibilities

of hermeneutics were developed with emphasis by philosophers such as John Caputo, first in his *Radical Hermeneutics*, in a number of other writings, and most recently in *Hermeneutics: Facts and Interpretation in the Age of Information*.

Perhaps no philosopher has developed the postmodern possibilities of hermeneutics more closely as an attempt to advance Gadamer's philosophical hermeneutics, however, than Gianni Vattimo. Vattimo aligns his hermeneutics with the postmodern possibility of the creation of new meaning in texts such as *The End of Modernity: Nihilism and Hermeneutics in Postmodern Culture*. Here, Vattimo argues that the postmodern possibility of the creation of new meaning demands what he describes as a '"weakening" of Being' that 'allows thought to situate itself in a constructive manner within the post-modern condition'.[32] In this, of course, Vattimo is no metaphysical realist who would use the term 'being' to refer to mind-independent reality. Rather, drawing on motifs in Nietzsche and Heidegger, he has in mind the predominant sense of being, in its many iterations, that has been passed down to us from the tradition of Western metaphysics and that remains in effect, often tacitly, in the deepest beliefs and practices of our modern times.

Vattimo argues that being, taken in this way, comes to be weakened through the 'attitude' – more precisely, a hermeneutical attitude – that we bring to this tradition and its effects on our beliefs and practices.[33] He describes the character of this hermeneutical attitude on the basis of a term used on occasion by Heidegger, *Verwindung*. This term is difficult to translate, but the word is often used in German in the context of health, in which it signifies the process of recovery from an illness. With this context of health in mind, it can be translated as 'recovering', 'getting over', or even 'convalescence'.[34] Vattimo, in view of this common usage as well as Heidegger's philosophical use of the term, introduces the term *Verwindung* to identify that hermeneutical attitude which will allow us to 'weaken' the Western-metaphysical sense of being and its continuing effects. He writes:

The essential meaning of this attitude may be found in its referral to the history of metaphysics (and thus also to modernity as the end result of metaphysics and Platonic/Christian morality). For it refers to this history in a way which is neither an acceptance of its errors nor a critique that tries to overcome them but merely ends up by prolonging them instead.[35]

For Vattimo, the postmodern possibility of the creation of new meaning requires that we take a new hermeneutic approach to the sense of being passed down from Western metaphysics. It is not enough to forward interpretations that simply trade on this sense of being as an unquestioned assumption. Nor is it enough to forward interpretations that purport to overcome this sense of being, as if its effects on our deepest beliefs and practices could so easily be identified and eradicated. Rather, what are called for are interpretations that acknowledge the effects that this sense of being continues to have, while, at the same time, exposing and working through these effects, both carefully and imaginatively, one step at a time.

It is not Vattimo's position that the postmodern possibility of the creation of new meaning remains a project for the future, one that can only begin after our recovery from the Western-metaphysical sense of being has been weakened completely out of existence. Rather, Vattimo's idea is that the postmodern possibility is constitutive of our interpretive efforts toward recovery in the first place. For Vattimo, interpretations that promote recovery are precisely those that create new meaning through their interventions in the Western-metaphysical sense of being and its continued effects. Indeed, such interpretations contribute to liberation, since the creation of meaning is not only new in the sense of a new trend or vogue, but, more radically, in the sense of something otherwise than Western-metaphysical.

Vattimo develops this postmodern possibility of hermeneutics, at least in part, on the basis of his own interpretation of Gadamer's attempt to advance Heidegger's ontological turn in hermeneutics. As we have seen, Gadamer's attempt culminates in a further turn toward language. In this, Gadamer maintains that participation in linguistic experiences, such as conversation and text interpretation, concretises our belonging to traditions. These linguistic experiences grant us access to the being of something from tradition in its truth. And, as we have moreover seen, Gadamer sums up this view in the motto, 'being that can be understood is language'.

Now Vattimo, for his part, goes on to explain his postmodern hermeneutics through his own interpretation of the relation Gadamer sees here between being and language. Vattimo argues that Gadamer increasingly recognises that being is no excess of language, as if being could exist as it were outside of or beyond linguistic experiences such as those of conversation and text interpretation. Rather, Gadamer comes to see that being is really nothing else than what we understand when we come to understand something in such linguistic experiences. Vattimo writes: 'Gadamer returns to, and elaborates, Heidegger's "connection" or "identification" between Being and language in a direction that stresses ever more emphatically the pole of language rather than of Being.'[36] For Vattimo, this emphasis on language thus leads Gadamer to view language as the arbiter of being. It is through linguistic experiences, such as those of conversation and text interpretation, that the being of something is determined in its truth. Indeed, insofar as such disclosiveness also grants the measure of ethical life, language is also the arbiter of the ethical standards of society. Vattimo continues: 'language is for Gadamer a locus, or a place of concrete realisation of the collective *ēthos* of a historically determined society, and thus it functions as a total mediation of the experience of the world'.[37] For Vattimo, Gadamer's emphasis on language makes our interpretations the final arbiter of being and value, rather than allowing being to be the final arbiter of our interpretations.

Vattimo, finally, argues that Gadamer's emphasis on language advances Heidegger's ontological turn, inscribing the hermeneutics of facticity with a more socio-historically determined notion of truth. Taking over Jürgen Habermas's description of Gadamer's philosophical hermeneutics as an 'urbanisation' of Heidegger, Vattimo writes that 'the "urbanization" of Heidegger's thought here appears in a very literal sense, namely as an acceptance of the more "external" rather than the intimate nature of truth on the part of a philosophy whose approach is originally an existentialist one'.[38] Gadamer's acceptance that language provides an 'external' measure of being and truth thus suggests a 'divergence between Heidegger and Gadamer', in which Gadamer's approach entails 'a bracketing of the more "existential" elements of Heideggerian philosophy (authenticity, the anticipatory decision for death, and so on). . .'.[39] Above all, though, for Vattimo Gadamer's emphasis on language demonstrates the postmodern possibility of hermeneutics to contribute to the 'weakening of being'. For, on Vattimo's account of Gadamer, it is ultimately our interpretations that determine being, not the other way around. Accordingly, interpretations undertaken in the spirit of recovery from the Western-metaphysical sense of being can, however incrementally, however piecemeal, effect shifts in the meaning of being itself.

Postmodern hermeneutics, and with it Vattimo's postmodern reconsideration of Gadamer, is an influential development of post-Gadamerian hermeneutics. Recently, however, postmodern reconsiderations such as Vattimo's have been challenged by Günter Figal's proposal of a 'realistic' hermeneutics. Figal's realistic hermeneutics is brought into focus in his *Objectivity: The Hermeneutical and Philosophy*.[40] Figal observes that Gadamer is now celebrated 'as the most significant German philosopher' of the post-war era.[41] But, as Figal believes, Gadamer's reputation is actually sustained above all by the 'effective history' of his thought in postmodern hermeneutics.[42] Within this context, the 'gesture'[43] of Gadamer's thought is celebrated as a contrast with more systematic, methodologically directed forms of philosophy:

Gadamer poses in discrete radicality the open, never conclusive 'conversation', in which one actually puts certainties into play. What has won everyone over in Gadamer's thought is above all his reservation against ultimate grounds and groundings; it is openness without the demand for system and without dramatization.[44]

Figal argues that this more postmodern-looking 'gesture' of Gadamer's thought has been fostered by philosophers such as Rorty and Vattimo, as well as by Habermas. From the viewpoint of Vattimo's approach to Gadamer, for example, it may appear as if the latter's philosophical hermeneutics 'could just as much be taken up . . . as a "weak thought" that renounces the claims of the metaphysical tradition'.[45]

Figal argues that although the postmodern image of Gadamer is an exaggeration, it nevertheless has a grain of truth in it. To be sure, Figal acknowledges that Gadamer makes claims that counter the possibility of interpreting him as postmodern. First and foremost, he implores that hermeneutical experience is not only open-ended, but, more originally, also always 'substantive' (*sachlich*).[46] Of course, Gadamer sometimes stresses that whenever we attempt to understand or interpret, our attempt is *about* something and, indeed, something that makes a claim of validity on us.[47] Even as understanding ultimately aims at self-understanding, even as the success of understanding always results in understanding otherwise, in new meanings, nevertheless: our attempts to understand and interpret are always driven first of all by our concern to understand or interpret something, a *matter* (*Sache*).

Yet, as Figal claims, Gadamer's insistence on the 'substantiveness' (*Sachlichkeit*) of hermeneutical experience is put in jeopardy by Gadamer's own account. Figal's point comes out in reference to the role Gadamer assigns to language in hermeneutical experience. Gadamer, we recall, holds that our pursuit of understanding only ever takes place in experiences of language, paradigmatically in conversation or text interpretation. This, however, has consequences that run against Gadamer's claims for the substantiveness of hermeneutical experience. For, Gadamer's view of the role of language in hermeneutical experience means not simply that we pursue understanding of a substantive matter through conversation or text interpretation. More fundamentally, his view suggests that conversation or text interpretation is what first allows the matter to appear as such. On this view, though, there may not be much about the matter that is substantive at all. Conversation or text interpretation is not so much *about* something that stands on its own, independently; rather, the conversation itself *determines* the matter in the first place. Figal writes: 'Gadamer develops the idea of the hermeneutically experienced matter in such a way that even as it is supposed to sustain conversation, it nevertheless only arises in the course of conversation itself.'[48] Despite Gadamer's insistence that our attempts to understand and interpret are always substantive, his consideration of the role played by language in hermeneutical experience implies the opposite. Gadamer's consideration of language leaves the impression, itself a precursor of his postmodern image, that a conversation or text interpretation does not simply pursue, but instead creates, its matter.

Figal develops his realistic hermeneutics as a reconsideration of Gadamer's philosophical hermeneutics that aims to make good precisely on the promise of the substantiveness of hermeneutical experience. Figal develops this concern for the substantiveness of hermeneutical experience programmatically under the auspices of objectivity (*Gegenständlichkeit*). By 'objectivity', Figal does not have in mind what the term usually signifies in the natural sciences, say, the quality of beliefs that are considered legitimate because they have been determined in accord with accepted norms and methods of research in the field.[49] Rather, with this term, Figal signifies that the matters which first elicit and then sustain hermeneutical experience are themselves exterior to, and thus independent of, our hermeneutical encounters with them. Figal writes:

The substantiveness of hermeneutical experience . . . belongs to its essence . . . In hermeneutical experience, one is concerned with something that one himself is not, with something that stands over against [*entgegensteht*], and, because of this, places a demand. Hermeneutical experience is the experience of the objective [*das Gegenständliche*] – of what is there in such a way that one may come into accord with it and that yet never fully comes out in any attempt to reach accord.[50]

For Figal, hermeneutical experience is not simply concerned with the postmodern possibility of the creation of new meaning. More originally (he says 'essentially'), our attempts to understand and interpret aim at something that stands on its own, over against us, such that it may demand our attention.

Figal, too, develops his realistic hermeneutics in reference to Gadamer's attempt to advance the ontological turn in hermeneutics achieved by Heidegger's discovery of the hermeneutics of facticity.[51] Figal's claim is that Gadamer's attempt fails fully to appreciate the objectivity of hermeneutical experience because he misses that our efforts to understand or interpret a matter involve 'the possibility to *maintain distance*' from that matter.[52] As Figal characterises such hermeneutical distantiation, understanding and interpretation have a 'referential sense':[53] they are oriented or directed toward something, they refer to a matter beyond themselves. Figal argues that Gadamer's attempt fails to appreciate this referential sense of understanding and interpretation because he retains the prejudice from Heidegger that understanding is not first of all referential, but, instead, the self-enactment of existence.

Heidegger, in his early writings, introduces the concept of facticity to argue that the being of our existence is not to be grasped in terms of a transcendental subject that grounds our experience. Rather, the being of existence is nothing else than the manner of the self-enactment of existence. With this, existence is 'ecstatic', in the sense that without a ground in the transcendental subject, the self-enactment of existence stands on nothing, and takes place in the exteriority of the situations we find ourselves in. For Heidegger, the being of existence therefore proves to be hermeneutical. It is constitutive of the being of existence that we attend to ourselves in the exteriority of the situations we find ourselves in; understanding names the enactment of such attentiveness. Figal explains:

Here is the point of departure for Heidegger's hermeneutics: it is for him not an art of interpretation, but instead a philosophical articulation of life in its 'sense of enactment' . . . The hermeneutics of facticity is an 'exceptional' realization of facticity itself; it is an explicit illumination of a being that is in itself illuminated and is only for this reason also able to darken.[54]

Heidegger achieves the ontological turn in hermeneutics through his claim that the being of existence is hermeneutical. But, as Figal points out, Heidegger here misses the referential sense of hermeneutical experience. On Heidegger's view, understanding and interpretation are the ways that we attend, that we come back to ourselves, from out of the groundless exteriority of factical life. Accordingly, understanding and interpretation are not ultimately referential; whatever they refer to, they are first of all an enactment of existence as such.

Gadamer, as we have seen, attempts to advance the ontological turn in hermeneutics through a 'concretisation' of Heidegger's hermeneutics of facticity. This 'concretisation' demonstrates that understanding and interpretation depend on tradition and language. Now, Figal recognises that Gadamer's 'concretisation' of the hermeneutics of facticity allows Gadamer to reinterpret the early Heidegger's idea of the groundlessness of existence.[55] Heidegger, in his early writings at least, characterises this groundlessness primarily in terms of our individual existence. Gadamer gives more concrete expression to this groundlessness in terms of the claim that our hermeneutical experience of tradition is ultimately 'ungroundable' and 'underivable'.[56]

Figal's objection to Gadamer, though, is that he fails to appreciate the objectivity of hermeneutical experience because he still retains the Heideggerian prejudice that hermeneutical experience is first of all an enactment. For Gadamer, our hermeneutical experience of the being of something from tradition does not ultimately have a referential sense. Now, it is true that the occurrence, or movement, of hermeneutical experience is initiated when something from tradition first appears as questionable to us. But, Gadamer characterises this experience of questionableness not primarily as a question *about* a matter that stands on its own, independently; instead, he conceives of such questioning as the initial moment *of* the enactment of tradition. The occurrence, or movement, of hermeneutical experience is an enactment of tradition precisely as the transmission of the being of something from the tradition in its truth through linguistic experiences such as those of conversation or text interpretation. Figal writes:

Heidegger, and, following him, also Gadamer, conceive of things exclusively on the basis of movement; for them, there is nothing that eludes, respectively, the movement of Dasein and the occurrence of inheriting something from the past. The attempt to distance oneself from the enactment of Dasein or from the occurrence of inheriting something from the past must itself accordingly be seen to belong to the enactment or occurrence.[57]

Gadamer, despite his insistence on the substantiveness of hermeneutical experience, reduces our hermeneutic distantiation from matters to nothing else than a moment of the enactment of understanding or interpretation.

Figal develops his realistic hermeneutics, then, through a reconsideration of Gadamer that has two sides. On the one hand, he aligns his programmatic concern for objectivity with Gadamer's insistence on the substantiveness of hermeneutical experience. In this, Figal endorses Gadamer's claim that our attempts to understand and interpret are always attempts to understand or interpret something that stands on its own, independently. On the other hand, however, Figal argues that his concern for the objectivity of hermeneutical experience requires him to develop this referential sense of hermeneutical experience against Gadamer's own reduction of such experience to a mode of enactment.

Within this context, Figal's realistic hermeneutics may be grasped as a systematic clarification and justification of just this referential sense of hermeneutical experience. While it is beyond the scope of the present enquiry to examine Figal's attempt in detail, it is possible to provide a schematic overview. In *Objectivity*, this attempt includes a consideration of the phenomenon of interpretation that brings its referential sense into focus and, on the basis of this, a comprehensive analysis of a complex of conditions – or, as he characterises it, the 'hermeneutical space' – that first makes such referentiality of interpretation possible. One of these conditions is language, and, in this, Figal argues that our experience of language does not *enact* the being of something in its truth, but, quite to the contrary, *refers* or directs us to something, so that it may show itself in distantiation from us precisely as an object. Finally, Figal also returns to the theme of life, definitive for hermeneutics since Heidegger's discovery of the hermeneutics of facticity. Yet, in this too, Figal argues that under-standing and interpretation cannot be reduced to the enactment of life. Rather, hermeneutical experience is part of a complex structure of life as a referential relation to what remains outside of us.[58]

Figal's realistic hermeneutics comprises an important develop-ment in post-Gadamerian hermeneutics. This is, first, because Figal's approach emphasises the compatibility of hermeneutics with real-ism, and, in this, puts hermeneutics into conversation with recent innovations in realism, such as the so-called new realism, specula-tive realism, object oriented ontology and related areas.[59] But, sec-ond, and especially pertinent for the discussion of post-Gadamerian hermeneutics, Figal's concern for the objectivity of hermeneutical experience brings into question whether a postmodern hermeneu-tics, such as Vattimo's, is plausible. Vattimo, we recall, argues that interpretations can foster recovery from the Western-metaphysical sense of being insofar as our interpretations can serve to weaken this sense of being through the creation of new meaning. For Vattimo, such a weakening of being is possible because interpretations, as enactments of language, ultimately serve to determine being. But, as Figal argues, the phenomenon of interpretation has a referential sense; it is only mistakenly described as an enactment that deter-mines being. If Figal is right, then Vattimo's hope for interpretations to weaken being are sorely misplaced.

Figal's realistic hermeneutics is not only important for new debates about realism or the critical questions it raises about post-modern hermeneutics, however. Figal's approach is also a powerful post-Gadamerian testament on behalf of the belief that hermeneu-tical experience is substantive, that it refers us to something out-side of ourselves, something that our attempts to understand and interpret can make accessible, but that nevertheless remains exte-rior to all such attempts.

The present enquiry comprises a distinct attempt to break further new ground within post-Gadamerian hermeneutics. The thesis here is that hermeneutical experience involves responsibility. In this, however, the present enquiry may be characterised as an attempt to advance the realistic approach in hermeneutics beyond the context of Figal's programmatic focus on objectivity. As we have seen, Figal introduces the notion of objectivity to emphasise the substantive-ness of hermeneutical experience. His concern for objectivity opens up a horizon of enquiry concerned with the 'referential sense' of hermeneutical experience, that is, the fact that hermeneutical experience does not simply have the 'sense of enactment', but, more originally, always refers us to something in its exteriority of all of our enactments. Yet, even as Figal's programmatic focus on objectivity opens up the horizon of enquiry into the referential sense of hermeneutics, this horizon is not enough to clarify the fuller stakes of this referential sense. For another horizon of enquiry is needed, namely, that of responsibility. The present enquiry therefore examines the responsibility involved in what Figal has called the referential sense of hermeneutical experience. There is more at stake than objectivity in the fact that hermeneutical experience refers us to things in their exteriority; there is also, and more originally, at stake the question of our responsibility to what we are thus referred to. If hermeneutical experience refers us to reality, this referral not only speaks to the objectivity of our experience: it also speaks to our responsibility to what is real.

*   *   *

The present enquiry unfolds in three parts. The purpose of Part I is to examine the character of the responsibility at stake in the referential sense of hermeneutical experience – that is, the responsibility to understand – in some detail. In Chapter 1, 'The Responsibility to Understand', I argue that the responsibility to understand comes into focus when we reconsider Gadamer's attempt to advance the ontological turn in hermeneutics in view of Heidegger's call for an 'original ethics' in the 'Letter on Humanism'. As I show, the responsibility to understand thereby appears in terms of an extreme, existentially motivated humanistic consideration of what I call the 'predicament of the exception'. In this, on the one hand, every hermeneutical situation places the demand on us to understand, without exception. Yet, on the other hand, no situation can be fully grasped in advance, because each situation is itself an event, and thus unique, exceptional in comparison to all other situations. In Chapter 2, I argue that the responsibility of this predicament of the exception demands of us 'The Capacity for Displacement'. In this, the responsibility to understand cannot be grasped foremost as a responsibility to reach agreement or achieve correct knowledge of something. Rather, the responsibility to understand is a responsibility to enact and cultivate a capacity to put one's prejudices – and thus oneself – into question, to remain open to the new in the face of self-interrogation, and, in consequence, to come to understand things and oneself differently.

The purpose of Parts II and III is to give further contours to the responsibility to understand in reference to contexts that are no less fundamental to hermeneutical experience than to the broader current interest in questions of responsibility. The division between Parts II and III follows a distinction Gadamer makes between two different, though interrelated, aspects of practical life. In a discussion of the notion of *praxis* from the interview mentioned above, Gadamer asserts in reference to Aristotle that the human 'form of life' is nothing less than defined by ethical and political endeavours. He writes: 'The word "praxis" points to the totality of our practical life, all our human action and behavior, the self-adaptation of the human being as a whole in this world. Thus it has to do also with one's politics, political advising and consulting, and our passing of laws. Our praxis, in short, is our "form of life".'[60] For Gadamer, as for Aristotle, the being of human beings is practical in character. In this, however, Gadamer distinguishes three aspects of *praxis*. He asserts: 'Our human form of life has an "I and thou" character and an "I and we" character, and also a "we and we" character. In our practical affairs we depend on our ability to arrive at an understanding. And reaching an understanding happens in conversation, in a dialogue.'[61]

The purpose of Parts II and III is thus to address the first two aspects of *praxis* that Gadamer identifies. Consideration of these first two aspects is indispensable to any examination of the responsibility to understand, as they concern, respectively, the intimacy of our encounters with one another and, second, our involvement in a shared world that is larger than these more intimate relations. The third aspect, which would concern among other things the role of hermeneutical experience in the arbitration of law, diplomacy and international political relations, though also important for a fuller account of the responsibility to understand, will have to wait for further study.[62]

Part II, then, focuses on contours of the responsibility to understand that are concerned with relations of 'I and thou'. Whereas Gadamer's remarks suggest that he holds a reductive conception of the 'thou' as another person (or text), I proceed, by contrast, on the basis of the claim that the 'thou' must be taken more expansively, and I elucidate the responsibility to understand at issue in our involvement with things, with animals, as well as with other human beings. Chapter 3, 'Things', focuses on the responsibility to understand involved in our everyday interactions with things. Although this is a topic not typically addressed within the philosophical study of ethics, I argue that our hermeneutical experience of things suggests the demand to cultivate a capacity to be displaced in what may be described as one of the most immediate, and so also intimate, contexts of our factical lives. In this, I argue that the hermeneutical experience of things demands that we not subjugate things to our wills, but enact and cultivate the capacity to involve ourselves with them as they are in their respective being.

Chapter 4, 'Animals', concerns the responsibility to understand involved in our relation with animals that are not human. Several important discussions about the relation of human beings and non-human animals have coalesced around points of difference between Heidegger and Derrida. Whereas Heidegger is criticised for propagating age-old prejudices about the radical difference between humans and animals, Derrida deconstructs the distinction of human and animal, leaving any final philosophical determination of the relation between the two in deferral. In Chapter 4, I argue that the responsibility to understand animals takes shape as a demand to enact and cultivate the capacity to displace the prejudice of such a divide, recognising, instead, the interplay of both our difference from and continuity with animals. Building on important but understated aspects of Gadamer's thought, I argue that such displacement requires that we recognise the shared aspects of our lives with animals based on the fact that both humans and animals participate in the hermeneutically significant experiences of play.

Chapter 5, 'Others', in turn takes up our responsibility to understand other persons. Gadamer, as I argue, holds that the ethical stakes of our relations with others are directed not at the other person in isolation from other others. Rather, for Gadamer, our relations to others take shape precisely in the larger context of the shared world in which we find ourselves and one another. Thus, for Gadamer, our responsibility to understand others is epitomised first of all by our relation to what he, in reference to Aristotle, designates as relations of friendship. From this viewpoint, our responsibility to understand others is not only a relation of 'I and thou', but marks a transition to our relations in a larger world. Building on Gadamer, I argue that our responsibility to other persons is to enact and cultivate the capacity to see the other in his or her difference from us, to come to understand and care for the other in our respective and also shared commitments, and, in this manner, to help the other understand herself and her life context otherwise and even better.

The focus of Part III is on contours of the responsibility to understand that are concerned with the relations of the 'I and we'. For Gadamer, these relations are not concerned directly with political phenomena such as the foundations of the state, the arbitration of law, diplomacy or international relations. Rather, for Gadamer, relations of 'I and we' focus, more originally, on the hermeneutical accessibility of our shared lives with one another that makes politics possible in the first place. This Part focuses, first of all, then, in Chapter 6, 'Solidarity', on our responsibility for the formation of solidarities with one another. For Gadamer, however, the formation of solidarities concerns not the determination of identities (racial or ethnic, gendered, religious, national, or otherwise). Rather, for him, it concerns our capacity to displace ourselves from our individuated interests in order to achieve a shared space of visibility in which we come into view for one another in our respective vulnerabilities and differences.

Chapter 7, 'Arts and Literature', considers contributions that can be made to our pursuit of the formation of solidarities by hermeneutical experiences of the arts and literature. It is a mainstay of hermeneutics that our encounters with arts and literature can displace our prejudices and lead us to understand otherwise than before. This chapter, however, stresses the responsibility that attends such displacement for the formation of a shared world of solidarities. Indeed, this stress on our responsibility to form solidarities brings into relief Gadamer's understated but significant concern for the role that the arts and literature can play not only within a given cultural tradition, but, more than this, in a global context. In this, I argue that our responsibility to form solidarities is fostered by the arts and literature because of their power to displace us even from the prejudices of our own traditions as such, allowing us to understand otherwise our participation in the transmission of meaning in the wider context of global life.

Chapter 8, 'Translation', focuses, finally, on contributions that can be made to our pursuit of the formation of solidarities by the hermeneutical experience of translation. Thus, again in this chapter, the concern is with a mainstay of hermeneutics – the idea that our experience of translation can displace our prejudices; this time, the very prejudices embedded in the language of one's speech or a text. In this chapter, I argue that this experience of displacement contributes to the formation of solidarities even with those from different linguistic traditions than our own. Moreover, translation, precisely as an extreme or limit-experience of language, underscores the ethical dimensions of Gadamer's attempt to advance Heidegger's ontological turn with a further turn to language. For here, as I argue, at the limits of language we find nothing else than a final emblem of the responsibility to understand as such.

PART I: THE RESPONSIBILITY TO UNDERSTAND

1 The Responsibility to Understand

In life no less than in our experience of the arts and humanities, we find ourselves responsible to understand. The character of this responsibility is recognisable – though it remains understated and perhaps even underdeveloped – in Gadamer's philosophical hermeneutics. It can be brought out, however, by a reconsideration of Gadamer's attempt to advance the ontological turn in hermeneutics achieved through Heidegger's hermeneutics of facticity. Gadamer affirms the basic claim of the latter: namely, that the study of hermeneutics concerns not first the art of understanding or methodological foundations of research in the arts and humanities, but, instead, the being or structure of existence (Dasein) itself. Our existence takes shape hermeneutically; our lives are lived understandingly and interpretively. In *Truth and Method*, Gadamer attempts to advance this ontological turn through a 'concretion' of the hermeneutics of facticity, focusing expressly on the role played in such hermeneutical experience by history and language. Yet, as I wish to show in this chapter, Gadamer's attempt to advance the ontological turn involves a further 'concretion' of Heidegger's hermeneutics of facticity. For, as we shall see, Gadamer attempts to make Heidegger more concrete not only in terms of history and language, but also, and just as importantly, in terms of responsibility.

Gadamer's attempt to concretise Heidegger's hermeneutics of facticity in terms of responsibility can be discerned in reference to Heidegger's 'Letter on Humanism'. This is a surprise, since, on first glance, it appears that Gadamer does not advance Heidegger's claims about humanism in the 'Letter' but instead simply disagrees with them. Gadamer, for his part, proposes an affirmative rehabilitation of several motifs of the humanist tradition, for example, in the first chapter of *Truth and Method*, Part I, 'The significance of the humanist tradition for the human sciences'.[1] Heidegger, by contrast, repudiates humanism.[2]

Gadamer's affirmative rehabilitation of motifs from humanism is, however, better grasped as part of his attempt to make Heidegger's hermeneutics of facticity more concrete. Heidegger, as we shall see, is motivated to disavow humanism because he believes every humanism is bound up with received ideas from Western metaphysics – specifically, metaphysically essentialist conceptions of the human being that, in turn, can be employed as normative standards for existence. Gadamer is in deep sympathy with Heidegger's motivation. But, as Gadamer's affirmative rehabilitation suggests, he disagrees with Heidegger that every humanism inherited from the Western tradition is reducible to metaphysical essentialism. Quite to the contrary, we shall see that Gadamer believes rehabilitated, non-metaphysical motifs from humanism can give concrete expression to the responsibility at issue in the hermeneutics of facticity. As I wish to show, this responsibility is what Heidegger calls 'originally ethical', and appears as a demand to address what I will call a 'predicament of the exception' that confronts us in all hermeneutical experience. In this predicament, we find ourselves, on the one hand, responsible to understand and interpret, without exception. Yet, on the other hand, we find that it is impossible to determine in advance how to make good on this responsibility, since every situation is unique, irreducible to any other, and thus exceptional.

The Possibility of a 'Curious', Non-metaphysical Humanism

Gadamer's admiration for the Western tradition of humanism, especially as it was carried forward from German classicism, is evident from *Truth and Method*. In Part I, he argues that the humanistic motifs of education (*Bildung*), *sensus communis*, judgement and taste provide the point of departure for his enquiry into the hermeneutical experiences of the arts and humanities.[3] It is not an exaggeration to say that these motifs provide the *entrée* for Gadamer's overall enquiry in *Truth and Method*, insofar as he develops Part II and Part III at least in part on the basis of the results of Part I. Indeed, Gadamer's admiration for the humanist tradition remains beyond *Truth and Method*. In his 1972 piece, 'The Incapacity for Conversation', he associates philosophical hermeneutics itself with a humanistic call to 'elevate' ourselves into our 'humanity' precisely through the enactment and cultivation of the 'capacity for conversation'.[4]

Gadamer's admiration for humanism appears, initially at least, to oppose Heidegger's celebrated disavowal of the tradition of humanism. Yet, Gadamer's admiration for humanism is no defence of traditional humanism. Rather, as I wish to show in this section, it is mediated by the possibility of a 'curious', non-metaphysical humanism[5] that accords with Heidegger's hermeneutics of facticity. As we shall see, Heidegger himself momentarily entertains the possibility of such a humanism, only to reject it almost as soon as he raises it.

The historical context of Heidegger's 'Letter' is widely known. Heidegger composed the 'Letter' in response to a request made by the French philosopher Jean Beaufret for Heidegger to clarify for a French readership the character and consequences of the analysis of existence he had presented in *Being and Time*. In France, Jean-Paul Sartre's essay 'Existentialism is a Humanism' had begun to receive acclaim, and it must have appeared to Beaufret as an opportune moment for Heidegger to introduce his thought to a French readership. Beaufret formed his request to Heidegger in a series of three queries: the first about humanism; the second about ethics; and, the third about the adventure of philosophical enquiry. Heidegger, in his 'Letter', begins with Beaufret's first question, 'How can we restore meaning to the word "humanism"?' Yet, in response, Heidegger provides no direct answer, instead refusing the premise of the question. He writes: 'The question proceeds from your [that is, Beaufret's] intention to retain the word "humanism." I wonder whether that is necessary.'[6] In this, Heidegger suspects that the word 'humanism', and with it the tradition of ideas it signifies, belongs among the empty '-isms' demanded by the 'market of opinion'.[7]

Heidegger's suspicion of the word 'humanism' is, at one level, a criticism of Sartre, insinuating that Sartre's association of existentialism with humanism was something of a sell-out. More deeply than this, though, Heidegger's suspicion is that the word 'humanism', and the tradition of ideas it signifies, obscure what he calls the 'claim' of being and the possibility to free ourselves for this claim in our existence. In the tradition of humanism, by contrast, what counts is the claim of the essence of the human being and the possibility to free ourselves for the claim of this essence in our existence. Heidegger writes: 'For this is humanism: meditating and caring, that human beings be human and not inhumane, "inhuman", that is, outside their essence. But in what does the humanity of the human being consist? It lies in his essence.'[8] For Heidegger, humanism recognises not the claim of being but only the claim of the essence of human being as a measure of existence. In this, human beings are taken to have a pre-given essence, a formal and final cause, that we can either realise or fail fully to realise in our existence. To realise our humanity, to be humane – this is nothing else than to free ourselves by living in accord with our essence as a human being. To fail to be fully human, to be inhumane – this is nothing else than to turn away from our essence as a human being.

Heidegger, for his part, maintains that the tradition of humanism is inseparable from metaphysics. He writes: 'Every humanism is either grounded in metaphysics or is itself made to be the ground of one.'[9] Heidegger recognises that over the course of the tradition of humanism it has taken many forms. In elucidation of this observation, he considers the definitions of the essence of human being found in the first humanism in the age of the Roman Republic, in Renaissance humanism, in Weimar humanism and even in Marxism; he observes, moreover, the broadly humanistic character of Christianity.[10] But, he writes, in each case, humanism is always based in the established metaphysical assumptions of the age. He writes:

However different these forms of humanism may be in purpose and in principle, in the mode and means of their respective realizations, and in the form of their teaching, they nonetheless all agree in this, that the *humanitas* of *homo humanus* is determined with regard to an already established interpretation of nature, history, world, and the ground of the world that is, of beings as a whole.[11]

Humanism, as Heidegger has it, is essentialism; but such essentialism is itself also always founded on metaphysics.

Humanism, in obscuring the claim of being and instead inserting the claim of a metaphysical essence of human being, is reductive of the possibilities of existence. In humanism, the concern is with the claim made on us by such an essence and our possibility

to free ourselves to live in accord with that essence. Yet, humanist freedom is constricted because the scope and limits of such
freedom are defined in advance as a return to a purportedly pre-
given essence. The concern to realise our humanity is nothing else
than the concern to realise, to make actual, an essence of human
being that already underlies, if only in the mode of potentiality,
our existence. Heidegger, of course, recognises that it is possible
for this essence of human being not to be realised in our existence. But, in humanism, all of the possibilities of our existence,
the possibility not to realise this essence as well as the possibility
to realise it, are determined in advance by that essence. And, as
many scholars of our times have made clear, the humanity/inhu-
manity dichotomy is also normative, and is often employed with
devastating consequences.[12]

Heidegger believes that his consideration of the claim of being,
by contrast, brings into focus that our existence is oriented by
something we are referred to in its exteriority from us. Focused
on humanism as a metaphysical essentialism, Heidegger writes:
'Metaphysics closes itself to the simple essential fact that the human
being essentially occurs in his essence only where it is claimed by
being. Only from this claim "has" he found that wherein his essence
dwells . . . Such standing in the clearing of being I call the ek-
sistence of human beings.'[13] And: 'What the human being is – or, as
it is called in the traditional language of metaphysics, the "essence"
of the human being – lies in his ek-sistence.'[14] Heidegger argues,
contra humanism, that human beings are not claimed by a metaphysical, pre-given essence that underlies existence, but, instead,
are 'essentially' claimed by being in our existence. By this, Heidegger means that human beings are, in their being, always already
in relation to, and thus also oriented and affected by, the being of
the things and others they find themselves involved with in a factically given, individual situation. Accordingly, the claim of being is
prior to any ground in the essence of the human being; it is also
contingent, in that being is not a ground but rather is co-given with
a respectively given situation. Heidegger's hyphenation of the word
'existence', and his use of the ancient Greek form of the prefix 'ek',
may be understood, at least in part, as an attempt to distinguish his
view from metaphysical conceptions of the essence/existence relation, and thus to capture the claim of being in this groundlessness

and contingency. In existence, as Heidegger's hyphenation emphasises, we stand outside, claimed by being, without anything to stand
on, as such being is granted to us just this once.

Heidegger argues that the claim of being frees us for a different possibility of existence than, as in humanism, the freedom for
the essence of human being. To Heidegger's mind, *contra* humanism,
freedom is a freedom to live in what he calls 'the truth of being'. By
this, he means our participation in being with care and attentiveness
as it is disclosed to us in its possibilities for enactment in a respectively given situation. He writes:

The human being is . . . 'thrown' by being itself into the truth of being, so
that ek-sisting in this fashion he might guard the truth of being, in order
that beings might appear in the light of being as the beings they are. Human
beings do not decide whether and how beings appear, whether and how
God and the gods or history and nature come forward into the clearing of
being, come to presence and depart.[15]

Here, the concern is not to realise our essence over and against
being, but, instead, to tend to being itself. We realise ourselves, or,
as Heidegger puts it, live in accord with what is proper to us,[16] when
we enact possibilities of being that are elicited by being as being
takes shape in a respectively given situation.

Heidegger describes this possibility to live in accord with what is
proper to us, then, not as a matter of realising ourselves, but, instead,
as a matter of remaining 'near' to being.[17] At the most basic level,
our relation to being is indissoluble; existence is encompassed by,
immersed in, being. Yet, our very participation in being nevertheless leaves us, time and again, initially remote from being. This is
because being is always only co-given with those things and others
in a respective situation; and, in this, being only comes into view for
us through our concern for those things and others. He writes: 'the
human being . . . at first fails to recognize the nearest and attaches
himself to the next nearest. He even thinks that this is the nearest.
But nearer than the nearest, than beings, and at the same time for
ordinary thinking farther than the farthest is nearness itself: the truth
of being.'[18] Heidegger, in turn, argues that our possibility to return to
the nearness of being takes shape as a 'call' to be responsive to being
in our existence, and thus to relate to being in terms of 'guardianship' and 'care'.[19]

Heidegger maintains that the human being, grasped in terms of such guardianship of being, is irreducible to definitions of the human being from the tradition of humanism. Referring to the definition of the human being from the first humanism of the age of the Roman Republic in particular, he contrasts his own view of the non-essentialist 'essence' of existence to that of a 'rational animal'. He writes, the 'essence of the human being consists in his being more than merely human, if this is represented as "being a rational creature"'.[20] Indeed, Heidegger argues that his interpretation speaks better to the 'dignity' of the human being than do the interpretations of the human being found in the tradition of humanism. Now, there are few ideas more central to the humanist tradition than that of the 'dignity of man'.[21] So, Heidegger's claim comprises about as direct an attack on the humanist tradition as can be distilled into a single word. He writes:

the human being, as the ek-sisting counterthrow [*Gegenwurf*] of being, is more than *animal rationale* precisely to the extent that he is less bound up with the human being conceived from subjectivity . . . human beings lose nothing in this 'less'; rather, they gain in that they attain the truth of being. They gain the essential poverty of the shepherd, whose dignity consists in being called by being itself into the preservation of being's truth. The call comes from the throw from which the thrownness of Da-sein derives.[22]

Heidegger, then, is himself concerned with the dignity of the human being. For Heidegger, our dignity is at the same time a humility. Our dignity derives from our possibility to orient ourselves toward – to guard, to care for, to shepherd – being, in the possibilities of being as they arise in a respectively given situation of things and others.

Heidegger doubts whether the dignity of our possibility to live 'near' to being can be made compatible with the tradition of humanism. It is true that he momentarily entertains the possibility of a non-metaphysical humanism that would accord with his interpretation of the being of human being as existence, or 'ek-sistence'.[23] For him, this is the possibility of a 'curious' humanism. He writes: '"Humanism" now means, in case we decide to retain the word, that the essence of the human being is essential for the truth of being simply as such. So we are thinking of a curious kind of "humanism".'[24] Heidegger suggests that this sense of humanism is curious because it requires us to invest the word with a significance that is more original than anything that belongs to the actual, historically inherited tradition of humanism itself. He describes this as 'the possibility of restoring to the word "humanism" a historical sense that is older than its oldest meaning chronologically reckoned'.[25] Heidegger acknowledges that while this possibility requires a redefinition of the word 'humanism', it does not for this reason reduce the word to a *'flatus vocis'* or empty sound.[26] Yet, as he argues, such a redefinition would indeed make of the word 'humanism' a *'lucus a non lucendo'*, a pun used by ancient Roman etymologists, we recall, to indicate a paradoxical word derivation.[27] Heidegger's point, it seems, is that to redefine the word 'humanism' is to coin a term that leaves the impression of referring back to the humanist tradition even when it does not.

Heidegger abandons the possibility of such a 'curious', post-metaphysical humanism as quickly as he raises it, however. In this, his discussion insinuates that to 'keep the name "humanism" for a "humanism" that contradicts all previous humanism'[28] is really something of a Faustian bargain. After all, the word 'humanism' carries prestige because of the venerable tradition from which it derives. But, if a curious, post-metaphysical humanism depends on a redefinition of the term, then any prestige carried over from the word itself would be ill-begotten. Moreover, this prestige would be bound up in confusion, since the prestige would entail an ambiguation of post-metaphysical and traditional humanism. Heidegger asserts that to retain the name 'humanism' would simply be 'to swim in the predominant currents, stifled in metaphysical subjectivism and submerged in the oblivion of being'.[29] Heidegger does not mention Sartre expressly in this passage, but is not difficult to imagine that Sartre, with his recent 'Existentialism is a Humanism', is the Faust that Heidegger has in mind. Be this as it may, Heidegger concludes that 'open resistance to "humanism"' is the best option.[30] In this, he calls for us to draw attention to the dignity of the human being not through the rescue of humanism from metaphysical essentialism, but, instead, through a disavowal of humanism, the 'shock' of which can 'for the first time cause perplexity concerning the *humanitas* of *homo humanus* and its basis'.[31]

Heidegger's suspicion about the prospect of retaining the word 'humanism' helps clarify Gadamer's admiration of motifs from the tradition of humanism. First of all, Gadamer's admiration of these humanistic motifs is not a simple disagreement with Heidegger. Heidegger, as we have seen, disavows humanism because he believes every humanism is bound up with metaphysical essentialism and, therefore, obscures the hermeneutics of facticity. But, Gadamer, too, is concerned with what Heidegger signifies by 'metaphysical essentialism', insofar as it contravenes his own attempts to advance Heidegger's hermeneutics of facticity. Gadamer's deep sympathy with Heidegger's concerns, in fact, forms the basis of his more specific disagreement with Heidegger. Really, that disagreement is over whether the word 'humanism' itself remains historically effective. Heidegger argues that the word 'humanism' can only be used to signify the possibility of a 'curious', post-metaphysical humanism if it is severed from the effective history of the word as it has been passed down to us from the tradition of humanism. Gadamer, it seems, begs to differ. Indeed, his approach suggests the belief that the historical effectiveness of 'curious', post-metaphysical motifs of the humanist tradition can be rehabilitated even after Heidegger's criticism of Western metaphysics. For Gadamer, the use of the word 'humanism' to signify such post-metaphysical possibilities of humanity is no redefinition that makes of the term a *lucus a non lucendo*. Rather, such a use of the word 'humanism' speaks to the richness of the effective history of humanistic motifs from the tradition.

It is true that Gadamer's admiration of humanistic motifs, even such 'curious', post-metaphysical motifs, leaves him as something of an outlier. Since the interwar period at least, many have perceived a 'crisis' in humanism, namely, that the challenges of modernity can no longer be adequately addressed by humanistic beliefs and the tradition that sustains them. Gadamer's admiration of humanistic motifs, even in the form of his affirmation of the possibilities of post-metaphysical humanism, cuts against the grain. It is true that, along with Gadamer, some other major figures in continental European philosophy, such as Sartre (as we have noted), but also Levinas and Arendt, take up motifs of humanism.[32] But, the trend-line is to relegate humanism as part of the Western tradition from which we are now called to twist free. In this, Gadamer's approach to humanistic motifs cuts against the grain not only of Heidegger before him but also of the broad critical concerns that have been raised in fields as diverse as continental philosophy, post-colonialism and post-humanism. Yet, if Gadamer's admiration of the motifs of humanism (and the possibility of a post-metaphysical humanism to which they speak) cuts against the grain, his approach should not be rejected for this reason. Indeed, it is perhaps better viewed as a counter-cut, one that warns not only against Heidegger's reductive conclusion about the word 'humanism' but, at the same time, against those who would fail to heed Heidegger's insight that the dignity of human beings is found precisely in our responsiveness to the claim being makes on us in our existence.

Responsibility in the Predicament of Exception

The responsibility to understand is itself a post-metaphysical, humanistically inflected concretion of Heidegger's call for us to be responsive to the claim of being. In this, Gadamer will characterise the responsibility to understand in a different idiom than that of Heidegger. Gadamer's notion of responsibility is captured by his appeal for us to elevate ourselves into our humanity through the enactment and cultivation of the 'capacity to converse'. In the next chapter, we shall consider the responsibility to enact and cultivate the capacity to converse as a capacity for what I will call hermeneutical displacement. Yet, as we shall see here first, this appeal is not for us to realise a pre-given essence of the human being. And neither is it an appeal for us to enact and cultivate a postmodern capacity for the creation of new meaning. Rather, this appeal is a concrete expression of the responsiveness demanded of us when we refer ourselves to individual situations in which we find ourselves. Gadamer introduces the term 'responsibility' to capture the character of this responsive referral in connection with Kant, as Gadamer believes Kant's notion of responsibility can be paired with elements of Aristotle's ethics. From this viewpoint, Gadamer's notion of the responsibility to understand will prove to concern what I shall call the 'predicament of the exception' involved in every individual situation.

Gadamer's hermeneutics has, of course, long and rightly been closely associated with practical philosophy.[33] Yet, his hermeneutics has not typically been associated with the responsibility to understand, much less with a sense of responsibility derived from Heidegger's call in the 'Letter' for us to be responsive to the claim of being. The horizon of enquiry that clarifies the connection of Gadamer's hermeneutics, practical philosophy and Heidegger's approach in the 'Letter' is brought into relief, however, through a provocative claim made by Dennis Schmidt in 'On the Sources of Ethical Life' and other essays.[34] This is Schmidt's claim that Gadamer's hermeneutics may itself be grasped as what Heidegger, in the 'Letter', calls 'original ethics'.[35] Schmidt argues that Gadamer's hermeneutics embraces Heidegger's appeal for ethics to become more original by returning from abstract debate centred on 'rules of conduct', 'the will and imperatives' and 'the juridical language of right and wrong' back to questions of 'comportment' and 'character formation' that remain close to the sources of our factical situatedness.[36] In this, Schmidt connects Gadamer's hermeneutics to Heidegger's concern for original ethics in reference to Gadamer's approach to the hermeneutical problem of application.

Schmidt, to be sure, acknowledges the intrepidity of his claim that Gadamer's hermeneutics should be treated as a response to Heidegger's call for original ethics; Schmidt himself characterises his own claim as a 'provocation' and even as an 'outrageous contention'.[37] Whether or not Schmidt's claim may be defended *in toto*, at any rate, he builds his case in reference to what he sees as the main idea of Heidegger's original ethics. Heidegger's concern is not to establish a novel ethical theory but, on the contrary, to return to the origins of ethical life by twisting free from what Schmidt refers to as 'the prejudices of metaphysics that have long governed ethical reflection'.[38] If Heidegger sees these prejudices as 'several', it is nonetheless the 'metaphysical partition of ontology and ethics, that is, the separation of theory and praxis, that Heidegger finds most in need of being overcome'.[39] Schmidt's point appears to refer to a claim Heidegger makes in the 'Letter'. Heidegger, as we have said, writes the letter in response to questions posed to him by Beaufret; the first question, as we saw, concerned the restoration of meaning to the word 'humanism'. His second question is about ethics: 'What is the relation between ontology and ethics?' Just as Heidegger challenges the wisdom of the first question, so too, here, he interrogates the metaphysical assumption that he takes to lead Beaufret's query. Again, Heidegger resists the customary procedure, characteristic of the discipline of ethics generally and within the humanist tradition in particular, by which, first of all, a theory of ethics is derived or abstracted from some purported ontology of the human being that, in turn, can be used as a guide for human practice.

Heidegger, by contrast, calls for ethics to become more original through the disavowal of this customary procedure in favour
of concern for our responsiveness to being. He addresses this concern in terms of what he calls the 'dwelling' (*Wohnung*) or, as his
German is intended to translate, the '*ēthos*' of human being.[40] With
this, Schmidt argues, Heidegger's call for original ethics 'undercuts
or deconstructs the theoretical/practical divide since it concerns the
formation of that character out of which both theoretical and practical relations to the world emerge'.[41] In view of this, Heidegger's call
for original ethics turns away from concerns in the discipline of ethics to establish, justify and adjudicate the validity of ethical systems,
positions or principles that, in turn, should be followed in practice.
The stress of original ethics, rather, is on the concern to enact manners of being that are appropriately responsive to each context we
find ourselves in, as well as on the cultivation of our ability thus to
involve ourselves responsively.

Schmidt recognises that although Gadamer addresses the affinity of hermeneutics and ethics along a number of related lines,[42] his
originally ethical concern for the issues of comportment and character come out in his consideration of what he refers to as the 'hermeneutical problem of application'.[43] Gadamer, as Schmidt observes,
recognises no less than Heidegger does that theory – ethical or otherwise – is defined by the 'impulse' of conceptuality toward 'universality and generality'.[44] Theory, in virtue of this impulse toward
universality and generality, is incongruous with ethical matters
because 'ethical life is lived out in the life of the idiom – in the realities of history, the sufferings of individuals . . .'.[45]

We may see Gadamer's idea of how theory can be made answerable to factical life if we distinguish between a received metaphysical idea of application and Gadamer's hermeneutical conception. On
the metaphysical conception, theory is grasped in terms of universalities or generalities that may be known to be true as it were prior
to and independent of all circumstances. Schmidt captures the crux
of this metaphysical conception of application as a '*post facto supplement*' to theoretical knowledge we already have.[46] But, he argues,
this metaphysical conception fails because, 'as a result of such an
approach, the questions of factical life, the real site of any ethics,
become secondary to *knowing* what is true'.[47] On Gadamer's hermeneutical conception of application, by contrast, application is not the

post facto imposition of universalities or generalities already known, but, instead, the process, or, event, by which we interpretively raise the ethical concerns at issue in our factical circumstances into articulation in the first place. With this, the hermeneutical conception of application does not concern universalities or generalities purported to be independent of all circumstances, but, rather, the achievement of an interpretation that draws out the ethical demands that otherwise remain diffuse or even only latent within the situation into which we find ourselves thrown.

Schmidt argues that understanding and interpretation, thus grasped in view of the problem of application, prove at bottom to concern our comportment to the world and to ourselves as well as the formation of character that sustains this comportment. 'Understanding', Schmidt asserts, 'is never found apart from factical life; it does not stand above it as a theory, but neither is it to be defined as a matter of praxis'.[48] Understanding cannot be grasped with reference to theory alone because it concerns not conceptuality for its own sake but rather only interpretation insofar as it answers to factical life by heightening and refining our awareness of and thus also our responsiveness to our factical circumstances. Understanding cannot be reduced to *praxis* either, however, if by *praxis* we have in mind an agent whose actions are oriented by intentions or ends conceived in terms of an independent will. Rather, understanding is to be grasped as a manner of being that remains in force and thus comes to define our disposition because it is always and again enacted, executed, performed. Schmidt explains: 'understanding is a continuous act that is renewed at every instant; it is a way of life that is informed by history, language, habits – all the realities of the situation of factical life'.[49] Understanding focuses not on a 'what' – neither what theory grants us knowledge of nor what intention or end we want to pursue. Instead, understanding concerns the 'how' of our comportment and the 'who' of our character. It speaks to the 'how' of our comportment through the achievement of conceptual patterns of articulation that guide our involvement with the world and ourselves; and, it speaks to the 'who' of our character as we come to be defined through the expression and development of these patterns.

Schmidt's examination of Gadamer's hermeneutics as an 'original ethics' is illuminative of Gadamer's relation to the practical-philosophical implications of Heidegger's 'Letter'. Schmidt's provocative claim suggests that Gadamer's concern for hermeneutical application is an attempt to give concrete expression to Heidegger's call for an originally ethical responsiveness to the claim of being. In light of Schmidt's provocation, Gadamer's association of understanding and interpretation with hermeneutical application is itself an attempt to specify that and how our responsiveness to respective, factically given situations actually takes shape. From this viewpoint, to understand and interpret requires hermeneutical application, but such application is itself nothing else than what is properly our mode of responsiveness to the facticity of existence.

Yet, as provocative as Schmidt's claim is, his provocation can be extended even further. Case in point is Gadamer's examination of Kant's notion of responsibility, as Gadamer couples this with elements of Aristotle's ethics, in 'On the Possibility of Philosophical Ethics' and other essays.[50] In this, Gadamer's introduction of responsibility serves to clarify the responsiveness of understanding. 'On the Possibility of Philosophical Ethics' begins – in light of Schmidt's provocation, not surprisingly – from Heidegger's critique of the reliance in the discipline of moral or ethical philosophy on the metaphysical assumption of the distinction between theory and practice. The question, as Gadamer formulates it in the context of his consideration of Heidegger, concerns how philosophy, whose 'métier' is 'reflexive generality', can 'do justice to the concreteness with which conscience, sensitivity to equity, and loving reconciliation are answerable to the situation'.[51] Gadamer claims that this dilemma may be resolved in reference to elements from each of Kant's and Aristotle's practical philosophies. In this, Gadamer is obviously not interested in a systematic interpretation of Kant's and Aristotle's positions. Nor, for that matter, is he interested in adjudicating Kant's and Aristotle's positions as representatives of so-called 'deontology' and 'virtue ethics'. Rather, to Gadamer's mind, Heidegger's dilemma is addressed by elements of Kant's and Aristotle's approaches that ground ethics in such a manner that serves to circumvent the usual distinction in ethics between theory and practice.[52] For Gadamer, Heidegger's dilemma is not addressed by either Kant or Aristotle on their own, but, taken together, each can contribute 'their parts'.[53]

In reference to Kant, Gadamer focuses on Kant's belief that ethics must be grounded in unconditional responsibility, recalling that Kant seeks to ground moral philosophy in what he sees as the apodictic 'fact of reason' that we are morally free beings.[54] Here, Gadamer does not believe Kant's moral philosophy is grounded first of all in the categorical imperative. Rather, as Gadamer interprets Kant, the categorical imperative is only unconditionally binding because we are already morally free beings. Gadamer argues that the character of responsibility comes into focus if we observe that all of our obligations are 'without exception'.[55] He suggests that we recognise the significance of this 'without exception' with particular lucidity *via negativa*, whenever we observe ourselves or another seek to deny 'a given duty's power to obligate' by engaging in what he calls a '"dialectic of the exception"'[56] and what in psychoanalytic terms is called rationalisation. Here, first, we 'admit the validity of the moral law', only, in turn, 'to underscore the exceptional nature of the situation' that we wish to exempt or excuse us from duty.[57] Gadamer suggests, however, that, more often than not, such efforts to deny the unconditionality of obligation simply serve to remind us that the fact of our freedom cannot be avoided. We are responsible, every time, without exception.

In reference to Aristotle, Gadamer focuses on Aristotle's belief that ethics must be grounded in the 'conditionedness' of human life in the *ēthos* of the community.[58] With this, Aristotle argues that ethical life cannot be guided by abstract theory but rather requires that we are able to bring the context of meaning provided by this *ēthos* to bear on the individual situations in which we find ourselves. Thus, ethical life requires not that we establish, justify and adjudicate ethical theories, but, rather, that we exercise and cultivate *phronēsis*, or, as Gadamer defines the term in this context, 'concrete moral consciousness . . . that finds expression in such unmeaning and all-inclusive concepts as what is "fitting," what is "proper," what is "good and right"'.[59] Gadamer, with Kant, recognises that responsibility is unconditional. Yet, with Aristotle, he also recognises that our enactment of our possibilities is guided by and constrained to operate within the contexts of social, political and interpersonal life that comprise the world within which we are called to understand and act. Here, Gadamer stresses Aristotle's idea of *phronēsis* as the ability to select and realise meanings derived from the *ēthos* of community in manners that are suited to individual situations. Although we can surely anticipate that our experience will present us with regularities and similarities between situations, Gadamer, following

Aristotle, sees that no two situations are really the same and, in virtue of this, no judgement from a past situation can be applied without qualification to the current one. But, because of this, Aristotle's approach suggests that every situation is exceptional because it cannot be reduced completely to any common wisdom or past experience.

Gadamer claims that, taken together, Kant and Aristotle help us come to terms with the dilemma in the study of ethics between the generality of philosophical enquiry into ethical life and the singularity of every factical situation. Yet, more than anything else, Gadamer's considerations suggest that this dilemma cannot so much be resolved as simply accepted in view of the predicament that Gadamer's treatment of Kant and Aristotle suggests. For, as Gadamer has it, we learn from Kant that our obligation is unconditional – without exception – because grounded in the fact of freedom. But from Aristotle we learn that because of the conditionedness of human being in the *ēthos* of community our ethical lives unfold only in the exception of circumstances that cannot be reduced to any theory or prior experience.

Gadamer's approach to Kant and Aristotle here further clarifies how his view of understanding concretises Heidegger's originally ethical concern for responsiveness to the claim of being. For Gadamer, understanding, grasped as a responsiveness to factical life, circulates precisely within the double bind of the predicament: at once, responsible without exception, and yet, at the same time, also always thrown into circumstances that remain exceptional as beyond anything we can be prepared to comprehend or control in advance. To be sure, in his hermeneutics Gadamer defines such freedom not in terms of an imperative grounded in a pre-given essence of reason; rather, his concern for such freedom filters through his attempt to advance Heidegger's ontological turn. But, for Gadamer, what Kant gets right is the unconditionality of such freedom in any case. And just as surely, Gadamer sees Aristotle's notion of conditionedness in light of his hermeneutics, and sees the *ēthos* of community as the result of meaning that has been transmitted historically in language. But, for Gadamer, what Aristotle gets right is that our ethical lives are conditioned through and through. Thus, Gadamer's approach to Kant and Aristotle bring into focus that we are responsible to understand, *without exception*, in every uniquely individual and thus *exceptional* situation in which we find ourselves.

Gadamer gives voice to the responsibility to understand in his appeal for us to raise ourselves up into our humanity. In fact, he suggests that the responsibility to understand at issue in this appeal to our humanity is perhaps a more urgent concern in our times than in any time before. In 'The Incapacity for Conversation', Gadamer articulates the urgency of our responsibility to understand in terms of the need to converse well with one another. He observes that our times are increasingly characterised by what he calls 'mono-logization'.[60] Posing a rhetorical question, he writes: 'Haven't we noticed an increasing monologization of human behaviour in the social life of our time?'[61] While he raises a series of questions about the cause of this monologisation, he observes that is it 'deplored' by some as an 'incapacity for conversation'.[62] Yet, as he argues, this monologisation, and, with it, the alleged spread of the incapac-ity for conversation, can be addressed even in the difficult times of the present. Indeed, as he suggests, the culture of monologue that permeates our times is in any case not due to a lack of knowl-edge, skill, or inborn talent. Rather, it is sustained by what, in light of Gadamer's analysis of Kant's notion of responsibility, we might call making an exception of ourselves. Here, in 'The Incapacity for Conversation', however, Gadamer gives expression to this respon-sibility to understand as an appeal to our humanity. This is not an appeal for a return to a metaphysical, pre-given essence of human being, however; nor is it an appeal to the postmodern creation of new meaning. It is rather an appeal to turn our attention from self-involvement toward the claims made on us in our respectively given situations. He writes:

Ignoring and mishearing occur for the same obvious reason: one who ignores or mishears is one who constantly listens to himself, whose ears are so filled from the encouragement that he constantly gives to himself and with which he pursues his drives and interests, that he is unable to hear the other. That is, I would insist, to some degree or other a character trait we all share. Nevertheless to become always capable of conversation – that is, to listen to the other – appears to me to be the true elevation of the human being to humanity.[63]

The appeal to elevate ourselves into our humanity is an appeal to remain responsive to the individual situations of factical life in which we find ourselves. Such responsibility is demanding, both because it is at issue in every situation, without exception, and because it is difficult to fulfil, since every situation is exceptional. Indeed, as Gadamer suggests, this responsibility thus demands of us that we 'always and again' enact and develop our capacity to understand, to converse. It is the purpose of the next chapter to examine just this capacity.

2 The Capacity for Displacement

The responsibility to understand, then, demands that we enact and cultivate the capacity to converse. This responsibility comes into focus as a 'predicament of the exception'. As we have seen, every situation we find ourselves in demands that we understand it, without exception. Yet, each situation is just as much exceptional because factically different from any other possible situation. In this chapter, I argue that the demand that we enact and cultivate our capacity to converse is, accordingly, really a capacity for displacement. This demand is *not* first of all directed by a concern to reach agreement, even if the capacity to converse is oriented toward or involves the pursuit of agreement. More originally, this demand is to be open for and to grapple with the displacement we experience in the predicament of the exception posed to us by every situation. The capacity to converse: this does not mean the capacity to reach agreement; rather, it means the capacity to become interpretively open by putting ourselves into question and holding ourselves in this openness in the face of the challenge it poses to even our deepest prejudices.

The claim that the capacity to converse concerns not agreement but displacement runs up against familiar criticisms of Gadamer's hermeneutics. Whatever else it is, the experience of displacement is a confrontation with alterity, the other or exteriority. Critics have long objected that Gadamer's hermeneutics affords too little credence to such exposure to exteriority.[1] A principle criticism is that in Gadamer's hermeneutics, displacement is not a definitive dimension of our experiences of understanding and interpretation but comprises only an intermediary phase of an occurrence, or event of understanding. Here, the experience of displacement is characterised as an interruption in our initial understanding of something. But, as this criticism goes, Gadamer believes that such interruption can (at least in principle, if not every time in practice) be superseded through the achievement of a novel, richer and deeper understanding. Accordingly, Gadamer's hermeneutics suggests that such interruption is provisional. Indeed, because he sees such interruption as provisional, his approach is said to emphasise not ultimately the importance of displacement, but, despite many of his own assertions to the contrary, the continuity of hermeneutical experience.

In this chapter, *contra* the customary criticism of Gadamer, I argue that displacement is, indeed, a definitive dimension of hermeneutical experience. As I wish to show, the claim that displacement is definitive of hermeneutical experience comes into focus when we recall that Gadamer's concern is for factical life, and, specifically, that his emphasis is on the whole of our factical lives as they are lived hermeneutically, and not simply with individual events of understanding.[2] Seen from the perspective of the whole of our factical lives, displacement is not an intermediary phase, as if our lives were somehow to conclude with the achievement of a final understanding! Rather, from the perspective of the whole of our factical lives, displacement is definitive: as the ubiquitous, recurrent exposure of exteriority that irrupts each time an event of understanding unfolds, from the first time in our lives when our prejudices become questionable to the time when we take our final breath. From the perspective of the whole of our factical lives, displacement is not provisional; understanding is. As our lives unfold, our achievement of understanding in one situation is inevitably interrupted by a new situation, and by the predicament of the exception with which this new situation confronts us. In life, it is not continuity, but precisely this exception, that is the rule.

Now, Gadamer's concern for the whole of our factical lives does not have to be seen as a challenge to his belief in our hermeneutical 'belonging to traditions'. With this, as we have seen, Gadamer believes that existence, in virtue of thrownness, always already finds itself within the context of historically inherited meaning. His concern for the whole of our factical lives will suggest, however, that this belonging signifies not that we find ourselves always and again at home within a pre-given tradition, but, instead, that tradition is itself a dynamic of pluralistic and even conflicted transmission through the experience of recurrent displacement. Gadamer's concern for the perspective of the whole of factical life sheds novel light on his idea that hermeneutical experience takes shape 'in the polarity of familiarity and strangeness' between a matter or 'object' under our hermeneutical consideration and 'tradition', and, thus, that '*The true locus of hermeneutics is this in-between*'.[3] From the perspective of our factical lives as a whole, this in-between is nothing other than the in-between of displacement.

Gadamer's concern for the whole of our factical lives has in any case remained underappreciated in debates about the credence his hermeneutics gives to exteriority. But, as we shall see, several philosophers in post-Gadamerian hermeneutics have drawn on this perspective of the whole of our factical lives to clarify that and how displacement is definitive of hermeneutical experience. In this, as I shall observe, three recent hermeneutical considerations of factical life stand out; all three stress that factical life is oriented by our exposure to exteriority that is and always remains insuperable and irreducible. Specifically, as we shall see, James Risser describes how the life defined by displacement takes shape as a form of *convalescence* without cure. Donatella di Cesare, in turn, maintains that the life defined by displacement takes shape as a *utopianism* without utopia. Günter Figal, finally, argues that the life defined by displacement is directed by a referential sense toward *objectivity* that can never master any object.

Together, each in different ways, these three post-Gadamerian developments in hermeneutics shed light on the definitive role that displacement plays in hermeneutical experience. Yet, as we shall see, Gadamer's concern for the whole of our factical lives focuses on the responsibility to enact and cultivate our capacity for displacement itself. Of course, insofar as factical life is defined by displacement, this responsibility is none other than a responsibility to live well.

Factical Life, or, Displacement

It is, then, from the perspective of Gadamer's larger concern for the whole of our factical lives that the definitive role played by displacement in hermeneutical experience comes into focus. Gadamer suggests that the concept of life defines his attempt to develop an account of hermeneutical experience that builds on, and, perhaps, even moves beyond, the limits of the elucidation of understanding found in Heidegger's analysis of existence in *Being and Time*. In this,

Gadamer argues that Heidegger's approach, right from the outset of his philosophical career, is motivated by the concern for life: like Dilthey, von Yorck and Husserl, Heidegger takes not the interests of modern science but concern for the context of life as the impetus for his consideration of understanding. Gadamer writes: 'The tendency which Dilthey and Yorck formulated as common to them, of "understanding in terms of life", and which was expressed in Husserl's going back behind the objectivity of science to the life-world, was characteristic of Heidegger's own first approach.'[4] If, as Gadamer claims, Heidegger's project is shaped by a concern for life that is shared by many of his contemporaries, however, Heidegger's pursuit of this concern through his analysis of existence comprises a decisive contrast with Dilthey and Husserl.[5] Per Gadamer, Dilthey's and Husserl's concerns for the theme of life leads them, each in distinctive manners, to elucidate understanding on the basis of epistemological considerations of the self-awareness of the subject. Heidegger's concern for life leads him, by contrast, to argue that understanding be grasped in ontological terms as the characteristic disclosedness or accessibility of our existence to the being of things, others and even ourselves.[6]

Gadamer observes that Heidegger, with this ontological turn, brings into focus that understanding takes shape as a concern for self-understanding that is bound up with facticity. We have discussed Gadamer's concern to 'concretise' Heidegger's hermeneutics of facticity. Now, we can begin to discern the stakes of Gadamer's concern in more detail. Heidegger, we recall, maintains in *Being and Time* that the human being, as existence, is distinguished from other beings by its concern about its being. He writes: 'Dasein is a being that does not simply occur among other beings. Rather it is ontically distinguished by the fact that in its being this being is concerned *about* its very being.'[7] Accordingly, our understanding is always guided by concern for our own being, whether our understanding is directed expressly toward ourselves, or toward our involvements with things and others. Yet, our concern for self-understanding can never be put to rest because understanding is at the same time bound up in facticity. As we have seen, this means that existence is ecstatic, in the sense that it has no basis in a transcendental subject, but is rather always already situated outside of itself. Dasein always finds itself already involved, or, as Heidegger also puts this in *Being and Time*, thrown, *geworfen*, into relations with the being of the beings. In this, Dasein finds itself involved in relations to being which it has neither chosen nor can fully control or comprehend. Thus, whenever we pursue self-understanding, by the time we attempt to understand, we find ourselves already confronted with an excess of being, a density or opacity of being, that we cannot make transparent. 'This', as Gadamer observes in a later essay, 'means that Dasein has to take itself up in a manner that is never penetrable to itself.'[8] Because our existence is bound up with facticity, we always arrive too late, with too little resource, to grasp who we ourselves are and whatever else is at stake in the situations into which we have been cast. In this same essay, Gadamer further clarifies facticity with an analogy between the facticity of existence and the condition of a litter of new-born kittens. This analogy suggests itself no doubt in part because, in German, the word that Heidegger associated with facticity, namely, thrownness (*Geworfenheit*), is echoed in the word for litter (*Wurf*), which in literal translation means 'throw'. Gadamer writes: 'one is thrown into the "there" just as kittens from the cat . . . In such a "litter" [that is, '*Wurf*', or, 'throw'] we are not even this single thing, and we do not even know who "we" are . . .'.[9] If, as Gadamer suggests, it is Heidegger's larger concern for life that guides his analysis of existence, then this context of life brings into focus that understanding is always indexed to facticity, and, thereby, to what is not and can never be made fully our own.

Gadamer's approach to hermeneutical experience builds from here. He takes up Heidegger's *Being and Time* formulation of the hermeneutical circle in order to clarify the 'historicity' of understanding, and thus also, as we may add, the linguisticality of understanding.[10] Gadamer tells us elsewhere that the notion of the hermeneutical circle originally refers to a 'rule' of interpretation that 'one must understand the whole from out of the individual and the individual from out of the whole'.[11] He recognises that Heidegger, for his part, adapts the notion of this circle in his analysis of understanding insofar as it belongs to the being of Dasein in its relation to being. Heidegger argues that although understanding takes shape as self-understanding, it is never autonomous, it is never freely pursued in a manner that is without interest and without prior tacit expectations. Rather, understanding remains conditioned factically by such interests and tacit expectations as what may be characterised as fore-structures of understanding. Gadamer observes that, in *Being and Time*, Heidegger elucidates such fore-structures in terms of what he calls fore-having, foresight or fore-seeing, and fore-grasping. In this, Heidegger means that understanding is conditioned, first, by fore-having, or, our prior understanding of relations of the beings amidst which we find ourselves. Understanding is conditioned, in turn, by fore-seeing, a first attempt to bring a definite interpretation to what is already held in fore-having. Finally, understanding is thus also conditioned by fore-grasping, or, the broader conceptuality that informs fore-seeing.[12]

Gadamer, in his elucidation of hermeneutical experience, characterises the fore-structures of understanding not with Heidegger's terms from his analysis of existence, however, but as a matter of prejudice (*Vorurteil*). With this shift, he stresses that the fore-structure of understanding is bound up with historicity and linguisticality. This fore-structure is informed by meanings, or, as the term 'prejudice' suggests, by preliminary judgements, that have been adopted ahead of time as a result of being transmitted historically through language. In his account, Gadamer stresses the contrast between the pretences of the programme of Enlightenment and his recognition of the limits of understanding implied by the facticity of existence. There is no universal rationality which would allow us to overcome all prejudices inherited from religion, custom and tradition. Rather, in consequence of the fore-structure of prejudice, understanding is made possible and limited by what Gadamer calls the 'principle' of the 'effectiveness of history'.[13] This means that hermeneutical experience, because it is conditioned by the fore-structure of prejudice, is never freed from historically inherited meaning, but remains always an effect of such inheritance. As such, he maintains, the prejudices which we have inherited and adopted historically through language determine 'in advance what appears to us as worthy of questioning and as an object of investigation'.[14] As a fore-structure of understanding, prejudice always makes possible, as well as limits, every effort to understand. There is, moreover, no bottom to our prejudice: even if our hermeneutical experience makes us aware of one of our prejudices or another, indeed, no matter how many of our prejudices we make transparent to ourselves, we nevertheless always again find that our further efforts to understand are made possible and limited by still other preliminary judgements. Thus, our concern for self-understanding never results in a universal perspective that overcomes all the prejudices we have inherited historically through language; rather, the concern for self-understanding poses an infinite task, one that unfolds as an interminable struggle against our prejudices in order to 'remain open to the meaning of the other person or text'.[15]

Gadamer suggests, albeit rather diplomatically, that his characterisation of the fore-structure of understanding as prejudice remains more true to Heidegger's concern for facticity than does Heidegger's own analysis of this fore-structure in terms of fore-having, fore-seeing and fore-grasping. Gadamer, to be sure, begins from Heidegger's idea that the fore-structure of understanding is to be grasped only secondarily as an epistemic condition of understanding, and is, more originally, constitutive of the being of human beings in their facticity. As he asserts, *'the prejudices of the individual, far more than his judgments, constitute the historical reality of his being'*;[16] or, again, as he puts it in perhaps even plainer terms in the 'Universality of the Hermeneutic Problem', 'it is not so much our judgements as it is our prejudices that constitute our being'.[17]

If Gadamer's characterisation of the fore-structure of understanding as prejudice captures Heidegger's concern for facticity better than Heidegger's own, this, Gadamer implies, is because his own approach to the fore-structure of understanding better guards against the lineaments of transcendental subjectivity that he worries remain operative in Heidegger's *Being and Time* analysis of existence.[18] As we have seen, Gadamer develops his hermeneutics as an attempt to 'concretise' Heidegger's hermeneutics of facticity in reference to tradition and language. With this, Gadamer means to imply that Dasein never fully achieves a ground in itself, never returns fully from facticity, not even in moments of inward, authentic insight, but rather remains always a participant in the facticity of history and language.

Gadamer, in any case, maintains that the hermeneutical experiences of understanding and interpretation must be grasped in terms of a logic of dialectic. He develops his approach in no small part with reference to Hegel. While Gadamer's considerations draw on Hegel's philosophy of history and of objective spirit, they are centred on motifs from Hegel's *Phenomenology of Spirit* account of experience. Even in this, however, Gadamer remains influenced by Heidegger, as his treatment of Hegel's account of experience is inflected by the analysis developed by Heidegger in his celebrated *Hegel's Concept of Experience*.[19] Gadamer takes his point of departure from Hegel because he sees in Hegel's notion of absolute knowing a figure of self-awareness or self-knowledge that is comparable to and thus can shed light on his own approach to hermeneutical experience. Hegel, too, recognises that self-knowledge is conditioned by the bequest of history. Gadamer writes: 'All self-knowledge arises from what is historically pregiven, what with Hegel we call "substance", because it underlies all subjective intentions and actions, and hence both prescribes and limits every possibility for understanding any tradition whatsoever in its historical alterity.'[20]

While Gadamer is drawn to Hegel's belief that self-knowledge is conditioned by historically inherited meaning, he nevertheless also asserts that there is a decisive difference between him and Hegel. Gadamer asserts this difference based on an interpretation of Hegel's notion of absolute knowing that has been brought into question in recent decades but that remains definitive for much of the late nineteenth and especially twentieth-century reception of Hegel. Gadamer believes that Hegel defines absolute knowing as a form of self-knowledge that is complete, or unconditional, because it is grounded in a full cognizance of the totality of historically inherited meanings which shape our awareness. Gadamer, for his part, asserts by contrast that self-understanding remains ineluctably incomplete, conditioned, because the effectiveness of history, or, with Hegel, of substance, always exceeds our cognizance. Gadamer writes: *'To be historically means never to arrive at self-knowledge.'*[21] Human beings, because they are defined more by their prejudices than by their judgements, can never become transparent to themselves.

In this context, Gadamer argues that hermeneutical experience is guided by a logic of dialectic based on what he calls Hegel's testimony that experience 'has the structure of a reversal of consciousness'.[22] He develops his notion of hermeneutical experience, with its logic of dialectic, by means of a contrast with a different notion of experience, one that typifies not only the methodological norms of the modern sciences but also has important philosophical precedents in Francis Bacon and even in Aristotle. This other notion of experience, Gadamer suggests, is guided not by a logic of dialectic but rather by a logic of 'induction'.[23] He means that from the perspective of this notion of experience as induction, experience

unfolds as a positive process by which we purport, at least, to discover universal laws, principles or concepts from out of the stream
of our individual sensations. Gadamer, unlike many contemporary
philosophers of science, is not concerned to demonstrate whether,
and, if so, why, the process of induction is epistemically justifiable.
Rather, what he wishes to point out is that on this notion of experience, it is presumed that experience is a matter of the positive accretion of knowledge: first, we discover one universal, then another
and again another, so that experience allows us to accrue an edifice of knowledge. Gadamer argues, by contrast, that hermeneutical
experience is guided not by a logic of induction but instead by a logic
of dialectic, by which our certainty in our beliefs undergoes a reversal. Gadamer writes that experience 'cannot be described simply as
the unbroken generation of typical universals. Rather this generation takes place as false generalizations that are continually refuted
by experience and what was regarded as typical is shown not to be
so'.[24] Hermeneutical experience increases our understanding not by
means of the abstraction of a universal from the stream of our individual sensations, but, rather, because experience confronts us with
something that compels us to reverse the certainty we have had in a
previous belief, recognising that what we believed to be the case is,
in fact, incommensurate with what we have encountered.

Gadamer's elucidation of hermeneutical experience in terms of
such a logic of dialectic allows us to bring into focus the definitive role
he believes displacement plays in understanding and interpretation.

Now, it is true, as Gadamer scholars no less than his critics would
agree, that his approach first of all demonstrates that, when it comes
to an individual occurrence of understanding, he takes displacement
to be only an intermediary phase. Gadamer's approach to this logic of
dialectic suggests that such an individual occurrence of understanding
unfolds in three phases, or, as we might otherwise be tempted to say,
with a term out of the Hegelian cloth from which Gadamer's account
is cut, three 'moments'. Gadamer suggests that an individual occurrence of understanding begins, first, on the basis of an initial phase, in
which the accessibility of a matter, such as a person or text, is shaped
by the authority of the fore-structure of prejudice. In this initial phase,
we begin with an unquestioning hermeneutic trust that the prejudices
we have inherited and adopted allow the matter to be disclosed in
its being as what it is. Next, however, in an intermediary phase, this

authority of the fore-structure of prejudice undergoes a reversal. Here we are confronted with the fact that the purported authority of our prejudices is unwarranted as we become aware that our prejudices do not disclose the matter fully in its being but rather only in an incomplete and distorted manner, only as it were through a glass darkly. This intermediary phase is characterised by displacement because, in this phase, the otherwise steady surety of our hermeneutical involvements is interrupted, and we find ourselves without the resources to understand, to grasp and deal with the matter.

Yet, in an individual occurrence of understanding, at least whenever such events are successful, displacement proves to be only an intermediary phase. For, Gadamer maintains, in a third phase, understanding is renewed. This renewed understanding results from a process of mediation, by which we work through our prejudices, that is, by which we reflect on our prejudices, deepen our understanding of their meaning, and reconsider their appropriateness to the matter under consideration. Here, Gadamer argues, our renewed understanding is transformative. He writes: 'understanding is not, in fact, understanding better . . . It is enough to say that we understand in a *different way, if we understand at all.*'[25] It is true that the renewed understanding, which results in this third phase, is not wholly other than the accessibility granted initially by the fore-structure of prejudice. No understanding arrives *ex nihilo*, completely unprepared, as if it were a flash of inspiration or epiphany; even when understanding is achieved through the disavowal of an initial prejudice, it remains dependent not only on that prejudice *via negativa*, but on other, as yet unrevealed prejudices. Gadamer nevertheless maintains that the renewed understanding is genuinely different from the access granted by our initial prejudices. In this, the renewed understanding involves, first, a transformation of our initial prejudices about the matter, from which we had been hermeneutically displaced. This is because renewed understanding results from a process of mediation that takes shape in reinterpretation, reconsideration and potentially even rejection of the validity of initial prejudices. He argues that this renewed understanding of a matter, is, second, indexed to a transformation in our understanding of ourselves. In this claim, it becomes evident just how much Gadamer's approach to understanding is guided by concern for the hermeneutics of facticity. For, as he suggests, the process of mediation, by which we attempt to grasp a matter, not only reminds us *that* we are constituted more by our prejudices than by our judgements but also leads us to reflect on *how* specific prejudices thus determine who we are, as well as to reconsider whether our concern for our being is exhausted by such a determination of ourselves.

Even as he argues that the renewed understanding of this third phase is transformative, however, he nevertheless also suggests that it represents a supersession of displacement. For, in an individual occurrence of understanding, at least whenever such an event succeeds, this success results from a process of mediation, by which the strangeness of a matter hermeneutically displaced is worked through, so that, however transformed our understanding is, the matter appears, once again, in familiarity.

Gadamer's elucidation of hermeneutical experience, when considered only through the narrow aperture of an individual occurrence of understanding, indeed lends itself to the criticism that he gives too little truck to exteriority. With this narrow approach, his account leaves the impression that while the event of understanding is occasioned by exteriority, our exposure to this exteriority is only provisional, ultimately to be superseded by a renewed, even if different, familiarity. Gadamer, however, also considers hermeneutical experience, and, so too, its logic of dialectic, from the wider perspective of the whole of factical life as it is lived through continual attempts to understand and interpret. With this shift to the larger perspective of the whole of factical life, displacement proves to be not merely an intermediary phase of an event of understanding, but definitive of hermeneutical experience as such. Gadamer's concern for the perspective of the whole of our factical lives suggests that displacement is definitive of hermeneutical experience in at least two interrelated regards.

The perspective of the whole of factical life suggests that displacement is definitive, first, because of the surplus, surfeit or excess of exteriority that characterises hermeneutical experience. Life, insofar as it is lived hermeneutically, takes shape in continual attempts to understand and interpret. Because every attempt to understand and interpret is conditioned by the fore-structure of prejudice, each begins in an authority of prejudices that, in an intermediary phase, turns out to be invalid. Yet, from the wider viewpoint of life, the achievement of a renewed understanding in a third phase is not so much a conclusion of an individual event of understanding as it is the preparation for a further event of understanding. In this, the renewed understanding leaves us right where we started, given over to the fore-structure of prejudice, the authority of which will, always and again, prove to be just as invalid as it has before. From the wider viewpoint of life, then, understanding and interpretation are bound up with displacement not merely as a provisional obstruction, but, more to the point, as the continual reminder of facticity, and, accordingly, a continual exposure to exteriority that cannot ever be mastered.

The perspective of the whole of our factical lives suggests that displacement is definitive, second, because this continual exposure to exteriority provides the recurrent impetus for hermeneutical experience. For Gadamer, the hermeneutical life is not lived in the stretches in which the accessibility granted by our prejudices suffices for us to grasp the situations we are involved in, others or texts. Although we are, of course, certainly still alive in these stretches, they are not lived hermeneutically because we are not confronted with the task of understanding and interpreting but, instead, carry on in absent-minded familiarity. Life becomes hermeneutical, always and again, whenever we are confronted with something that brings this familiarity into question: an unexpected insecurity about a carefully cultivated ability of ours, a surprising response from an old friend to a new shared experience, or a line from a text read many times that now appears unintelligible. Life, insofar as it is lived hermeneutically, takes shape not in the stretches but in the shifts; Gadamer, with William James, suggests that 'life is in the transitions as much as in the terms connected; often, indeed, it seems to be there more emphatically . . .'.[26] From this larger viewpoint of life, then, the continual exposure to exteriority is not merely a provisional obstacle to the satisfaction of a desire to understand. Rather, this continual exposure proves to be the abiding impetus for us always and again to undergo transformative understanding, to understand ourselves, and the matters we are involved with, differently.

Horizonal Displacement

Gadamer's consideration of hermeneutical experience from the perspective of the whole of our factical lives, then, brings into focus the definitive role played by displacement in that experience. Accordingly, his concern for the wider viewpoint of life is of important consequence for our grasp of a number of the central concepts he develops in order to expand and deepen his elucidation of hermeneutical experience. Of these concepts, perhaps none puts into starker relief the difference that Gadamer's concern for the whole of factical life makes than his claim that hermeneutical experience involves a 'fusion of horizons'.[27] For many critics, Gadamer's notion of the 'fusion of horizons' has become an emblem of his reduction of the displacement involved in our exposure to exteriority to a provisional, intermediary phase of hermeneutical experience. Yet, as I wish to show, when considered from the viewpoint of Gadamer's concern for the whole of factical life, his notion of the fusion of horizons actually underscores the definitive role that is played in hermeneutical experience by displacement.

Gadamer introduces the notion of the fusion of horizons in *Truth and Method* to deepen and expand on his view that understanding, in that it is conditioned by the fore-structure of prejudice, remains always historically effected.[28] In his account, he builds on the definition of the notion of horizon, which he associates especially with Nietzsche and Husserl, as a larger context of meaning that stakes out the possibilities and limits for specific meanings within that larger context to become apparent. He writes:

The horizon is the range of vision that includes everything that can be seen from a particular vantage point. Applying this to the thinking mind, we speak of narrowness of horizon, of the possible expansion of horizon, of the opening up of new horizons, and so forth. Since Nietzsche and Husserl, the word has been used in philosophy to characterize the way in which thought is tied to its finite determinacy, and the way one's vision is gradually expanded.[29]

According to Gadamer, we find ourselves always already with a horizon – itself always a matter of prejudices that have been historically inherited – that shapes the possibilities and limits of our relation to ourselves, the situations we find ourselves in, and the matters we encounter. Gadamer maintains, however, that horizons are not to be understood as closed systems but rather as more or less coherent arrangements of meaning that are thus able to accommodate the introduction of new meaning or link into other arrangements of meaning. He writes:

A person who has no horizon does not see far enough and hence overvalues what is nearest to him. On the other hand, 'to have a horizon' means not being limited to what is nearby but being able to see beyond it. A person who has an horizon knows the relative significance of everything within this horizon, whether it is near or far, great or small. Similarly, working out the hermeneutical situation means acquiring the right horizon of enquiry for the questions evoked by the encounter with tradition.[30]

In every situation, we find ourselves within horizons that give orientation to our hermeneutical encounters, typically for Gadamer, encounters with texts and others. But, it is not as if these encounters involve two discrete, closed systems of meaning – one that belongs to 'me' and one that belongs to the 'other'. It is not as if understanding involves only that we 'transpose' ourselves, as it were relinquishing our horizon in favour of the horizon of the other. Rather, in such encounters, one finds that the situation is permeable, and admits of multiple possible horizons. Hermeneutical experience, therefore, takes shape as a process by which our horizons are interpenetrated by other possible horizons of the situation, such as those of a text or person, so that horizons infuse one another to the point of fusion, which reveals that a more 'universal', or, as it may also be put, encompassing horizon had already been in the offing when the hermeneutical encounter began.[31]

To be sure, Gadamer's notion of the fusion of horizons, considered through the narrower aperture of an individual event of understanding, may seem only to reinforce the impression that he fails to give enough due to the insuperability and irreducibility of displacement. Considered from the viewpoint of an individual event of understanding, the fusion of horizons appears simply to represent the supersession of a provisional disorientation that accompanies the diffusion of one's own horizons as they interpenetrate and are interpenetrated by other horizons.

Parenthetically, before moving forward with the argument, we should pause to note that Gadamer's approach to the 'fusion of horizons' clarifies the anxiety of disorientation that results from the diffusion of one's horizons, even when considered from the viewpoint of an individual event of understanding. This anxiety is very real, and existentially significant. Gadamer's notion of the disorientation involved in the diffusion of one's horizon is reminiscent of Nietzsche's celebrated description of the erasure of a horizon through the purported death of God. This Nietzschean example may seem to be an extreme one. While some of our horizons are as profound as those concerned with a belief in God, not all of them are. Yet, the anxiety of disorientation revealed by this extreme may nevertheless also form a basis for grasping the lesser anxiety of disorientation felt when less profound horizons become diffuse. In a famous passage, Nietzsche expresses the anxiety of disorientation felt with the loss of horizon of belief in God through the voice of a 'madman'. The madman suggests that the loss of this horizon 'unchained this earth from its sun', leaving him to ask 'Whither is it moving now? Whither are we moving? Away from all suns? Are we not plunging continually? Backward, sideward, forward, in all directions? . . . Do we not feel the breath of empty space . . .?'[32]

Gadamer, as we have said, does not believe that all of our experiences of displacement are as profound as the one that Nietzsche treats. But, his account, like Nietzsche's, suggests that the diffusion of one's horizons involves an anxiety of disorientation because it leaves us, even if temporarily, without a measure; it leaves us uncertain about which way is up and which is down. Given Gadamer's idea that our horizons are comprised of prejudices as these are historically inherited and adopted, he stresses that this disorientation is, crucially, the detachment from tradition. Even so, as critics might point out, if his notion of the fusion of horizons is grasped only from the narrow viewpoint of an individual event of understanding, this disorientation appears only to be a provisional interruption that yields to reorientation.

Gadamer's concern for the perspective of the whole of factical life, by contrast, brings into focus that even the notion of the fusion of horizons speaks to the definitive role that his account grants to displacement. Considered from the perspective of life that is lived hermeneutically, the fusion of horizons signifies not simply the completion of an individual occurrence of understanding, but clarifies the larger dynamic of hermeneutical experience. Gadamer suggests that the hermeneutical life concerns the expansion of horizons. Although, as we have seen, he disavows the Enlightenment pretence of knowledge that is freed from prejudice, he nevertheless maintains that we may become more reflective and judicious in the context of meaning that comprises our prejudices through the pursuit of extensive and variable hermeneutical experiences. In this, he emphasises the importance of hermeneutical experiences of tradition, characteristically texts inherited from the past, as encounters with such texts provide an especially intensive possibility to become reflective about our prejudices.

Based on his concern for the expansion of horizons, Gadamer's notion of the fusion of horizons not only refers to the coalescence of an encompassing horizon in the completion of an individual occurrence of understanding, but, moreover, clarifies that the hermeneutical life takes shape in the continual loosening of our horizons through the infusion of meaning from other horizons, in particular, horizons of past life. With this, the hermeneutical life concerns not simply the establishment of horizons that will provide an orientation for our lives, but a movement that oscillates always and again between orientation and disorientation, fusion and confusion. He writes: 'The historical movement of human life consists in the fact that it is never absolutely bound to any one standpoint, and hence can never have a truly closed horizon.'[33] Accordingly, as he develops this idea a few pages later, 'in a tradition, this process of fusion is continually going on, for there old and new are always combining into something of living value . . .'.[34] From the viewpoint of our factical lives as a whole, Gadamer's notion of 'fusion' points above all to a dynamic that entails not only fusion, but also infusion, diffusion, confusion and fusion again. While this dynamic is suggested by the family that surrounds the English root word 'fusion', it is perhaps captured even better by the German word that 'fusion' translates, *Verschmeltzung*. In German, the word derives from the verb *verschmelzen*, which means to fuse, to merge, to amalgamate. But, as especially the root *schmelzen* makes apparent, the word connotes that such fusion takes shape as a process of melting together. Accordingly, we may venture, Gadamer's notion stresses that the fusion of horizons concerns the continual challenge of dissolution, the continual heating, softening and liquefying that allows for our prejudices to become permeable and combine in novel manners. Life, as Gadamer's notion of the fusion of horizons indicates, calls neither for the rigidity of certitude, nor for the conceit of technical mastery, nor even for the will to exhaustive comprehension, but, rather, for the capacity always and again to soften, to allow our prejudices to become more fluid and to commingle in novel manners.

Variations of Displacement

Gadamer's concern for life remains underappreciated, and, indeed, this is at least in part because he leaves the notion of life underdeveloped. It is perhaps also because of this that his elucidation of hermeneutical experience remains susceptible to criticisms. There can be little doubt that Gadamer believes the viewpoint of the whole of factical life to be decisive for his elucidation of hermeneutical experience; as we have seen, he identifies concern for life as the motivation of Heidegger's development of his hermeneutics of facticity, which Gadamer, in turn, treats as a basis for his own treatment of hermeneutical experience. There can also be little doubt that Gadamer invokes the notion of life throughout his considerations of hermeneutical experience. Yet, despite the significance of his concern for life, and his repeated return to the theme, his treatment of the notion remains less a fully developed account than a provocative suggestion.

If Gadamer's concern for the whole of our factical lives is thus as significant for his considerations of hermeneutical experience as it is underdeveloped, the hermeneutical import of the theme of life has not, however, been entirely overlooked. Quite to the contrary, some of the most significant recent developments within post-Gadamerian hermeneutics have taken their point of departure from the perspective of life and the accent this perspective affords to displacement. Indeed, current research in hermeneutics is also distinguished by several figures who have developed Gadamer's concern for the larger viewpoint of life in distinctive directions, offering novel perspectives on the definitive role played in hermeneutical life by displacement.

One of the most significant Anglophone contributions to recent discussion is James Risser's *The Life of Understanding: A Contemporary Hermeneutics*. In this work, Risser develops what he calls a 'contemporary hermeneutics after Gadamer' on the basis of the 'hermeneutical insight . . . that understanding is inseparably tied to the life situation'.[35] Risser maintains that 'factical life',[36] the life lived hermeneutically, may be grasped at least in part as a form of convalescence, for which, however, there is no cure. He argues that the life of understanding, as a life of continual hermeneutical experiences, is conditioned by memory, which he defines as the recovery of meaning from tradition, and by language, which he identifies as the weaving, albeit the threadbare weaving, of such meaning. He claims that the life of understanding is a form of convalescence because, in its dependence on memory, such life is not homeostatic but rather chronically in need of the recovery of meaning from tradition, as such meaning has either been forgotten or become hidden in its very familiarity and obviousness. Yet, in the life of understanding, this chronic need of recovery is never overcome. This life, as a form of convalescence, admits of no cure.[37]

Donatella di Cesare, by contrast, in her recently translated *Utopia of Understanding: Between Babel and Auschwitz*, argues that in the hermeneutical life displacement takes shape as a utopian impulse. Despite the impression that her use of the term 'utopia' may leave, however, she does not mean that hermeneutical experience arrives at an absolute horizon of understanding to supersede all horizons. Rather, her notion of 'utopia' hews closely to the etymological sense of the word as 'not a place' or a 'no place' at which, as she maintains, we are never able to arrive. She suggests that hermeneutical experience is utopian in the sense that our pursuit of understanding never results in the completion of actual understanding but, rather, remains always only possible as still to come. Thus, she suggests that life, insofar as it is lived hermeneutically, turns on a form of displacement, in which hermeneutical experience is guided by an aim – the completion of actual understanding – that such experience is nevertheless, in principle, unable to reach. For di Cesare, the definitive role played in hermeneutical life by displacement means that this life bears a fractured, even exilic relation to tradition and language.[38]

The hermeneutical theme of life, and the displacement that characterises it, is also treated by Günter Figal in his recent *Objectivity: The Hermeneutical and Philosophy*. Figal maintains that human life, as hermeneutical, is indexed to objectivity. By this, however, he does not mean that human life is to be guided by the methods and standard practices of the modern natural sciences that we have come to associate with the notion of objectivity. Rather, as we have seen, Figal's approach comes into focus in reference to connotations of the German word translated here as 'objectivity', namely, '*Gegenständlichkeit*'. Thus, human life is oriented by the exteriority of 'something that one himself is not', by 'something that stands over against [*entgegen steht*] and, because of this, places a demand'.[39] Yet, as Figal argues, the objectivity of whatever we encounter as objective is inexhaustive; thus, on his view, we find ourselves always and again oriented toward the objectivity of something which we can never reduce to a fully comprehended and masterable object. Figal's elucidation of the hermeneutical significance of objectivity is systematic, and, indeed, has become the impetus for further enquiries into artworks, taken as an epitome of the conspicuousness of objects, and recently, of inconspicuousness. He maintains, in any case, that human life takes shape in continual reflective conduct that strives to achieve an equilibrium, or a rapprochement with whatever appears to us in its objectivity. In this, human beings are called to take measure for their conduct not from their own wills, from their own prejudices and interests, but instead from the orientation provided by what stands over against them in its inexhaustive exteriority. Thus, Figal's approach suggests that human life, as hermeneutical, takes shape in the unending effort to relate to, adjust to and deal with the displacements brought about by our encounters with what is not our own.

The Capacity for Displacement

The approaches to the theme of life developed by Risser, di Cesare and Figal not only stand as significant developments in their own right for the philosophical study of hermeneutics, they also give voice to the richness for further enquiry of this theme and, with it, of displacement. Gadamer's concern for the hermeneutical life, even if it offers less a fully formed position than a positive suggestion, nevertheless recommends that hermeneutical experience is ultimately to be grasped in ethical terms. As we have seen in the previous chapter, Gadamer disavows that the ethical demands placed on us in our hermeneutical experience can be addressed in advance by any ethical theory, system, code or pre-given principles. He maintains that the ethical demands placed on us in hermeneutical experience call for us to exercise and develop what he describes in post-metaphysical humanistic terms as a capacity to converse. Now, with Gadamer's concern for the whole of our factical lives in view, we are in a position to recognise that this capacity is, above all, a capacity for displacement.

Gadamer elucidates the belief that the hermeneutical life demands such a capacity for displacement with the example of one who has achieved this capacity through expansive and varied hermeneutical experiences – the 'experienced person'.[40] His description of this exemplary figure opposes the ideal of epistemic certitude and technical mastery that are today often associated with the image of the natural scientist or expert; Gadamer's example is characterised, rather, in terms of readiness for and openness to what is incalculable, unmasterable. It is, accordingly, reminiscent not only of motifs of the humanist tradition but, especially, of Aristotle's notion of the one with practical wisdom, the *phronimos*. Gadamer introduces the example of one who has the capacity for displacement in order to clarify the ethical consequences of the fact that hermeneutical experience is guided by a logic of dialectic. He maintains, as we have seen, that hermeneutical experience takes shape not as a positive accretion of knowledge through a 'logic of induction', but, on the contrary, as a dialectical process. In this dialectical process, our self-understanding, as well as our understanding of the situations, others and texts we are involved with, increases through the negation of our prejudices as these involvements prove them to be invalid. Yet, given that this dialectical process is unending, hermeneutical experience never concludes in absolute self-transparency, epistemic certitude or technical mastery, but, on the contrary, always and again proceeds to further displacement. Accordingly, as Gadamer maintains, 'the perfection that we call "being experienced"'[41] – or as we might also put it, the virtue or excellence of being experienced – is not a matter of acquiring knowledge and expertise that would bring all perils of further displacement to an end. On the contrary, it is a matter of intensifying our openness to and readiness for such displacement. He writes:

The experienced person proves to be . . . someone who is radically undogmatic; who, because of the many experiences he has had and the knowledge he has drawn from them, is particularly well equipped to have new experiences and to learn from them. The dialectic of experience has its proper fulfillment not in definitive knowledge but in the openness to experience that is made possible by experience itself.[42]

Gadamer's concern for the whole of our factical lives leads him to the ethical consideration that the excellence of such a life is its openness to what brings our prejudices into question, what loosens our horizons, and what thus, in turn, allows always for new interpenetration and fusion with other horizons. Gadamer's larger concern for life also suggests that, ethically, what matters most in hermeneutical experience is not only or even foremost what we have called the third phase of events of understanding, the renewal of understanding from out of displacement. For, although this third phase comprises the completion of an individual event of understanding, the excellence of a life lived hermeneutically depends on the range and depth of the encounters we have had with the second phase of hermeneutical experience, displacement. For Gadamer, the ethical demand of the hermeneutical life is not to acquire knowledge but to be open and ready, and this openness and readiness can only be won through a deep and abiding acquaintance with displacement.

Gadamer, finally, recognises that the life of the person of experience – one who has achieved a capacity for displacement – leads not only to an openness and readiness for more displacement but also to what may be described as a tragic sensibility about hermeneutical experience. This is because, with the capacity for displacement that comes through expansive and varied hermeneutical experiences, one is exposed to the fact that every experience is punctuated by a phase of painful disorientation and confusion. In this, Gadamer observes, the one who has achieved a capacity for displacement has thereby come to see the wisdom of the Aeschylean dictum that human beings learn through suffering (*pathei mathos*).[43] He writes: 'experience is the experience of human finitude. The truly experienced person is one who has taken this to heart.'[44] Gadamer's concern for our factical lives as a whole suggests that the stakes of hermeneutical experience are greater than any individual supersession of displacement. The hermeneutical life, rather, circulates entirely within the prospects for growth and the inevitability of pain that arise from such displacement.

PART II: I AND THOU

3 Things

As we have seen, Gadamer's attempt to advance the ontological turn in hermeneutics promises an original possibility for the philosophical study of ethics, one that rehabilitates the weightiness of responsibility experienced by us in factical life. This is a responsibility to understand. But, as we have seen in Part I, such responsibility is not first of all a responsibility to seek out and achieve mutual understanding or agreement with others. Rather, the responsibility to understand calls for us to cultivate and enact a capacity for displacement. The purpose of Part II is to examine the contours of this capacity for displacement in terms of what Gadamer calls practical relations of 'I and thou'. These contours concern the capacity to be displaced in our intimate, everyday affairs. Yet, the scope of the role that this capacity plays in our intimate, everyday relations is not fully captured by Gadamer's construal of the 'I and thou'. Whereas Gadamer leaves the impression that 'I and thou' relations are restricted to encounters with other persons (or texts), the displacement at issue in our intimate, everyday affairs in fact also extends to encounters with other kinds of being. These include, for example, encounters with things and animals as well as other persons and texts.

The purpose of the present chapter is to examine the responsibility to understand that is at issue in our interactions with things. This is a topic not typically addressed within the philosophical study of ethics. However, as I wish to show, even our intimate, everyday interactions with things confront us with hermeneutical demands.

As we shall see, our interactions with things demand that we displace our prejudice to subjugate things to our subjective wills, instead enacting and cultivating the capacity to 'correlate' ourselves with them as they are in their respective being.

Gadamer suggests that the hermeneutics of facticity is what Husserl would call a 'correlation', but one that extends beyond the transcendental subject's relation with itself to things.[1] Now, Gadamer himself will not develop the responsibility at stake in such correlation with things in any detail. Thus, in order to develop the possibility of responsible correlation with things, we shall consider two views closely related to Gadamer's concerns. In the first section of this chapter, we shall focus on some of Heidegger's reflections on things to develop the sense of displacement at issue in our intimate, everyday relations with them. Heidegger's approach suggests that such displacement takes shape as what he calls 'letting-be' (*Gelassenheit*). In the second section, we shall focus on what I will call an addendum to Heidegger suggested by Figal's recent hermeneutical realism. Figal, reading both with and against Heidegger, suggests that the achievement of correlation between human life and thing is ultimately made possible by the exteriority of what we encounter. In the final section, I will argue that responsible correlation is best grasped as a dialectical movement of displacement that oscillates between letting things be and exposure to their exteriority. In this, responsible correlation is a living back-and-forth, one that calls for us to appreciate things even as they time and again exceed and even resist our projects.

Factical Life, or, Correlation with Things

As Gadamer observes, the 'ontological turn' in hermeneutics is achieved through Heidegger's discovery of the hermeneutics of facticity. Heidegger recognises that existence itself is hermeneutical, a matter of understanding and interpretation of the situations into which we find ourselves thrown. In this, however, Gadamer argues that the need for Heidegger to introduce the hermeneutics of facticity is discernible already from an ambiguity found in Husserl's notion of the 'life-world'. For Husserl, phenomenology reveals that rigorous knowledge of the human condition is not reducible to claims made about human beings in the sciences, but originates in lived experience. Yet, paradoxically, Husserl maintains that our experience of the life-world is itself a phenomenological correlation grounded in transcendental subjectivity. For Gadamer, this paradox 'threatens to burst the framework' of Husserlian phenomenology.[2] For, as the very idea of life suggests, correlation is not grounded in the transcendental subject, but in the facticity of things that makes all experience possible in the first place.[3]

Gadamer, in *Truth and Method*, turns first of all to Count von Yorck in order to develop the notion of life as correlation. Yet, it is really with Heidegger that the question of correlation with the facticity of things is brought fully into focus. Heidegger, as we know, maintains that the relation to being is definitive of the being of existence. For us to exist means to belong to being, and to take our measure for our existence from being. Thus, in his own way, Heidegger stands among the philosophers who reject the position of figures such as Protagoras, for example, that 'man is the measure of all things'.[4] Heidegger, however, does not reduce fundamental being itself to the status of a being, such as, say, a Platonic idea. Accordingly, he does not reduce the measure of existence to the normative implications of such a being. Rather, he believes being is an event, always contingent and thus singular, and that we only ever encounter being as the being of *something*. Thus, moreover, we encounter the measure of our existence in our involvement with such a something.

Heidegger, in fact, upholds that our exposure to the event of being and the measure it provides can occur through our involvement with numerous kinds of beings. In several writings, for example, he stresses that our encounters with artworks (when these encounters are successful) make accessible the being of whatever they bring into focus and make valid.[5] With nearly as much emphasis, however, Heidegger also suggests in several writings that we may be exposed to being through our involvement with what he simply refers to as 'things'.[6] Scholars such as Walter Biemel have suggested that Heidegger's consideration of things undergoes important transformations over the course of his philosophical career.[7] Be that as it may, it can in any case be said that Heidegger's concern for being leads him to maintain an abiding concern for our relation to things over the entire arc of his life. He thereby stresses that our relation to being is at stake not only in our encounters with the works of great poets and artists – though, certainly, he recognises a special kinship between being and art – but also and crucially in the nearness of things in our everyday lives.

Heidegger's conviction, then, is that our belonging to being and the measure it provides for existence is at once profound and quotidian. He draws this point out in the 'Letter on Humanism' in an important discussion of Aristotle's report of foreign visitors who went to meet with Heraclitus. Heidegger takes up Aristotle's report to clarify the stakes of Heraclitus' celebrated dictum, *ēthos anthrōpōi daimōn*. Heidegger's concern, as we recall, is more specifically to open a path to a more original ethics though a consideration of the sense of the word *ēthos*, itself the etymological origin of the word ethics, on the basis of Heraclitus' use of the word *ēthos* in his dictum. Thus, if Gadamer's concern for the responsibility to understand can be grasped as a response to Heidegger's call for an original ethics, then this concern must, building on Heidegger, also address precisely our relation to things.

Heidegger ties the question of Heraclitus' dictum to our relation with things in his recounting of Aristotle's report. As he puts this in the context of the 'Letter', 'the word names the open region in which man dwells. The open region of his abode allows what pertains to man's essence, and what in thus arriving resides in nearness to him, to appear.'[8] That what appears in nearness are first of all things is brought out for Heidegger by Aristotle's report. Heidegger cites the relevant passage from Aristotle's *Parts of Animals*:

The story is told of something Heraclitus said to some strangers who wanted to come visit him. Having arrived, they saw him warming himself at the stove. Surprised, they stood there in consternation – above all because he encouraged them, the astounded ones, and called for them to come in, with the word, 'For here too the gods are present.'[9]

As Heidegger interprets Aristotle's report, the foreign visitors are astounded because 'they believe they should meet the thinker in circumstances which, contrary to the ordinary round of human life, everywhere bear traces of the exceptional and the rare and so of the exciting'.[10] Yet, the visitors discover just the opposite. 'Instead of this', Heidegger states, 'the sightseers find Heraclitus by the stove. That is surely an insignificant place.'[11] For the visitors (Heidegger calls them sightseers!), this proves to be a 'disappointing spectacle'.[12] As Heidegger stresses, Heraclitus' invitation for the foreign visitors to enter, and in particular his final pronouncement, suggest the contrary. Here, for Heraclitus, *ēthos* is nothing else than our dwelling as this appears in such 'insignificant', familiar places. Moreover, such intimate, everyday settings are characterised by our likewise quotidian involvement with the things that we find in such familiar haunts. Heidegger states, 'χαί 'ενταῦθα, "even here", at the stove, in that ordinary place where every thing and every circumstance, each deed and thought is intimate and commonplace, that is, familiar [*geheuer*], "even there" in the sphere of the familiar, εἶναι θεούς, it is the case that "the gods come to presence"'.[13] For Heidegger, our relation to being, while weighty, is not first of all a matter of the rare, the extraordinary or the exciting. Rather, even if we are astonished by this fact, our relation to being is precisely in the context of ordinary life, in familiar haunts, in our involvement, or correlations, with everyday things.

Yet how, more precisely, are we to understand our relation to being as this comes through in our intimate, everyday correlation with things? Heidegger's idea is that we achieve a relation to being when we involve ourselves with the thing *qua* thing. This means that we participate in an event by which a world (or, as this may be put perhaps too cursorily, a context of meaning) gathers together so as to enact the thing, allowing it to come into presence and remain present for a while as what it properly is. From this standpoint, the being of a thing does not appear as the cause of the thing or as something that underlies it; neither, then, does the thing appear as something merely present, whether this is grasped as a substance with properties, a bundle of what is sensuously given, a composite of form and matter, or otherwise.[14] Rather, our access to and thus relation with being takes shape as the culmination of a movement that brings out certain possibilities of the context of meaning we find ourselves in, putting them into relation and making them actual, so that they coalesce to convey something into presence in the first place. In this event, both world (context of meaning) and thing *result* in the presence of a thing, but are not themselves merely present; they are, together, the movement by which something comes into presence and remains present for a while. In order to stress the point, Heidegger assigns a strong verbal sense to both world and thing that would have been captured in ancient Greek with the middle voice. In the event of being, he tells us, 'the *world worlds*' and the 'the *thing things*'.[15]

Heidegger argues that this event, by which a thing is enacted, must be understood as a whole round of activity. In his celebrated essay, 'The Thing', he observes that the complexity and dynamism of this event may be discerned in the etymological origins of the modern German '*Ding*' and in the Old German words '*thing*' and '*dinc*'.[16] These words signified 'affair', or 'matter of pertinence', and are related to the notion of a 'case'.[17] Heidegger believes that, grasped properly in light of the event by which it comes to be, the thing takes on the sense found in these older words. The thing is an affair in the sense that it is not something simple or static but rather a progression comprised of multiple and often intricate relations, activities, twists and turns. The thing is a case not only in the sense that an affair may itself be taken to be a case, but, moreover, because the movement that comprises such an affair is always unique. Things, as Heidegger suggests, do not admit of commonalities that would allow us to see them as a class of particulars; they are, rather, singular, and so must be understood on a case-by-case basis.

In 'The Thing' and elsewhere, Heidegger attempts to elucidate the event by which the thing is enacted under four aspects, or, as he calls this, 'the fourfold'.[18] Heidegger's elucidation of the fourfold is difficult, not least because it also brings into focus the subtlety and layers of his engagements with Hölderlin. As Andrew Mitchell stresses, though, Heidegger introduces this idea above all to get at 'the utter relationality of worldly existence'.[19] Heidegger describes the event that allows something to be enacted as a convergence, intersection or gathering of interrelated folds within which all beings make their appearance – namely, earth, sky, divinities and mortals. Elucidating the significance of each of these in detail is beyond the scope of this chapter,[20] but what can be drawn from Heidegger's introduction of the fourfold, for our purposes, is the insight that the event by which a thing is enacted is comprised not only as a unique constellation of relations and contexts, but, in this, also by ontological multiplicity, and thus richness and concretion.

Crucial, in any case, is Heidegger's stress on the claim that this event does not simply allow the thing to come into presence and remain present, but to come into presence and remain present as what it *properly* is. This event, whether it is cast in terms of the fourfold, or as an affair or a case, may therefore be understood as appropriative.[21] The event transpires so as to bring into effect those aspects of the context of meaning that allow the thing to come into presence and remain present for a while. At the same time, the event leaves out of effect those aspects that would stultify or even stop the thing from coming into presence as what it properly is. Heidegger says that the event of appropriation that succeeds in allowing the thing to be enacted thus allows the thing to exist in its 'independence', and, trading on the German word for independence, *Selbstständigkeit*, he describes a thing in its independence as something that 'stands on its own', or is 'self-supporting'.[22]

Heidegger recognises that our exposure to being is not guaranteed by things, however. Quite to the contrary, he dedicates much attention to the possibilities of involving ourselves with things precisely so as to foreclose the access to being that our correlation with them might otherwise offer. Although Heidegger's examination of the possibilities of such foreclosure is nuanced, he describes such foreclosure, in part, in terms of correlations that diminish the independence of the thing. In this, he focuses on correlations that reduce things first to objects and then to what he calls standing-reserve.

Heidegger maintains, first, then, that we foreclose access to being through the reduction of correlation, such that things no longer appear in their being independently but, instead, are reduced to 'objects'.[23] He believes that research in the modern sciences is typified by the tendency to reduce things to objects; in a rather dramatic passage, we recall, he asserts that scientific knowledge, though 'compelling within its own sphere, the sphere of objects, already had annihilated things as things long before the atom bomb exploded'.[24]

Heidegger argues that we disregard the being of a thing when we represent it as an object and, thus, as he suggests, 'annihilate' it *qua* thing. As he develops his concerns in his writings on Ernst Jünger, his 'Bremen Lectures', the Nietzsche volumes and elsewhere,[25] the tendency of the modern sciences to reduce things to objects is bound up with a certain metaphysics of the will. Here, our disregard for the being of things – for what they are on their own terms and, thus, how they are properly to be treated – enables us to run roughshod over the measure they may provide for our lives and conduct, instead pressing them into the service of whatever our wills urge. To disregard the being of a thing in this manner means to detach ourselves from the event that would otherwise allow the thing to enact itself. This displaces the thing from the event that had sustained it, replacing the fullness of meaningful relations that comprise it with the much more impoverished relation of subject and object. This detachment, Heidegger suggests, takes shape above all as a compression of the temporality of our encounter with things into mere presence. When we comport ourselves properly to the event that allows a thing to show itself, we find ourselves involved in a larger course of relations; when, on the other hand, we treat something merely as an object, it is reduced to standing across from us in mere presence, devoid of any robust relationality.[26]

Heidegger's contrast between a proper correlation to things as 'independent' and a reductive relation to things as 'objective' is evoked again here by the original German words used. Our proper correlation to things allows a larger context of meaning to be brought into focus by our involvement with a thing that stands on its own, *selbstständig*. By contrast, the correlation to things in objectivity is reductive, taking shape not through a larger complex of meaning that brings something into focus on its own terms, but rather through a truncation of that larger context that results in an restricted, bivalent relation of subject and object – that is, a correlation that posits a subject, on the one hand, and the thing as an object, something over and against, on the other, *gegenständlich*.[27] Here, what remains is something that we stand across from and against, not in a richness of involvements, but instead in the opposition of an impoverished, detached presence.

Heidegger, secondly, expands on his concern that we turn away from being as it unfolds through our correlation with things in his celebrated discussions of modern technology.[28] Here, we recall, he suggests that common ideas of technology as a human activity or as a means are derivative of the ontological significance of technology taken as a mode or manner of revealing.[29] He maintains that technology, as a form of what the Greeks called '*poiēsis*', is originally a manner of knowing or understanding; it is a manner of bringing a thing forth (*Hervorbringen*) that allows it to come into being as what it is.[30] Yet, he suggests, in turn, that *modern* technology is itself a perversion of technology in this original, Greek experience of it. Heidegger captures this idea with his celebrated claim that modern technology does not allow things to be brought forth as they are but distorts them through 'enframing' (*Gestell*). Although his elucidation of 'enframing' is subtle and nuanced, he means, first of all, that modern technology frames things out in advance in a manner that precludes us from the experience of them as things in their independence.

Heidegger, once again, refines his point through the connections among the German words he chooses to use. Technology in the original Greek sense reveals things, as we have said, in that it simply *brings* them forth as they independently are, *hervorbringt*. Technology in the modern, distorted sense, by contrast, frames our correlation to things out in advance, and, indeed, in such a manner that does not simply *bring* things out as they are but is a 'challenging' of them, *Herausfordern*.[31] Here, the German suggests that modern technology does not just bring things out, but demands of them that they come out. In view of this, Heidegger argues that modern technology allows neither for a correlation with a thing in its independence, as something that stands on its own or by itself, nor even for a reductive correlation to the thing as an object, as something that thus stands across and against. Instead, within the frame of modern technology, our relation to things is reduced to that of a standing-reserve of commodities or resources (*Bestand*).[32] Here, things are reduced always to something that is able to be quantified with common metrics and is determined, exclusively and in advance, in terms of instrumentality. Thus, when framed out by modern technology, our correlation to things does not allow things to stand on their own or by themselves independently, *selbstständig*, nor even allow things to stand at least as objects, *Gegenstände*, across or against. Rather, under modern technology, our correlation with things reduces them to something that simply stands there, as *Bestand*, ready for instrumental deployment. With this, everything is reduced to a sort of purely instrumental *materiel*, always already 'set in order', that is, always already subjected to quantification, exploitation, distribution and exchange.[33]

Heidegger contends that modern technology, like modern science, is typified by the tendency to turn a blind eye toward the event that would otherwise allow a thing to be enacted. Yet, he believes, modern technology may be said to represent an advanced stage of our turn away from being in favour of our own wills. For, although modern science wrests a thing from the larger context of meaning and event that would allow for a correlation with what it properly is on its own or by itself, even once the thing is thus treated as an object it nevertheless retains at least a trace of its independence. The reduction of a thing to an object retains a trace of independence insofar as an object continues to stand against, to resist our efforts to grasp, manipulate and control it. In modern technology, the reduction of our correlation to things goes even further: 'Whatever stands by in this sense of standing-reserve no longer stands over against us as object.'[34] Here, all pretences of the independent being of the thing are covered over.

One of Heidegger's important concerns in this context is that once the measure granted by being through our correlation with things gets washed over to this degree, nothing remains to orient us except our wills – a *will-to-will*.[35] Our wills increasingly become the arbiter of our correlations with all we encounter, reducing everything to mere fodder for our inclinations and desires.

But, what, precisely, does Heidegger believe it takes for us to enter into correlation with a thing as it properly is, and, indeed, thereby circumvent the modern tendency to subjugate things to our wills by treating them as objects or a standing-reserve? How, in short, does Heidegger believe we come into proper correlation with things? He comes to identify this proper correlation perhaps more than anything else with what he calls releasement or letting-be (*Gelassenheit*). The access we may be granted to the event of the being of a thing – that is, what allows a thing to come into presence and remain present for a while as what it properly is, in its independence – requires that we let it be.

The challenge Heidegger poses with this idea, as Bret Davis argues, is to grasp the relation of letting-be neither as a will not to will nor even as a specific or special manner of willing but, instead, as a relation to things that is otherwise than all of the forms or modes of willing.[36] Heidegger thus asks us to think of letting-be as something otherwise than the will not to impose our will on a thing, a mere abnegation of the will that leads us to disengage from the thing and become indifferent toward it. On the contrary, Heidegger thinks that to let a thing be is to involve ourselves with it in a special manner: in letting a thing be, we do not as it were leave it alone out of respect; rather, we look over it, tend to it, so as to bring it out into the open and bring it to bear in our situation as what it properly is. At table, for example (of course, everyone familiar with Heidegger's essay on 'The Thing' will recall that this is his example), we let a jug be not by ignoring it, but by allowing it to come into presence and remain in presence as something that allows us to share wine or water there. This means, among many other things, that we allow it come into presence and remain in presence as something that helps to enact the conviviality and even community in the use we make of it to pour wine or water for those with us.[37] Heidegger's use of the term *Gelassenheit* is highly nuanced.[38] But in this context his idea is perhaps drawn into special focus by the family ties between the German words for involving ourselves with something and letting something be. To involve oneself, in German, is *sich einlassen*; to get involved with something properly, Heidegger's German suggests, requires that we attend to the thing in letting it be what it is, in *Gelassenheit*.[39]

Heidegger, then, suggests that we conceive of letting-be otherwise than as a specific or special form or mode of the will. If letting a thing be is a matter of getting involved in a certain manner, this getting involved is not a wilful activity. Rather, letting-be must be a manner of correlation with things that holds out and stays with them as it were on their own terms.[40]

Objectivity Reconsidered

Heidegger's consideration of letting-be illuminates an important dimension of our proper correlation with things. Yet, taken on its own, Heidegger's approach is incomplete. His account can leave the impression that we experience things in their exteriority only when correlation with them is improper and they resist us due to being treated as objects or a standing-reserve. But such mistreatment does not seem to be the only reason that we experience things in their exteriority, since it is also the case that things resist us even when they are treated properly. This, at least, is the recent proposal from Günter Figal's hermeneutical realism. For Figal, such a relation to a thing can transpire, for example, when the beauty of a thing exceeds and therefore interrupts all technological enframing, so that even 'in the midst of technology and the technologically influenced world, it is possible to take a stand instead of allowing oneself to be pulled forth by the possibilities opened by technology'.[41] For Figal, this can also happen in our practical affairs that lead us to involve ourselves with things. In such affairs, we are sometimes caught out by what we take the possibilities of a thing to be. We go to open the stove door, and we are surprised that the door sticks; we do not yet realise that the rusted hinge requires us to wiggle the handle in order to open it; or, we are taken off guard by the sudden memory of an older parent's arthritic hand unable to open the door just as we are unable to now. Despite every familiarity, we can be surprised by any number of ways in which the thing can thing.

The exteriority of things we experience in our intimate, everyday practical affairs is the focus of this chapter. This exteriority is brought into focus, in particular, by Figal's considerations of objectivity. His approach contributes to our examination of the capacity to be displaced by things an important addendum to Heidegger's call for letting-be.[42] Figal first of all follows Heidegger's idea that to live properly or fully is to involve ourselves with things in their independence – genuinely to come into correlation with them – and not to subjugate them to our wills. He thereby also follows Heidegger's conviction (or, at least, the later Heidegger's conviction) that our very possibility for correlation with things depends on an openness that allows them to enact themselves and not on our ability to subject them to our purposes.[43] One of Heidegger's names for the achievement of this openness is, as we have seen, letting-be. Yet, Figal emphasises that letting-be, though it is a manner in which we comport ourselves to things, is ultimately dependent on precisely the 'objectivity' of the things we involve ourselves with.[44] Now, with his introduction of this notion of 'objectivity', Figal initiates a discourse that diverges from Heidegger's. For Figal, 'objectivity' refers first of all to the exteriority that accompanies our encounters with things: in our involvement with them, they always retain an excess of the context of meaning to which they otherwise belong and through which they enact themselves. Figal thus suggests that there is a 'more' of things that remains as it were in wait, latent, even as it allows them to enact themselves as what they properly are.

Figal, here, obviously develops the term 'objectivity' in manner different from Heidegger; in terminology familiar to us from Gadamer, he refers to his approach as a 'rehabilitation' of objectivity.[45] On the one hand, Figal, like Heidegger, trades on the connotations of the German word for 'objectivity', *Gegenständlichkeit*, as the character of something that stands in opposition or over against. Yet, on the other hand, in contrast to Heidegger, he indicates that the tendency of modern science to reduce things to objects represents a merely derivative sense of these connotations. Indeed, in order to signify this derivative sense of objectivity, Figal sometimes uses the Latinate *Objektivität*.[46] He maintains that the more originary sense of objectivity – *Gegenständlichkeit* – bespeaks the exteriority of whatever we encounter.

Figal suggests that this rehabilitation of objectivity not only forms the basis for a critique of modern science and technology but, moreover, that it has a 'critical edge' against consanguineous philosophical tendencies as well.[47] He thus holds that his rehabilitation helps to expose 'that modern philosophy as a whole appears as a large-scale enterprise of de-objectification'.[48] His basic claim is that much of modern and especially late nineteenth and early twentieth-century philosophy turns on a desire to reject any final significance of exteriority. 'To this enterprise', as he puts it, 'belong the different notions of increased dynamism and of fluidity, which wish to admit nothing that is steadfast, standing on its own, and which wish to displace everything into movement.'[49] He thinks that philosophers as diverse as Nietzsche and Wittgenstein contribute to this enterprise. But, he suggests, it takes shape especially in two central patterns of modern thought: in dialectical thinkers, such as Hegel, Marx and Simmel, who typically interpret objectivity as a form of alienating objectification; and in figures associated with phenomenology, such as Husserl and Heidegger, who typically interpret objectivity in terms of an objective presence that conceals living relations.[50]

Figal's rehabilitation of objectivity, however, not only complements Heidegger's critique of modernity but also has implications for our understanding of the independence of things. Figal, no less than Heidegger, believes that it is only because of our openness to things that they may come into presence and remain present for a while in their independence. Yet, there is an important difference of emphasis between them. Heidegger, for his part, underscores that our possibility to enter into correlation with something in its independence requires something of us – namely, that we comport ourselves properly to it, letting it be instead of subjugating it to our wills. Figal would not disagree. He does, however, stress that our prospects for correlation with a thing in its independence concern more than letting the thing enact itself as what it is. Rather, he believes that to come into correlation with a thing in its independence is to expose ourselves to its exteriority. His idea may be elucidated in terms of a distinction he initially makes in a different context between enactment (*Vollzug*) and reference (*Bezug*).[51] We come into correlation with a thing in its independence not through our involvement in an event by which the thing is *enacted*, but when we stand in a *referential* relation to the thing in light of its 'accessibility' or availability (*Zugänglichkeit*) for being enacted in the first place.[52] For Figal, then, our correlation to the independence of a thing is not first of all a matter of the (always contingent) *actualisation* of what it properly is; instead, this correlation with a thing in its independence turns on the thing's excess of *possibilities* – that is, those possibilities that remain exterior to the context of meaning to which the thing belongs and in which it can become actual. Since the possibilities of the thing also mark its limits, Figal's idea is that correlation with a thing in its independence turns not only on how we properly comport ourselves to a thing in our involvement with it, but, more originally, on possibilities that the thing itself can properly admit of or abide.

While Figal takes up the question of our correlation with things in their independence in several contexts, the connection he draws between this correlation and the availability of things comes perhaps most readily into focus in his discussion of practical action. In practical action, he observes, we often conduct ourselves in accord with a plan, and, as he puts it, 'to plan means: to project possibilities, and this, in turn, means: to think of schemata for action and to arrange individual steps of action as well as to connect and coordinate various schemata of action with one another'.[53] He notes that if our plans require us to come into correlation with things – as they characteristically do – then it is not enough simply to let them enact themselves. Rather, we must also first consider things in their availability, whether they are suited to our plans, and, if so, which ones and how – and, if not, how we must change our plans to accord with their possibilities and limits. As may be familiar to us from our own conduct, and as Figal notes, our correlation with things in their independence often comes into view precisely when we have failed to appreciate them in their availability, that is, when 'something resists, something does not submit to use or something gets in the way as a hindrance'.[54]

Figal, then, conceives of our correlation with things in their independence in a somewhat different manner to Heidegger. Certainly, both Heidegger and Figal suggest that correlation with a thing in its independence is a matter of involving ourselves with the thing in terms of its own possibilities. But they characterise this relation to possibilities in different ways. Heidegger, for his part, thinks of our correlation to a thing in terms of its own possibilities as a matter of enactment – for him, we correlate with a thing in its independence when we let it be, which means that we involve ourselves in the event by which it enacts itself in the right way. Figal, by contrast, thinks that our correlation to a thing in its own possibilities is matter of reference – for him, we correlate to a thing in its independence when we refer ourselves to the excess of the thing's possibilities from out of which we might involve ourselves in its enactment at all.

Responsibility Toward Things

If Gadamer aligns the project of philosophical hermeneutics with the notion of life as correlation, then Heidegger, and in turn Figal, both shed light on the possibility of a proper correlation with things. For both of them, if in different manners, our lives are defined in no small part by the possibility of a proper correlation with things, allowing them to appear in their independence of us and taking them as a measure for our own conduct instead of relating to them improperly by subjugating them to our wills through the rationalities of modern science and technology. In this, both recognise, in different ways, that our lives always take place amidst things and, moreover, are shaped by involvements with them – from our simplest involvements, such as Heraclitus' warming himself by the stove, to the multiplicity of our obsessions with them and our sanctifications, exploitations and destructions of them.

Figal's proposal, as we have seen, takes shape as an at least partial objection to Heidegger's. In this, Figal suggests that our correlation to things in their independence is a referential relationality that stresses the exteriority of things from the contexts of their enactment. For him, it would seem, this represents a more phenomenologically adequate description of our correlation to things in their independence than Heidegger's account of our correlation with things in their independence through letting-be. Yet, we may suggest, treated under the auspices of Gadamer's hermeneutical consideration of life as correlation, Figal's approach appears not so much as an objection to Heidegger as an addendum to Heidegger's account.

From this point of view, Figal's concern for the exteriority of things and Heidegger's concern for letting-be identify reciprocal aspects of our responsible correlation with things in their independence. For, with Figal, we may agree that to come into correlation with a thing in letting-be first requires that we have encountered the thing in its exteriority. Yet, in counterpoint, we might also reaffirm, with Heidegger, that our correlation with a thing in its exteriority only comes fully into focus in consequence of our involvements with things in which we let them be. This description, though circular, has nothing vicious about it. On the contrary, it helps to capture the hermeneutic circularity of properly living with things. To relate properly to a thing is neither simply to comport ourselves to it in a certain manner nor to become exposed to its exteriority, but, rather, to take part in a movement that circulates in both letting-be and exteriority; it is to involve ourselves with a thing in the oscillation or back-and-forth between both of these.

In living responsibly with things, then – that is, in coming into correlation with them in their independence and not subjecting them to our wills – letting a thing be and being exposed to its exteriority may be understood to condition one another. First, as we have seen, Figal suggests that to comport ourselves to a thing properly in letting it be requires that we already be exposed to its exteriority. In letting a thing be, we involve ourselves in the event by which it enacts itself. But, as Figal believes, it is only possible to come into correlation with a thing in this manner if we involve ourselves with it in light of the fact that its possibilities to be enacted exceed the context of meaning that allows it to enact itself. In order to involve ourselves with the event by which a thing enacts itself, we must already have a sense for the availability of the thing. Yet, it may equally be said that our correlation to a thing in its exteriority requires that we comport ourselves to it in letting it be. For, it is only insofar as we first involve ourselves in the event by which a thing enacts itself that any concern about its availability comes into focus. Unless it is our concern to let a thing be, to allow it to enact itself in its independence, there is no impetus for our correlation to the exteriority of a thing to come into play in the first place.

The repeated circularity involved in living responsibly with things, then, is hermeneutic and not vicious. The correlations with things under consideration in this chapter – that is, relations in which we come into correlation with things in their independence – are, *per definition*, rarely if ever casual or transitory. Rather, it is part and parcel of such relations that we become familiar with a thing, even intimately acquainted with it, as no doubt Heraclitus was with the stove that kept him warm in his home. But, this kind of correlation does not characteristically occur all at once: it unfolds as part of the larger movement of factical life. It requires, first, that we involve ourselves with a thing so as to let it be. Yet, no matter how open we are to it, the exteriority of the thing inevitably puts up resistance against our efforts to treat it as it is. This resistance, in turn, confronts us with the exteriority of the thing and requires of us that we consider it in its availability before we further involve ourselves with it. And, so on – back-and-forth – for however long our involvement with the thing lasts: we comport ourselves to it so as to let it be until it resists us, and this, in turn, exposes it in its exteriority and leads us to consider it in its availability until, once again and anew, we let it be.

4 Animals

Gadamer, as we have seen, aligns the responsibility to understand with an affirmative rehabilitation of motifs from the humanist tradition. Indeed, he encapsulates this responsibility with the entreaty to 'elevate' ourselves into our 'humanity' through the enactment and cultivation of our 'capacity for conversation'. Yet, this hermeneutical entreaty concerns much more than our relations with other humans alone. In the previous chapter, for example, we saw that it concerns even our intimate, everyday relations with things. Now, in this chapter, I wish to show that this entreaty moreover concerns our interactions with animals.

Building on important but understated themes in Gadamer, I argue that the responsibility at issue in our interaction with animals comes into focus as a question of *belonging (Zugehörigkeit)*.[1] We have already seen that Gadamer develops the notion of 'belonging to tradition', and, further, the hermeneutical experience of language, as part of his attempt to 'concretise' Heidegger's early hermeneutics of facticity. Here, Gadamer's notion of belonging will be taken up in the context of his ontological considerations of the human and animal. On the one hand, Gadamer's position indicates that human belonging is distinguished from that of animals by the hermeneutical experience of language. He will, however, describe this distinction as a specific or relative, not an absolute, difference. On the other hand, Gadamer's approach will allow us to suggest that the characteristically human, hermeneutical experience of language is itself based in a mode of enactment that is shared by humans and animals alike. This, as we shall see, is the enactment of *play*.

Accordingly, the responsibility at issue in our interactions with animals requires us to displace the polarity of two extreme prejudices about animals – which, as extremes, may be called the Scylla and Charybdis of our hermeneutical experiences of animals. First, this responsibility requires that we displace the increasingly common prejudice that humans and animals are, for all relevant intents and purposes, ontologically compatible. As Gadamer's consideration of the hermeneutical experience of language will indicate, the being of human beings is distinguished by participation in historically transmitted language, and, with this, is bound up with the transmission of world-disclosive written texts, paradigmatically religious, juridical and literary texts. Yet, at the same time, our responsibility toward animals likewise requires us to displace the opposite, 'anthropocentric' prejudice of an absolute ontological divide between human and animal. For, as Gadamer's approach suggests, the ontological distinction of human and animal is itself only relative, a difference in continuity, underlain by the commonality that the being of both human and animal is enacted in play.

Displaced from this polarity of extreme prejudices about animals, we make ourselves available for an interaction with animals that respects difference and recognises our common belonging together with animals within a world, or, if not a world, then at least the shared space opened by our respective participation in play.

In Chapter 1, we saw that Gadamer's entreaty for us to elevate ourselves to our humanity through the enactment and cultivation of the capacity for conversation is part and parcel of his attempt to develop a 'curious', because post-metaphysical, humanism. Now, we see that the consequences of such a 'curious' humanism for our interactions with animals are themselves every bit as curious. Typically, within the humanist tradition, the entreaty for human beings to elevate themselves into their humanity is at the same time a call for human beings to detach themselves from any animal nature. Thus, the humanist tradition not only re-inscribes the anthropocentric prejudice of an absolute ontological divide between human and animal but, moreover, purports to establish the normative superiority of human being over animal being. With Gadamer's 'curious' humanism, by contrast, the entreaty for human beings to elevate themselves into their humanity is a call for us to recognise our difference-in-continuity with animals, and, with this, to pursue responsible interactions made available in the space opened by that difference-in-continuity. To Gadamer's mind, the entreaty to elevate ourselves into our humanity does not aim at our separation from other kinds of beings. Quite to the contrary, for him, to elevate ourselves into our humanity is to increase our capacity for displacement and, thereby, to allow ourselves to become involved with all kinds of beings, including animals.

Gadamer's curious humanism thereby also brings into focus the novelty of his approach toward animals among major figures within continental European philosophy. This possibility of a Gadamerian contribution to the question of animals has largely been overlooked in the literature, other than by Alain Beauclair. As Beauclair observes, 'Contrary to contemporary critiques of logocentrism and its alleged tendency to inscribe, codify, and rigidify certain metaphysical concepts, Gadamer offers a phenomenology of language that seeks to unravel these prejudices'; accordingly, 'Gadamer's analysis powerfully articulates humanity's potential for inhabiting a shared world'.[2] Gadamer's curious humanism, in any case, first of all brings into relief his contrast with Heidegger. Heidegger, we recall from his 'Letter on Humanism', disavows the tradition of humanism because he believes every humanism is an essentialism. Yet, as many scholars have observed, in his 1929–1930 lecture course, *Fundamental Concepts of Metaphysics: World, Finitude, and Solitude,* Heidegger draws a distinction between humans and animals that appears to reinscribe the human/animal divide that typifies that same humanist tradition. Heidegger, we recall, maintains that while human beings are 'world forming', animals are rather 'poor in world' (and, as he goes on, inorganic beings are 'worldless'.)[3] Moreover, as we know, figures such as Jacques Derrida and Giorgio Agamben have, if for different reasons and in different manners, each questioned Heidegger's distinction.[4]

Gadamer, however, will neither fully reject nor fully accept Heidegger's distinction. On the one hand, his approach will broadly align with Heidegger's claim that human beings are 'world-formative'. Heidegger's claim is based on the conviction that human beings are distinguished by the disclosedness of existence made possible through their participation in language – that, for human beings, language is 'the house of being'. Gadamer, notwithstanding the differences between his and Heidegger's considerations of language, will also claim that human beings are distinguished from animals by their participation in language. On the other hand, though, in Gadamer this claim does not lead to a reiteration of any absolute human/animal divide. For, as we shall see, our participation in language is, more originally, participation in an experience that is common to both humans and animals:

that of play. Thus, for Gadamer, humans are distinct from animals, but not absolutely different; in our experience of animals, as in all herme-neutical experience, we are confronted with something in between strangeness and familiarity.

Belonging and Language

Philosophers as diverse as Derrida and Kelly Oliver have incorporated into their enquiries about animals testimony of their own intimate, everyday experiences of animals – and, in the case of both, in fact, tes-timony of their experiences of their cats.[5] The specific question of com-mon human and animal belonging is perhaps also brought into sharp relief, however, in testimony given by Annie Dillard of an intimate, everyday encounter with an animal while walking in a forest near her home. Just after sunset, while leaning against a tree, she looks down and is surprised by a weasel just next to her:

The weasel was stunned into stillness as he was emerging from beneath an enormous shaggy wild rose bush four feet away. I was stunned into stillness twisted backward on the tree trunk. Our eyes locked, and someone threw away the key.

Our look was as if two lovers, or deadly enemies, met unexpectedly on an overgrown path when each had been thinking of something else: a clearing blow to the gut. It was also a bright blow to the brain, or a sudden beating of brains, with all the charge and intimate grate of rubbed balloons. It emptied our lungs. It felled the forest, moved the fields, and drained the pond; the world dismantled and tumbled into that black hole of eyes. If you and I looked at each other that way, our skulls would split and drop to our shoulders. But we don't. We keep our skulls. So.

He disappeared. This was only last week, and already I don't remember what shattered the enchantment . . . He vanished under the wild rose. I waited motionless, my mind suddenly full of data and my spirit with plead-ings, but he didn't return.

Please do not tell me about 'approach-avoidance conflicts'. I tell you I've been in that weasel's brain for sixty seconds, and he was in mine.[6]

Dillard's testimony of her encounter is, to say the least, rich in impli-cation. It raises any number of matters – metaphysical, epistemo-logical, ethical and perhaps also spiritual. Among the many matters, though, it also raises the question: how far does our sense of belong-ing extend? In referring to the locked eyes between her and the weasel, to the 'enchantment' that followed, and in asserting that she had 'been in that weasel's brain for sixty seconds, and he was in mine', Dillard suggests that our sense of belonging extends not only to other human beings but also to the animals among which (or whom?) we find ourselves – or, at least, that our sense of belonging can extend to the animals in extraordinary moments. How can we interpret such testimony?

Certainly, many, maybe even most, contemporary philosophers would remain sceptical of Dillard's account. Perhaps some of the most obvious scepticism would be from those, such as Thomas Nagel, who might object that Dillard's testimony is misleading because human beings cannot inhabit the mind of a weasel, that we cannot know what it is like to be a weasel.[7] Yet, such scepticism may in truth be a symptom of a more encompassing alienation. From this viewpoint, the contemporary philosophers' scepticism of Dillard's claim of 'enchantment' is more accurately a symptom of their own disenchantment about our possibilities for belonging. Since the Age of Goethe at least, many major figures of continental European philosophy and literature have argued that modernity has resulted in a condition of what the early Hegel simply calls 'division',[8] in which we experience the severance of our belonging not only with nature, but with our fellow humans, and even with ourselves.[9] Within this modern context, we are told that it is a fallacy – a 'pathetic fallacy' – to presume any form of common belonging that would entitle us to ascribe human experiences to animals or other non-human beings.

But, what if we remain sceptical of such scepticism? What if we treat the scepticism as a symptom of modern alienation, and instead take Dillard's testimony at face value? What does this testimony tell us about whether, and, in turn, to what extent, our sense of belonging is shared in common not only with humans but also with animals?

It is not at all irrelevant to these questions that Gadamer, in his celebrated 'Universality of the Hermeneutic Problem', introduces his conception of philosophical hermeneutics first and foremost as a response to what he calls 'experiences of alienation' that confront us in our 'concrete existence'.[10] Accordingly, Gadamer builds on Heidegger's questioning of modern science and technology, some of which was discussed in the previous chapter. And, thus, both Gadamer and Heidegger can be associated with the tradition of continental European philosophy since the Age of Goethe concerned with modern alienation.

In this, Gadamer may be said to recognise the increasing prevalence of our experience of alienation since the inception of the revolution in science and technology in seventeenth-century Europe. Although Gadamer does not elucidate the legacy of this revolution explicitly in 'The Universality of the Hermeneutic Problem', the broader contours of his concerns are familiar. The hallmark of this revolution is the ascendancy of the modern interpretation of reason as instrumental. Under this modern interpretation, reason is no longer understood in reference to language as the disclosedness or accessibility of being. Instead, reason is grasped in reference to the will as a calculative instrument for the measurement, manipulation and transformation of nature. For Gadamer, like Heidegger before him, the ascendancy of this modern interpretation results in the experience of alienation because it distorts and obscures our originary relation to language. As the modern interpretation of reason as instrumental has come to take on global proportions and encroach ever further into our concrete existence, our experience of ourselves, the world and other beings becomes ever more alienated.

Gadamer indicates in his 'Universality of the Hermeneutic Problem' that such experiences of alienation are epitomised by and coalesce around our loss of a sense of beauty and of history in particular.[11] He thus suggests that, together, these experiences of alienation clarify that and how modernity has robbed us of our sense of belonging. Gadamer, we recall, elucidates our experience of alienation from beauty in terms of what he calls 'aesthetic consciousness'.[12] No doubt taking inspiration from Kant, he maintains that the experience of beauty shows us that we belong in the world. Yet, his conception of the experience of beauty no doubt owes more debts to Heidegger, Hegel and Plato. Gadamer suggests that works of art, insofar as they deserve the name, are characterised by beauty. He identifies the experience of beauty first of all with the captivation that artworks can hold for us, and, in turn, believes that this captivation is a testament to the authority of a claim to truth made on us by the artwork about the world. Thus, on Gadamer's view, the experience of beauty is at the same time an experience through the artwork of the hold that this truth claim about the world already has over us even before we begin to think about it or judge it. In aesthetic consciousness, he maintains, we are alienated from this original hold that the truth claim made by an artwork has over us. In this, the experience of beauty in artworks is an epitome of the hermeneutic experience of beauty more generally.[13] Gadamer describes aesthetic consciousness as a derivative form of consciousness, in which we take ourselves to have a sovereign authority to accept or reject an artwork based on its 'expressive power and validity'.[14] He writes:

> The consciousness of art – the aesthetic consciousness – is always secondary to the immediate truth-claim that proceeds from the work of art itself. . . . This alienation in aesthetic judgement always takes place when we have withdrawn ourselves, and are no longer open to the immediate claim of that which grasps us.[15]

Under the auspices of aesthetic consciousness, our relation to artworks is derivative, becoming reduced to an instrument that allows us to measure and assess. The more that this form of consciousness prevails, however, the more we become alienated from the experience of the original hold that the truth claim made by an artwork has over us, and, thus also, the belonging to which this original hold speaks.

Gadamer elucidates our experience of alienation from tradition in terms of what he calls 'historical consciousness'.[16] By historical consciousness, Gadamer has in mind the attitude of objectivity or critical distance that characterises not only the nineteenth-century intellectual movement of historicism but also and more broadly the modern attitude about the past. Whereas this form of consciousness is often celebrated for its conformity with the norms and methods of the modern sciences, Gadamer argues that it is nevertheless alienated because it calls for epistemological independence from the very traditions that in any case sustain all of our understanding and interpretations. As Gadamer puts the point, 'Historical science . . . expresses only one part of our actual experience – our actual encounter with historical tradition – and it knows only an alienated form of this historical tradition.'[17]

Gadamer's attempt to 'concretise' Heidegger's hermeneutics of facticity is, in part, also an attempt to clarify our prospects for recovery from the modern experience of alienation epitomised by aesthetic and historical consciousness. Gadamer, as we have seen, argues first of all that our experience of facticity is concretely to be grasped as a matter of 'belonging to tradition'. With this, he maintains that understanding and interpretation are historically effected, that is: the achievements of understanding and interpretation are never fully liberated from reliance on meaning that has been inherited from the past but, on the contrary, remain always effects of such inheritance. In virtue of this, all achievements of understanding and interpretation are made possible by prejudices and remain prejudicial. But, as we have also already seen, Gadamer further 'concretises' belonging to tradition in terms of the hermeneutical experience of language. In this, we recall, he argues that belonging to tradition is itself experienced as the hermeneutical belonging of being and truth. This more original belonging of being and truth takes shape in specific, concrete pursuits of understanding as these occur in individual experiences of language (for example, individual hermeneutic interactions, conversations or text interpretations).

Gadamer, then, indicates that the prospect for recovery from modern alienation depends on a form of belonging that is made concrete through participation in tradition, and this, in turn, thanks to the hermeneutical experience of language. The question all but suggests itself: does Gadamer's consideration of the prospect for recovery re-inscribe the anthropological prejudice of an absolute ontological divide between human and animal? After all, Gadamer hangs the hat of our prospect for recovery on an experience of language, the phenomenon that, more than any other in the Western tradition of thought, has always served as a marker of the ontological divide between human and animal. Is Gadamer's consideration of the prospect of recovery part of this dubious legacy? If so, the dark irony would also be hard to miss – Gadamer's position on the prospect of human *recovery* from modern alienation would prove to be a claim that trades on the *alienation* of humans from animals through the anthropocentric prejudice.

Indeed, if anything, Gadamer's hermeneutics involves a notion of language that looks as if it demarcates humans from animals more robustly than many theories of language. This is because hermeneutics focuses on a possibility of language that appears to colour human existence as much as it remains insipid in animal life.[18] By now, we are familiar with the fact that some animals, indeed many, engage in a variety of linguistic activities. But Gadamer focuses on the possibility of language to shape the world, or context of meaning, as this is passed down historically in occurrences of linguistic enactment such as conversations and text interpretations. Moreover, he observes that this possibility of language to shape the world itself reaches a certain summit in the experience of the *written text*.

Gadamer develops what he calls a 'hermeneutical perspective' on the written text in essays such as 'Text and Interpretation' and 'On the Truth of the Word'. For him, this hermeneutical perspective is concerned not with grammar or linguistics but rather with what the written text says.[19] Accordingly, the hermeneutical perspective focuses on interpretation, and it comes into play whenever 'the meaning-context of what is fixed in writing is disputable and one needs to attain the correct understanding of the tidings in the document'.[20] Thus, from a hermeneutical perspective, it is ultimately the need for interpretation that distinguishes what a written text is in a strict sense, and, moreover, clarifies that this need for interpretation defines what a written text is.[21] He writes: 'Accordingly, we must say that a text is not an object but a phase in the fulfilment of an event of understanding, of a *Verständigungsgeschehen*.'[22] For Gadamer, experiences of language are concrete occurrences of the transmission of tradition that shape, or can shape, the world; in the interpretation of a text, this occurrence takes shape in reference to a written text, grasped not as something that as it were stands over and against us, but rather as something that enables the historical transmission of meaning.

Yet, in this, even as such a 'phase' of interpretation, the written text is nevertheless also something that stands on its own. In 'On the Truth of the Word', Gadamer argues that the '"authentic" word'[23] is exemplified by the written text. By the 'authentic word', he means the form language takes when the truth claims made in it are able to endure. He writes of the 'authentic word' that it embodies 'the distinguishing characteristics that make a word truly "a word": that *it stands* and that one *stands by it*. Obviously this already contains the idea that the word, along with what it says or does in saying, making a lasting claim to be valid.'[24] He argues that the 'authentic word' is exemplified by the written text because, in such texts, something is said whose claim to validity abides. In conversation, what is said can make a claim to validity, too, but what is said disappears no sooner than it is spoken. In the written text, by contrast, what is said makes a claim to validity that remains and, insofar as the written text is such in the strict sense, so, too, the need to interpret the claim remains as well.

Indeed, Gadamer argues that written texts cannot be grasped reductively as transcriptions of actual or possible oral conversations. In conversations, the horizon for understanding is comprised by the present interpretive situation, in all of its historical, practical and other dimensions. In the interpretation of texts, by contrast, this horizon of understanding includes not only the present interpretive situation and those of the historical period of the written text; it can also include the horizon carried forward by the written text itself. He states:

> In writing, the openness that is implied in seeking the words [in oral conversation] cannot be communicated because the text is written. Therefore a 'virtual' horizon of interpretation and understanding must be opened in writing the text itself, a horizon that the eventual reader has to fill out. Writing is more than fixing something spoken in writing.[25]

From the hermeneutical perspective, it is ultimately as a phase of interpretation that the written text is to be grasped. Yet, within this context, the written text is nevertheless also something that endures, remaining available beyond any one reading, and thus allowing us to return time and again to what it says, not only in the claim that it makes, but even in the horizon for understanding and interpreting this claim.

Gadamer brings into focus the possibility of the interpretation of written texts to shape the world in his attempt to clarify what a written text is in the 'eminent' sense. For Gadamer, written texts, as texts, comprise what he refers to as an '*Aussage*', a German word that can be translated as declaration or statement.[26] But, for Gadamer, *Aussage* refers to what a text says, including the 'virtual horizon' it as it were carries with it. He suggests that eminent texts are distinguished from other kinds of texts by the autonomy of the interpretive enactment and, thus, the transmission of the *Aussage* they contain. He believes that eminent texts are most exemplified by literary texts, and clarifies his position through a tripartite distinction he draws between 'the religious, the juridical, and the literary text'.[27]

Gadamer argues that religious texts, such as the Hebrew Bible and the New Testament, contain an *Aussage* as a 'promise' (*Zusage*).[28] But, the authority of the promise – as, namely, the putative author who authorises the promise, God[29] – is grasped as exterior to the text. In view of this, the text's promise cannot be enacted and thereby transmitted through interpretation of the text alone. He writes: 'in the *Zusage* language goes beyond itself. In the Old Testament or the New Testament, the promise does not fulfill itself in just being made . . . a promise in a way finds fulfillment in its acceptance in faith – as indeed every promise becomes a promise only if it is accepted.'[30] Gadamer, in turn, holds that legal texts, such as the formulation of a law or a juridical verdict, contain an 'announcement' (*Ansage*).[31] Here again, however, the authority – this time, the legal authority – of the text is exterior to the text. Gadamer observes that we sometimes personify the authority of the law in phrases like 'in the name of the Law . . .'.[32] What comes to expression in such turns of phrase is that the legal authority of the law depends on something outside of the text, whether a magistrate, judge or, as this can be conceived in republican governments, the citizenry or populous. So, in the case of the legal text, too, its enactment and thereby its transmission cannot be achieved through the text alone. Gadamer writes, 'a juridical text, formulating a law or a judgment, is binding as soon as it is enacted, but it is fulfilled as enacted not in itself but in being carried out or enforced'.[33] The enactment and thereby the transmission of religious and legal texts are not fully autonomous but rather dependent on authorities outside the text.

Things are different, Gadamer argues, with the literary text. For Gadamer, poetry is perhaps the epitome of the literary text, but he believes that the literary *Aussage* appears in different forms, such as 'the poetic word, the speculative sentence of the philosophers, and the basic logical unity of the predicative judgement'.[34] What distinguishes the literary text, in any case, is that no external authority is required for the enactment and thereby transmission of its *Aussage* and, with this, the 'virtual horizon' needed for its interpretation. To be sure, Gadamer understands that such texts have authors. But, in the case of literary texts, it is not the author (in familiar parlance, it is not the 'author's intent') that as it were authorises an enactment and thereby a transmission of the text. Rather, it is the text's *Aussage*. Referring to the authorities of written texts as 'ideal speakers', Gadamer writes:

one may note that there is a wide variety of ideal speakers: there is the one who makes a *religious* promise to you, or the one who speaks to you in the name of the *law*, or . . . Yet at this last 'or' one hesitates, one is brought up short. Should we really say: 'those who as poets speak to someone'? Would it not be more appropriate if one only said that *the poetry speaks*?[35]

The only authority requisite to interpret a literary text, Gadamer argues, is the text itself. In this, the transmission of a literary text turns not on any external authority, but only on repeated interpretations.

Gadamer's considerations of the eminent text are, of course, significant for a number of reasons. For the purposes of the present chapter, however, we recall that Gadamer associates our prospects of recovery from modern alienation with the possibility of language shaping the world as this is passed down historically through participation in understanding and interpretation. Moreover, as we now see, this possibility of language finds definitive expression in the interpretation of written texts, such as religious, legal and literary texts. Indeed, in the case of what Gadamer calls the eminent text – namely, the literary text – this possibility of language to shape and pass down the world is encompassed by the resources of the text as such. Yet, in view of this, Gadamer's vision of our recovery from modern alienation turns on what seems to be an especially human experience of language. After all, the interpretation and transmission of written texts appears, at least, to play a much more important role in human linguistic activities than in those of animal life.

Human and Animal Play

Do Gadamer's considerations of our prospects for recovery from modern alienation, then, turn on a hermeneutical experience of language that re-inscribes an absolute ontological divide between human beings and animals? Does Gadamer's very conception of belonging, which is made possible by these considerations of language, at the same time attest to our apartness from animal and other beings born of the earth? I believe that the answer to these questions is 'no'. It is true that Gadamer's considerations bring into question the opposite prejudice that humans and animals are, for relevant intents and purposes, ontologically the same. His account of the definitive role played in human life by the enactment and historical transmission of written texts, I think, brings this prejudice into question. Yet, neither is his account a new iteration of the old anthropocentric prejudice of an unbridgeable ontological gap between human and animal. That Gadamer's account charts a course between this Scylla and Charybdis comes into focus through his recognition that the human difference from animals – namely, humans' participation in hermeneutic experiences such as text interpretation and transmission – is itself bound up in a continuity with animal life. For Gadamer, the continuity of the human participation in such experiences of language and animal life is *play*.

Gadamer treats the notion of play in a number of contexts within his philosophical hermeneutics. No doubt, his most extended treatments appear in his examinations of the hermeneutical experience of art,[36] but the notion of play is also important for his hermeneutical considerations of language. This becomes evident perhaps especially in his *Truth and Method* discussion of what he calls the 'speculative structure' of language.[37] This discussion is significant not only because it represents a culmination of his considerations of language within *Truth and Method*, but also because it centres on a hermeneutical experience of language that he squarely associates with the literary text, namely, the 'speculative sentence of the philosophers'.

Gadamer's claim, in any case, is first of all that in the hermeneutical experience of language, matters are presented through a movement which, as the etymology of the word 'speculative' indicates, involves a relation of reflexivity or back-and-forth mirroring.[38] Gadamer clarifies the speculative character of our hermeneutic experience in reference to Hegel's notion of the speculative sentence.[39] As he reminds us, Hegel contrasts the speculative sentence with sentences that predicate something of something else. In predicative sentences, the copula expresses a relation between a concept in the subject position and something else, another concept in the predicate position. In speculative sentences, by contrast, the copula expresses a movement of negation, in which the concept in the subject position is not related to something else, but, instead, comes to be explicated. As Gadamer puts it, a speculative sentence 'does not pass over from the subject-concept to another concept that is placed in relation to it; it states the truth of the subject in the form of the predicate'.[40] This reflexive, mirroring relation of the speculative sentence finds an example in the sentence, 'God is one'.[41] In this sentence, the copula does not relate the concept of God to another, distinct concept. Rather, it unfolds the concept of God, expressing that intrinsic to God is that God is one. Here, our understanding of the concept of God is expanded not through the connection of the concept of God to another concept, but through a reflexive, mirror relation, in which the subject is reflected upon itself in novel terms.

Gadamer believes that all hermeneutical experience of language involves the reflexive, mirror relation at issue in Hegel's notion of the speculative sentence. Crucially, however, he maintains that in the hermeneutical experience of language, this reflexive relation admits of no end point or closure. In this, he diverges from Hegel's view (or, at least, a view commonly attributed to Hegel) that speculation ultimately allows the subject of a speculative sentence to be definitely (or 'absolutely') reflected back on itself. Accordingly, in our hermeneutical experience of language, our attempt to reflect a matter back on itself does not work toward a final destination but rather remains ultimately suspended in play. For Gadamer, all of our attempts to reflect matters back on themselves are conditioned by prejudices, since such prejudices are given by our factical situatedness. But our attempts are not therefore determined by prejudices; rather, they involve 'leeway'.[42] As Gadamer makes the point in reference to the aspect of Hegel's approach to language he wishes to retain, this leeway is granted by 'the way language playfully determines thought . . .'.[43] For Gadamer, it is precisely this playfulness of language that characterises our attempts to reflect something back on itself, so that 'the finite possibilities of the word are oriented toward the sense intended as toward the infinite'.[44] In the hermeneutical experience of language, our attempts to understand and interpret are speculative, and this means participation in a playfulness of language that allows us always and again to approach the being of a matter, that is, its infinity of interpretive possibilities, without conclusion.

If Gadamer maintains that human life is defined in no small part by the hermeneutical experience of language, then this experience is itself characterised by a form of play. Yet, he holds that it is not only this definitely human experience of language that involves play. So too does animal life. In his hermeneutical considerations of life, Gadamer is cognizant of research in animal behaviour that blurs received distinctions between human and animal, and, in this, he resists what he refers to as 'the dogmatic Cartesian philosophy of self-consciousness'[45] that, as we know, underwrites Descartes' conviction that human life is bound up in an ontological order completely alien to animals. Really, Gadamer can be understood to take his point of departure rather from an Aristotelian gesture that human and animal belong to the same 'genus' but have specific differences. This Aristotelian gesture, as Günter Figal observes, comes into focus if we recognise that human beings and animals alike are living beings. He writes:

Whenever we speak of life we think not only of human beings. The concept of life speaks of the context in which we are associated with other living beings. In conceiving of ourselves as living beings, and not as 'sub-jects', 'Dasein', or 'consciousness', we know that we are not separated from plant and animal as if by an abyss. Despite this proximity, not all differences between living beings dissolve with the concept of life. Precisely these differences are addressed by a thought that to this day is still convincing, namely, Aristotle's proposal that a living being be defined in terms of the peculiar expression of life proper to it.[46]

If this is correct, then Gadamer's approach suggests that although human beings and animals are differentiated by the respective expressions of life proper to them, these differences arise within the shared context of being alive; and, of all the elements that comprise being alive, perhaps none illuminates their commonality more than the impulse toward play.

Gadamer, as we have seen, believes that play is part of the definitively human hermeneutical experience of language. He argues that for animals, by contrast, play takes shape without language as a form of free self-movement. Gadamer's conception of animal life obviously more or less follows the Aristotelian idea from *De Anima* that animals (*zōē*) are distinguished from inanimate beings by their power to move themselves.[47] Gadamer's central claim about animal play is that it takes shape as a form of self-presentation (*Selbstdarstellung*); whatever else an animal engages in when it engages in play, it gives heightened expression to its own capacity for self-movement. In this, he maintains that because animal play is free self-movement, it comprises a token, or self-expression, of nothing other than the animal's very capacity for self-movement as such. He writes that in animals 'play appears as a self-movement that does not pursue any particular end or purpose so much as movement *as* movement, exhibiting so to speak a phenomenon of excess, of living self-presentation'.[48] Animal play, as play, takes shape as free movement; as a self-movement without language, however, animal play is as it were self-referential, it does nothing less than give expression to what it is to be an animal in the first place.

Gadamer, in fact, goes further still in his claims about the continuity between human beings and other kinds of beings. Indeed, he goes so far as to suggest that not only human beings and animals, but even what we can call the other beings born of the earth – what are typically called beings of inanimate nature and the elements – also share in the free movement of play. The play of such beings born of the earth appears as 'the to and fro of constantly repeated movement' and is evoked in 'certain expressions like "the play of light" and the "play of the waves" where we have such a constant coming and going, back and forth, a movement that is not tied down to any goal'.[49] Although Gadamer acknowledges that we use the term 'play' in an apparently metaphorical sense in the context of inanimate and elemental nature, he suggests that this use is nevertheless apt, since such a back-and-forth strikes us, at least, as a kind of movement for its own sake, devoid of any reason or orientation toward an end or purpose.[50]

In this, Gadamer's description of the play we observe in inanimate and elemental nature may resonate less with current scientific explanations than with motifs of *Naturphilosophie* found in Germany at the turn of the nineteenth century. We find a precursor of Gadamer's description, for example, in Eckermann's report of what Goethe took to be a 'great law' that 'pervades all nature and on which all life and the joy of life depend'.[51] This is the 'law of required change' (*Gesetz des geforderten Wechsels*).[52] To Goethe's mind, the universe is guided by the demand that all things not remain what they are but rather change, shift from one state to another. This law equally guides not only the natural order, whether in the play of light or of the waves, but also the world of art. In illustration, Goethe mentions the demand in dance for music that alternates major and minor keys, and the demand in Greek tragedy for the shift from chorus to episode and back.[53] It is true that Gadamer, in contrast with Goethe, does not expressly elevate his observations of play among beings born of the earth to the status of a general law. He nevertheless suggests that the structure of play we observe among beings born of the earth – free movement – is consanguine with the play found in human and animal experience alike.

Belonging Beyond the Human

Gadamer's considerations of the human being's difference-in-continuity with animals, and, indeed, perhaps even with other beings born of the earth, suggests that belonging extends beyond the sphere of the human. To be sure, his considerations are inflected differently than Dillard's. Dillard, as we might read her testimony, proposes that in extraordinary moments, at least, our encounters with animals involve, or can involve, a profound communion with them. Indeed, her testimony makes it no stretch to see such a communion in religious, even mystical terms. In this, Dillard's perspective may be situated within a tradition that includes figures such as Aldo Leopold, John Muir and perhaps some English and German Romantics; her perspective appears also to resonate, somewhat more remotely, with figures such as St Francis of Assisi.

Gadamer, too, suggests that our encounters with animals are or can be profound. He speaks not of religious or mystical communion, however, but of a distinctive possibility of belonging. And as we have seen, he identifies our recovery from modern alienation with belonging. This belonging is first of all the belonging to tradition we achieve through participation in the interpretation and transmission of meaning. As we have also seen, Gadamer suggests such belonging to tradition reaches a certain summit through our participation in the interpretation and transmission of written texts, eminently, literary texts. In this, he associates our prospects for recovery from modern alienation with participation in some of the most definitively human possibilities of what, in the Western tradition at least, has most defined the human being, namely, language. Yet, if for Gadamer our recovery from alienation thus takes shape in a belonging to tradition through participation in hermeneutical experiences of language, this recovery does not, in turn, imply an alienation of human from animal. Quite to the contrary, our participation in hermeneutical experiences of language, even experiences of the interpretation and transmission of written texts, speaks to a fuller scope of belonging that includes human, animal and perhaps also other beings born of the earth. For, in our participation in such hermeneutical experiences, we also participate in play, a mode of enactment not only essential to human life but also shared by animals and other beings born of the earth. Accordingly, belonging concerns not only belonging to tradition, but belonging to something deeper and wider: the back-and-forth movement of life, maybe even of all things.

Gadamer's approach thus also allows the initial outlines of our hermeneutical responsibility toward animals to come into view. To be sure, this responsibility cannot be reduced to a position on our duties toward animals or provide a code of conduct for the ethical treatment of animals. Our hermeneutical responsibility toward animals, like every responsibility to understand, is not concerned with the establishment, clarification or adjudication of ethical systems or principles. Rather, the responsibility to understand takes shape in the displacement of prejudices that allows us to become more open to the ethical stakes of the factical situations we find ourselves in and of the matters at issue within them. In the case of our hermeneutical responsibility toward animals, such displacement begins with the displacement of a polarity of prejudices – what we have called the Scylla and Charybdis of our hermeneutical experiences of animals. These are the prejudices, first, that humans and animals are for all intents and purposes ontologically the same; and, second, that there is an absolute ontological divide between human and animal. This polarity of prejudices comes to be displaced whenever our hermeneutical experience draws attention to the difference-in-continuity of humans and animals suggested by the phenomenon of play. When we interpret a text, we participate in play; when we encounter an animal at play, with us or with other animals, we recognise that, notwithstanding our differences, humans and animals participate together in something deeper and wider than what differentiates them. In turn, this hermeneutic displacement of our polarity of prejudices about animals through the recognition of our difference-in-continuity with them frees us up for possibilities to understand and interpret animals in ways that respect them in the context of our deeper, wider belonging with them. Given the experience which first makes this deeper, wider space of belonging available to us, it seems reasonable to call it a space of play.

5 Others

The purpose of Chapter 5 is to examine the contours (or at least one of them) of the responsibility to understand at issue in our 'I and thou' relationships with other persons. It is a remarkable fact that one of the most significant formulations of this responsibility is found in an analogy Gadamer makes between our experience of tradition and that of another person. As he famously puts it, in our encounter with tradition as it is passed down in language, tradition 'expresses itself like a Thou'.[1] Gadamer introduces this analogy in order to clarify 'the openness to tradition characteristic of historically effected consciousness'.[2] But, by invoking our relationships with other persons as a normative ideal of our relation to tradition, he also reveals the embryo of his claims about our responsibility to other persons. He writes: 'In human relations the important thing is . . . to experience the Thou truly as a Thou – i.e., not to overlook his claim but to let him really say something to us.'[3]

Gadamer, as we shall see, finds an important antecedent for such responsibility in what Heidegger, in *Being and Time*, calls authentic solicitude. And, perhaps in consequence, Gadamer's view of our recognition of other persons has been criticised on the grounds that it fails to account for forms of recognition we owe to those with whom we have no personal 'I and thou' relations.

Yet, for Gadamer, our responsibility to other persons, while personal, is not heedless of what we can call 'other others', that is, those others with whom we are unfamiliar. Quite to the contrary, he maintains that our responsibility to the other person is itself our *entrée* to the larger world of others in which both we ourselves and the other person participate. In this, as I shall argue, Gadamer further clarifies the significance of our relations with other persons through motifs from Plato's and Aristotle's notions of friendship. Our mutual relations with the other, or friendship, will thus prove to be essential for our 'self-love', grasped not as self-absorption, but as an expression of life that helps us to recognise the limits of our self-knowledge – that is, to recognise our prejudices. Friendship allows us better to grasp not only ourselves but also the larger world in which we find ourselves and, thereby, marks a transition to the formation of more expansive solidarities.

Indeed, as I shall argue in the conclusion to this chapter (in transition to our Part III discussion of the responsibilities to understand at issue in our 'I and we' relations), the importance of friendship as an *entreé* to our larger world is brought into relief by what Gadamer sees as the alienated mediation of our relation to the world through mass media.

Let the Other Say Something!

Gadamer, then, introduces his conception of our responsibility to understand other persons in his attempt to examine our openness to tradition. As many have noted, he presents authentic openness to tradition as the highest of three gradations, which he elucidates on the model of three moral gradations of our hermeneutical recognition of another person. In view of the purpose of the present chapter, I shall focus not on the consequences for tradition of Gadamer's considerations, but only on his treatment of the three gradations of our hermeneutical recognition of the other.[4]

Gadamer begins with the lowest of the three gradations. This is characterised by the maximum of our 'self-absorption' (*Selbstbezüglichkeit*),[5] which, accordingly, allows for only the most minimal recognition of the other. Here, we recognise the other not as a person with her own voice, but, instead, purely as a means to our ends. Our recognition of the other is thus reduced to our *instrumentalisation* of them. Gadamer associates this gradation of hermeneutical recognition with generalisation, and, thus also, with the norms of modern scientific enquiry. This is 'a kind of experience of the Thou' concerned with 'human nature', and that 'tries to discover typical behaviour in one's fellowmen and can make predictions about them'.[6] In the reduction of our interests in other persons to the predictable, general aspects of their behaviour, they come to be recognised as no different from any other phenomenon. Accordingly, our interest is not to recognise others in their own voices, in their own testimony about the meaning of their desires and actions. Instead, we recognise others only in what is generally predictable about them, regardless of their own voice, for the sake of some end or other that we wish to impose. To be sure, we can claim that our end is also in the other's interest, as when, for example, economists call for the implementation of tax incentives that they predict will promote healthy behaviour among individuals under the relevant tax regime. But, even here, our end is not to take the other's own testimony as arbiter of the other's ends; it is rather to impose our end on the other, using what is generally predictable about the other to do so. It is perhaps no surprise that Gadamer evokes Kant to indicate that and how this lowest gradation of hermeneutical recognition is morally deficient. It 'contradicts the moral definition of man' that, according to Kant, 'the other should never be used as a means but always as an end in himself'.[7]

Gadamer maintains that self-absorption continues to characterise the second gradation of our hermeneutical recognition of the other, but here at least 'the Thou is acknowledged as a person'.[8] In this gradation, we recognise the other as a person with an independent voice, but, instead of allowing them to say something of their own, we demand that they confirm the validity of what we have to say. Our recognition is thus reduced to a dialectical struggle oriented by a will to *subjugation*; a struggle in which 'To every claim there is a counterclaim . . . One claims to know the other's claim from his point of view and even to understand the other better than the other understands himself.'[9] Gadamer, as he acknowledges, has Hegel's notion of the struggle for recognition in mind,[10] and his account of this second gradation can be grasped as a hermeneutical reconsideration of Hegel's view. Gadamer maintains that while our recognition of the other through subjugation remains morally deficient, it is nevertheless not as deficient as our recognition of the other through instrumentalisation. For, in order to recognise the other through subjugation, we must at least admit the independence of that other's voice; whereby, we not only betray the contradiction of our pursuit, but anticipate its resolution.

Gadamer maintains that, in the highest of the three gradations, we recognise the other fully as a person. That is, we recognise that others have a voice of their own. Whereas in the second gradation we recognise the other's voice only insofar as it confirms the validity of what we have to say, in this third gradation we recognise that what the other has to say may be valid in its own right. In this highest of the three gradations, then, our recognition is characterised by the openness of *listening*. Now, for Gadamer, to listen (*zuhören*) is not 'to have command over' (*überschauen*)[11] what the other has to say, as if listening were about achieving an actual mastery of the validity of the other's claim. Nor, however, is it immediately to accept the validity of the other's claim, as if 'to pay heed to someone' (*auf jemanden hören*) were actually to 'do blindly what the other desires'.[12] After all, as Gadamer observes, 'we call such a person slavish' (*hörig*).[13] In listening, our recognition is not primarily concerned with the *actuality* of the validity of the other's claim at all; listening treats this validity neither as an actual matter for us to master nor as a matter for us slavishly to follow. Rather, in listening, our recognition is oriented by the *possibility* of the validity of the other's claim.

To listen means to be open, in the sense that we are freed by our encounter with the other enough to put aside our self-absorption and genuinely entertain the possible validity of the other's claim. Such entertaining can, perhaps, be described as a free suspension of our self-absorption, one that is held open by the tension of a challenge posed and a promise elicited by the other. Openness to the possible validity of the other's claim poses a challenge because it requires us to consider that the other's claim may be right and that we may therefore have to change our minds, and even ourselves. This challenge is at the same time a promise, however, because the possibility that the other's claim may be right is likewise the opportunity for a deeper, richer understanding and transformative growth. Gadamer writes: 'Openness to the other, then, involves recognising that I myself must accept some things that are against me, even though no one else forces me to do so.'[14] In listening, we do not reduce the other to a voiceless instrument, but neither do we any longer subjugate the other's voice to our demand that they confirm the validity of what we have to say. Rather, in listening, we hold ourselves in a free suspension, precisely in the tension of challenge and promise that comprises our openness to the possible validity of the other's claim.

Gadamer's treatment of our hermeneutic recognition of other persons as a model for our openness to tradition expressly draws upon Kant's and Hegel's contributions to moral philosophy. In his later essay, 'Subjectivity and Intersubjectivity, Subject and Person',

Gadamer suggests that he also takes important orientation from Heidegger's *Being and Time* account of authentic solicitude. Gadamer's
purpose in this later essay is to question the validity of the concept
of intersubjectivity, which, he believes, requires also that we question the concept of subjectivity on which it is based.[15] He argues that
Heidegger's analysis of existence not only successfully demonstrated
that the concepts of intersubjectivity and subjectivity are derivative,
but also helped to clarify the more original structures of existence
that these concepts are supposed to get at. Behind the concept of
intersubjectivity, then, is the more original existential structure of
solicitude (*Fürsorge*); in turn, behind the concept of subjectivity is
the more original existential structure of care (*Sorge*).[16]

Gadamer suggests that his approach to the hermeneutic recognition of other persons as a model for our openness to tradition
originates in Heidegger's existential analysis of solicitude. As he
states:

in Heidegger's approach the concept of subjectivity is replaced by the concept of care. Here it becomes clear that the Other does not remain only at
the margins, seen only from a biased perspective. Heidegger speaks, then,
of care and also of solicitude. Solicitude receives a particular accent when
he calls real solicitude 'freeing solicitude'. The word indicates what its significance is. True solicitude is not to care for the Other, but rather to let the
Other come freely into one's own being [a] self.[17]

For Gadamer, the highest gradation of hermeneutical recognition
is listening, grasped as the openness to the possible validity of the
other's claim. This, however, can be described as a further aspect of
Gadamer's 'concretisation' of Heidegger – this time, of Heidegger's
notion of authentic solicitude. For, as his description of Heidegger's
view makes clear, Gadamer's conception of openness to the possibility
of the other's claim can be grasped as nothing else than the concretion
in conversation or text interpretation of precisely Heidegger's analysis
of authentic solicitude as letting others come freely into their own.

Yet, Gadamer maintains that his own account of openness to the
other as a model for openness to tradition affords the other a more
fundamental role than we find in Heidegger's analysis. He rejects
Heidegger's notorious claim in *Being and Time* that being-with-others
is irrelevant for our experience of being-a-self in authentic being-
towards-death. Heidegger, as we recall, argues that when, in our

existence as Dasein, we are 'imminent' to ourselves in relation to death as the 'possibility of no-longer-being-able-to-be-there', our Dasein 'is *completely* thrown back upon its ownmost potentiality-of-being. Thus imminent to itself, all relations to other Dasein are dissolved.'[18] In other words, when it comes to the possibility of our own death, the other has no valid claim. Gadamer, by contrast, maintains that there is no experience, not even the experience of the possibility of our own death, that can 'dissolve' the possible validity of the other's claim. Here, we may call to mind Albert Camus's considerations on what he describes as the 'one truly serious philosophical problem, that of suicide', in his 'The Myth of Sisyphus', as a classic example of the contemplation of one's own death.[19] From the viewpoint of Heidegger's analysis of existence, contemplation of our own suicide is and can only be our own affair; there is no possible validity to the other's claims about whether we should commit suicide or not. For Gadamer, by contrast, even in our experience of something so extremely individualising as the contemplation of our own suicide, the other still counts; and we are responsible for entertaining the possible validity of the other's claim about the matter. Gadamer writes:

I was trying, in opposition to Heidegger, to show how the understanding of the Other possesses a fundamental significance . . . To allow the Other to be valid against oneself – and from there to let all my hermeneutic works slowly develop – is not only to recognize in principle the limitation of one's own framework, but is also to allow one to go beyond one's own possibilities, precisely in a dialogical, communicative, hermeneutic process.[20]

While Gadamer's account has its origin in Heidegger's analysis of authentic solicitude, for him, nothing can quash the possible validity of the other's claim – and not only when this claim is made by another person but also when, as Gadamer's analogy between openness to others and openness to tradition suggests, this claim is made on us in an encounter with tradition.

In his turn to hermeneutical recognition as a model of our openness to tradition, Gadamer reveals the embryo of his vision of our responsibility to other persons: that we allow the other to say something to us – entertaining the possible validity of the other's claim – and that nothing, not even our relation to our own death, can dissolve this demand.

What About Other Others?

Gadamer's approach to the hermeneutical recognition of other persons is not without its critics. One concern has been that his approach falls short because it focuses not on the recognition of all others but rather only on others with whom we are already familiar or are in the process of becoming familiar. Gadamer's account, so goes the concern, has little purchase for recognition of others who are unfamiliar to us – others, in other words, who in one way or another are otherwise than the others with whom we are already familiar or are becoming familiar.

Gadamer's hermeneutics has, in fact, been confronted with this criticism for some time, and from different quarters. From one quarter, he has been criticised by philosophers such as Derrida and Caputo, who focus on our responsibility to others as 'radically' other, that is, others so unfamiliar that our hermeneutical horizons are unable to allow them to appear, or unable to allow them to appear except in distortion. Here, Gadamer's approach is said to fall short because it excludes from consideration the recognition of those so 'radically' unfamiliar that they cannot unproblematically appear to us in the first place.[21]

From another quarter, Gadamer has been criticised by philosophers associated with critical theory who are concerned with the recognition of unfamiliar others within the context of the highly mediated relations of social communication characteristic of modern societies. This concern is with recognition not of the 'radically' unfamiliar other, but with the unfamiliarity of our social interactions with others in society at large, and perhaps especially the unfamiliarity of the unavowed other we encounter in modern social interactions – say, in an encounter with someone or other on a commuter train or over the phone with a representative of our health care provider (if we are fortunate enough to have one!). Here again, Gadamer's approach to hermeneutical recognition is said to fall short, though this time because it excludes from consideration the lion's share of our interactions with others under the typical conditions of modern life.[22]

Criticisms that Gadamer's approach excludes from consideration the recognition of both 'radical' others and 'social-communicative' others have filled plenty of pages of scholarly literature. What I wish to draw attention to, however, is the implication of these criticisms that

Gadamer's approach is restricted in being relevant only to our relations with others already familiar to us. This concern is brought into
focus with emphasis in recent literature by Axel Honneth in 'On the
Destructive Power of the Third: Gadamer and Heidegger's Doctrine of
Intersubjectivity'. Honneth's essay originally appeared in a celebratory
volume for Gadamer's 100th birthday.[23] In it Honneth forwards a version of the criticism that Gadamer's approach to hermeneutical recognition excludes from consideration 'social-communicative' others. He
argues that the recognition of such others requires the mediation of a
'third', namely, an impartial normative conception of human being.[24]
In this context, he argues that Gadamer rejects such a possibility
because of a 'normative pre-decision'[25] against such normative generalisation, a pre-decision that, indeed, derives from Gadamer's proximity to the early Heidegger's analysis of being-with-others. Gadamer,
on this view, remains averse to generalised normative conceptions of
the human being because they comprise what Heidegger referred to as
the inauthentic being-with-others characteristic of '*Das Man*', or 'the
they'.[26]

To bring his point home, Honneth takes issue with Habermas's
celebrated laudation of Gadamer for his achievement of an 'urbanisation' of Heidegger's philosophy. As Honneth reports, 'According
to Habermas, Gadamer was able to urbanise the philosophy of
Heidegger decisively inasmuch as he removed its "obstinate and
idiosyncratic character" . . . by means of the hermeneutic opening
to the other, and thus, through a lessening of distance . . . placed it
on firm ground.'[27] Yet, per Honneth, Gadamer maintains his normative pre-decision against generalised conceptions of the human
being precisely because of his closeness to Heidegger. Accordingly,
as Honneth puts it, Gadamer's approach of hermeneutical recognition is not an 'urbanisation' (*Urbanisierung*) that puts Heidegger
on better grounds. Rather, it is much more an attempt at the 'rec-
lamation' (*Urbarmachung*) of the ground already established by
Heidegger's analysis.[28]

Honneth, in any case, concludes that Gadamer's approach, because
of its Heideggerian pre-decision against the possibility of normative
generalisations of the human being, is of restricted relevance. For Honneth, Gadamer's conception of recognition is not universal in scope,
but rather 'is already justifiable in a conditioned way only with respect
to close personal relations'.[29] Honneth observes that our encounters

with others range from involvements with those we know well to interactions that take place in the anonymity of modern societies. But, as he argues, 'With expanding distance between interaction partners, the possibility diminishes of viewing openness toward the claims of the other as the only morally appropriate behaviour.'[30] Accordingly, in our encounters with others in the anonymity of modern societies, what is 'morally appropriate' is not 'to meet' the other 'with an attitude of hermeneutical openness'.[31] Rather, what is called for is 'to treat him or her according to the universal principle of respect'.[32] Indeed, for Honneth, Gadamer's conception of hermeneutical recognition applies to close, personal relations in only a qualified manner. For, as Honneth argues, even in our relations with others close to us, our interactions take orientation from and depend on a 'third', that is, on some normative generalisation.[33]

Honneth's criticism comprises an innovative iteration of the objection that Gadamer's approach to hermeneutical recognition excludes from consideration our interactions with 'social-communicative' others. Moreover, his argument helps clarify the charge that Gadamer's approach is relevant only for our relations with those familiar to us. Yet, Honneth's charge of restricted relevance, and others like it, fail to appreciate the broader compass of Gadamer's considerations of our responsibility to understand and interpret other persons. Gadamer's approach to hermeneutical recognition reveals that our responsibility is to let the other say something to us, that is, to entertain the possible validity of the other's claim. However, our experience of this responsibility not only orients every 'I-Thou' relation, but, more than this, is *embryonic*. That is, this responsibility to let the other say something, to entertain the validity of the other's claim, fosters the growth of our relations with others, and thereby, in turn, allows us to expand our possibilities of recognition to include not only those familiar to us, but other others – the others that are not familiar to us – as well. For Gadamer, as I wish to argue in what remains of this chapter, our responsibility to let the other say something to us grows, first of all, into friendship. As we shall see, though, he grasps friendship not simply as a feature of private life, but, more than this, as an *entreé* to the larger world in which both friends participate. In Part III, we will consider Gadamer's view that this initial outgrowth of friendship is itself already a transition to the further, even more expansive outgrowth of solidarity.

Self-love and Friendship

Gadamer presents his notion of friendship in a number of essays, and his approach, as David Vessey observes, focuses on several discrete features of relations between friends.[34] While Gadamer's concern is principally with the significance of friendship in the context of modern life, he develops his approach mainly on the basis of motifs from ancient practical philosophy, especially that of Plato and Aristotle. Within this context, Gadamer's conception of the significance of friendship is drawn out by his claim that friendship is a form of 'self-love' (*Philautia*).[35] He recognises that for us, no less than for members of ancient Greek society, this word has a 'bad ring' to it.[36] In common parlance, now and then, we do not typically associate friendship with 'self-love'; if anything, 'self-love' sounds closer to the 'self-absorption' that, as Gadamer himself indicates, constricts our ability to recognise the other. He observes that in Greek comedies, for example, 'self-love' concerns just such self-absorption: 'The often comical and certainly tremendous vice of humans . . . that they always only think of themselves and not what the Other is and what is for the Other.'[37] Yet, against such common views now and then, Gadamer follows the claim he finds in Plato and Aristotle that self-love is necessary for the achievement of the good life.[38] In this, he affirms what he calls the 'bold thesis' that 'friendship must exist first and foremost with oneself'.[39] Accordingly, as Gadamer maintains, true self-love cannot be reduced to self-absorption, but, instead, represents genuine concern for one's own being.

Yet, Gadamer also maintains that true self-love, as friendship with oneself, quickly leads us to friendship with others. For, as both Plato and Aristotle recognise, such self-love turns on our ability to achieve self-knowledge. Such self-knowledge cannot, however, be a matter of general concepts of human nature that will allow us to predict our own behaviour; in this, we would not be a friend to ourselves but would, as it were, only instrumentalise ourselves. Rather, by self-knowledge, Gadamer has in mind the need for us to recognise the limits of our self-understanding. As he explains in reference to ancient Greek religion:

One knows the famous 'know thyself', this saying of the Delphic oracle that always impresses itself on the human mind. 'Know thyself'. That means, notice that you are only a man and not an appointment of divine providence or a particularly charismatic one of the Lord's anointed, so to speak, to whom privilege, victory, and success are given on this side of and beyond all human commitments.[40]

Self-love, genuine concern for our own being, requires Delphic self-knowledge. But, unlike the Gods, we are not self-sufficient, and our fortunes in life are not guaranteed. Indeed, as I wish to clarify in what follows, for Gadamer human beings are not even self-sufficient in their pursuit of the self-knowledge required to fare as well as we humanly can. For this, human beings must rely on one another, first of all, through friendship. Accordingly, self-love leads us to form friendships that make us familiar with one another. But, as a form of self-love, such familiarity does not leave us at ease. Quite to the contrary, friendship helps us to experience the limits of our grasp of ourselves and the world, and, thus, to displace ourselves through exposure to the unfamiliar within us as well as without.

Gadamer's concern for human finitude is ubiquitous within his thought. After all, his philosophical hermeneutics is an attempt to 'concretise' Heidegger's discovery of the 'hermeneutics of facticity' – itself an articulation of the radical finitude of existence. In Gadamer's consideration of self-love and friendship, however, his concern is foremost with the significance of finitude for practical life, and he draws this significance into focus especially through Aristotle. To Gadamer's mind, Aristotle's 'speculative genius' lies in his 'sense for the multiply conditioned' character of human life.[41] Because of this, Gadamer believes that precisely in Aristotle 'an answer [emerges] to the question that has been plaguing us: namely, how a philosophical ethics, a human doctrine of the human, is possible without requiring a super-human self-transcendence'.[42] While Gadamer's treatment of Aristotle's ethics is extensive and ranges over a number of issues, his concern for the finitude of practical life can be discerned from his considerations of the Aristotelian motifs of *ēthos* and *phronēsis*. A discussion of these motifs will set the stage for a consideration of how self-love leads us to friendship, or, in Aristotle, *philia*.

Scholars such as Christopher P. Smith have demonstrated that Gadamer's conception of the task of practical philosophy comes into focus in his association of the political and ethical significance of tradition with the notion of *ēthos*.[43] One of the principal tenets of Gadamer's philosophical hermeneutics is that understanding arises in dialogic encounters that depend crucially on the transmission of inherited prejudices.[44] Because of this, understanding never attains an absolutely self-reflexive 'view from nowhere', but rather always remains within a horizon of convictions, sensibilities and dispositions carried over from the past. This does not mean that Gadamer's emphasis on tradition has to be taken as a form of cultural conservatism. He certainly realises that understanding always involves the transformation of a traditional inheritance, and, as Hans-Helmut Gander has put it, he also realises that tradition itself 'does not proceed in a linear course or evenly across its surface, but rather as a history of breakdowns and fractures, of the forgotten and subterranean paths'.[45] Gadamer's principal point is that hermeneutical understanding achieves not an infinite form of transcendence but only a finite one. It does not follow from this that our understandings are condemned to the simple reiteration of a monolithic past.

Gadamer's view does imply, though, that practical philosophy turns not on the establishment of transcendent laws, but on the interpretation of ethical values immanent to a historical milieu. Because practical philosophy relies on hermeneutical understanding, it cannot achieve the self-reflexive standpoint that would be necessary to establish *a priori* grounds of moral values. Rather, the principal task of the practical philosopher, like anyone who is engaged in practical life, in fact, is to reach an understanding about what to do within what Gadamer refers to as a 'living network of common convictions, habits, and values – that is to say, within an *ēthos*'.[46] Practical life concerns not the establishment of and adherence to transcendent moral principles that would regulate our affairs, but focuses instead on the interpretation of inherited ethical resources of the past to address the real needs of the present.

It requires no great stretch to see why Gadamer would associate the fulfilment of this task of ethical understanding with Aristotle's notion of *phronēsis*.[47] Since there are no transcendent principles that guarantee us success in ethical life, 'the rationality that guides practice' centres on prudent judgement, ethical imagination and the wisdom that accompanies experience.[48] Gadamer associates ethical understanding with Aristotelian *phronēsis* in a number of his later essays. Some of the most important stakes of the connection he makes may also be discerned, however, in his discussion in *Truth and Method* of what he refers to as 'the hermeneutical relevance of Aristotle'.[49]

Here, Gadamer turns to Aristotle's practical philosophy to elucidate his notion of hermeneutical understanding. Yet, as Risser has argued, Gadamer's intention is also to pose philosophical hermeneutics as an heir to 'the classical tradition of practical philosophy itself'.[50] Because of this, his approach to the 'hermeneutical relevance of Aristotle' may be seen to contribute to 'an authentic description of the conditions of our practical life'.[51]

Gadamer sheds light on the relationship between understanding and *phronēsis* in his discussion of the problem of 'hermeneutical application'. For him, this problem refers to the difficulty our understanding faces in our practical efforts to bring a general ethical standard, norm or law of our inherited *ēthos* to bear on a concrete situation of action. Gadamer refers to *phronēsis*, in turn, as our capacity to discharge this task of application in a manner that befits the demands of our concrete situation. Yet, the fulfilment of this task differs from the implementation of a predetermined methodological plan or procedurally guided process that typifies technical production (*technē*). As Risser writes, the achievement of understanding as 'application is not simply a matter of following a procedure as one follows a recipe in cooking, but is a matter of perceiving what is at stake in the situation'.[52] Here, the understanding required for application turns not only on a familiarity with our *ēthos* and the ethical standards, norms and laws embedded in it, but also on the judgement, the discretion and the creative insight required to remain sensitive to the ethical demands of the concrete situation in which we find ourselves.

Although Gadamer's practical philosophy leads him to eschew any transcendent basis of critique, his association of understanding with *phronēsis* nevertheless suggests the critical force of his view. It is true that for Gadamer, ethical standards, norms and laws embedded in our *ēthos* are 'valid only as schemata. They are concretised only in the concrete situation of the person acting. Thus they are not norms found in the stars, nor do they have an unchanging place in the moral universe.'[53] On this view, our attempts to apply our ethical inheritance take shape in what we have already called the 'predicament of the exception'. Application guided by *phronēsis* cannot unfold as a mindless reiteration of and thus adherence to tradition. Rather, it involves an interpretive distance opened up by our attempts to apply the tradition in a new way, one that is prescient for and responsive to the requirements of our particular situation. As Gadamer puts it, the *phronēsis* involved in application achieves a certain critical distance in its achievement of a hermeneutical 'leeway'.[54]

Gadamer illustrates the interpretive distance of play implied by *phronēsis* in reference to the phenomenon of carrying out orders. He conceives of following orders as an example of application, and he no doubt introduces it as an extreme case that would appear not to require interpretive 'leeway' at all. He suggests, however, that precisely this extreme case of application puts the ineluctability of the need for judgement and discretion into relief:

> An order exists only where there is someone to obey it . . . To understand an order means to apply it to the specific situation to which it pertains . . . It is given its real meaning when it is carried out and concretized in accord with its meaning . . . The comic situation in which orders are carried out literally but not according to their meaning is well known. Thus there is no doubt that the recipient of an order must perform a definite creative act in understanding its meaning.[55]

Even following orders, an extreme case of application, demands the *phronēsis* that takes shape in the interpretive leeway we need to bring the order to bear in the concrete situation. Indeed, without taking recourse to this leeway, we make ourselves laughable.

It is in the context of this association of understanding with the Aristotelian themes of *ēthos* and *phronēsis* that Gadamer elucidates the practical import he assigns to *philia*. As we have seen, his conception of *ēthos* indicates that practical philosophy and practical life are guided not by transcendent principles but rather by our ethical inheritance. He interprets *phronēsis*, in turn, as the ability to apply the bequest of our *ēthos* in a fitting manner that remains sensitive to the ethical needs of concrete life. Within this context, Gadamer sees *philia*, our friendships with others, as essential to the formation of our beliefs, judgements and actions. In his essay entitled, 'Friendship and Self-knowledge: Reflections on the Role of Friendship in Greek Ethics', he writes: 'Through exchange with our friends, who share our views and intentions but who can also correct or strengthen them, we draw nearer to the divine, which possesses continually what is possible for us humans only intermittently: presence, wakefulness, self-presence in "Geist".'[56] For Gadamer, Aristotle's approach to *philia* comprises a statement of the power we may draw from each other when we form bonds of friendship.

Even though Gadamer associates friendship with the augmentation of our practical abilities, he believes we need friends precisely because of our finitude. This is a point he elucidates in reference to a distinction he sees in Aristotle's discussion of friendship between self-sufficiency (*autarkeia*) and self-love (*philautia*). To Gadamer's mind, Aristotle rejects the idea that human beings are capable of any kind of 'self-possession' that absolves them of the need for friends.[57] Instead, he argues, the self-love that guides friendship turns on the insight that our efforts to reflect on ourselves and also on our practical affairs require the aid of others.[58] For Gadamer, human finitude may render complete self-sufficiency impossible, but he believes that friendship countervails our limits; the friend may understand us better than we understand ourselves, and, because of this, is indispensable to us as we work to understand ourselves and come to an understanding about what we should do.

Gadamer appreciates the important role friendships play, above all those friendships characterised by proximity and intimacy, in bolstering our efforts to flourish in our particular and personal lives. Whereas Honneth suggests that Gadamer's emphasis on this kind of intimacy betrays a provincialism incompatible with present conditions of political life, however, Gadamer maintains that friendship answers to a vital political need in our times perhaps more than ever. Indeed, he argues that we are prompted to return to the Aristotelian themes of *ēthos*, *phronēsis* and *philia* at the present historical juncture precisely to address the collapse of modernity's optimism at the outset of the twentieth century. He originally turned to Aristotle, he asserts, because 'after the liberal period's optimism about progress was shattered following the catastrophe of the First World War, we needed to construct a new understanding of human (and also civic) community'.[59]

For Gadamer, the promotion and expansion of close, personal friendships within society is decisive because friends supplement our *phronēsis*. Here, friendships help us not only to realise our private ends, but also and crucially to augment our ability to deliberate and decide about what to do in the larger world we share with others. 'Ethics', as Gadamer puts it in reference to Aristotle, 'proves to be part of a politics'[60] because in friendship we are concerned not only with what is advantageous for our more private concerns but also with what is virtuous in our engagement in the larger world.

Gadamer writes that friendship 'flows into the full stream of self-forming commonalities in which one begins to feel and recognize oneself . . . it signifies a real embedding in the texture of communal human life'.[61] Within Gadamer's philosophical hermeneutics, one of the principal tasks of our shared lives in common is the application of inherited ethical standards, norms and laws to present societal needs. Yet, he believes that human beings are exposed to the same finitude in the political sphere that they encounter in their personal lives: for him, there is no blueprint or script, nor for that matter any institution of procedural justice, which will guarantee that the application of ethical standards, norms and laws embedded in an *ēthos* will succeed. We must rely, rather, on the *phronēsis* of all in our shared world, and we all may draw strength from *philia*, our friendships, to augment our capacities to do so.

Friends, Culture and the Media

Gadamer maintains that the pursuit of friendships is as relevant for modern life as ancient philosophers such as Plato and Aristotle believe it is for all human life. Indeed, he suggests that the pursuit of friendship is perhaps made even more urgent by the conditions of modern life. In order to illustrate the relevance of Gadamer's conception of friendship for modern life, I shall focus in this section on the urgency for friendship that he believes has been created by the rise of mass media in modern society. Gadamer makes some of his most important observations about this urgency in his essay, 'Culture and Media', which appears in a volume dedicated to Jürgen Habermas on the occasion of his sixtieth birthday (and which, interestingly enough, was co-edited by Axel Honneth). Gadamer's larger concern in 'Culture and Media' is what he sees as the 'frightening anonymity life has acquired' under modern conditions of bureaucratically administered society.[62] Under this larger rubric, however, he focuses on the effects that the mass media of such modern societies has on the culture of our times, and on our capacities for deliberation and opinion-formation.[63] Gadamer insists, however, that he does not take up this theme to join in the 'usual tirades of cultural critique', but instead aims to understand how to 'deal with our fate of living' under the concrete conditions of our times.[64]

To this end, his approach suggests, perhaps nothing is more press-ing in modern life than the preservation of our close, personal rela-tions with others and the strength we draw from them. Gadamer's concern is with the influence that mass media has over culture not only in European civilisation but also in all of the regions of the world that have come to rely on these media. In 'Culture and Media', he defines culture in terms of the institutions and practices of society that aim at the achievement of new understanding through the cre-ative preservation, development and even transformation of beliefs and values transmitted from the past. Culture is thus the name for those activities of society concerned with deliberation and opinion-formation 'that open up the space within which something can be done and exclude what perhaps ought not to be done'.[65] Thus, Gadamer's enquiry concerns the effects that the rise of mass media has had on our larger social and political lives.

No doubt for Gadamer one of the most palpable consequences of the mass media, like many conditions of modern life, is the isola-tion that results from it; under the mass media, our encounters with one another occur not in person but rather at a quite depersonalis-ing distance.[66] Gadamer emphasises the potential of such isolation and loneliness to stifle the kinds of growth, change and independent thought that can arise from face-to-face experiences. Above all, he asks whether modern society has not presented us with an 'excess of mediations'[67] that diminishes our opportunities to form relations with others through dialogical experience. 'Nothing', he asserts, 'has become as difficult in such a pervasively regulated civilisation as having experiences – a fact that marks our entire social life.'[68]

Living under such 'structures of a thoroughly rationalized soci-ety'[69] that pre-empt experience, there is no task more pressing than to engage in activities that allow us to encounter the world and others directly. To describe the character of such direct experience, Gadamer invokes the language of immediacy and spontaneity. To be sure, his point is not to gainsay his hermeneutical view that all expe-rience is conditioned by the inheritance of ethical standards, norms and laws embedded in an *ēthos*. Rather, he associates such direct experience with immediacy and spontaneity as part of a polemic against the specific kinds of mediation that impose themselves on experience under conditions of bureaucratically administered soci-ety. He writes: 'In view of the infinite mediation controlling our entire life, we wish as much as possible to protect immediacy. As spontaneity, it permits immediate access to reality and, in particular, to the otherness of the other, of the fellow human being.'[70] For Gadamer, the conditions of modern life call for what might be described as the urgency of the face-to-face, the urgency of an affirmation of the shared life and experience that fosters growth in resistance to the isolation and loneliness of modern society.

In 'Culture and Media', in any case, Gadamer focuses in particular on the consequences of the mass media for deliberation and opinion-formation. Because he associates culture with the activities that aim at these processes, he warns that the mass media involve complex forms of mediation which stultify the awareness of shared concerns, the creativity, and the flexibility characterising the relation of self and other. He writes:

we must recognize that all institutions and undertakings that start from the formation of public opinion and that pursue their tasks through the mass media contain an apparatus of endless mediation and intrication; thus the immediacy of spontaneous judgement and of spontaneous address is threatened again and again.[71]

Due to the excessive mediations of the mass media, the processes by which we undertake the tasks of deliberation and opinion-formation with others risk becoming rigid and unresponsive. The imposition of such mediations endangers our capacities for practical life.

Although Gadamer does not ignore the improvements to our lives achieved through the mass media, he nevertheless points to the dangers of the depersonalisation involved in the kind of communication carried out through such media. He first invokes the history of the notion of communication to underscore the political stakes of his concern for the mass media. 'Communication', he reminds us, 'is an old Roman term for urban public affairs (Gemeinwesen), the handling of which took place in living conversation and in speeches before the assembled masses.'[72] Perhaps the greatest problem with communication facilitated by the mass media, by contrast, is that the excessive mediation it produces robs us of the strength we draw from friendships forged in the face-to-face context. There can be no question of the awesome power of the mass media to interconnect all regions of the globe in an unrelenting exchange of information. What Gadamer reminds us of, however, is that these media not only connect us to each other but also threaten to cut us off from the help we can give one another in our deliberations and formation of opinions – they threaten to cut us off, in other words, from the lessons we might learn through friendship.

At stake is nothing less than our experience of otherness. For Gadamer, the imposition of impartial standards – whether normative, bureaucratic or otherwise – threatens to interrupt our capacities for judgement, discretion and ultimately play that are required for deliberation and opinion-formation. By contrast, these capacities are fostered and augmented not only by the similarities we share with our friends but above all by the questions our friends can pose to our convictions precisely in their otherness from us. Gadamer writes: 'our experience is enriched whenever we are challenged to understand the unexpected, the uncalculated, the uncalculable – in short, the other. This is the only way we can learn from our experiences'.[73] For Gadamer, practical life – whatever else it may be – is a sphere in which we are called to understand what is best for us to do in the face of our irresolute finitude. Gadamer's approach suggests that we may find help in this endeavour from our friends.

PART III: I AND WE

6 Solidarity

Part III of the present enquiry addresses the contours of the responsibility to understand in the dimension of our lives that we live in common. This Part is therefore concerned with what is usually designated by terms such as 'the political sphere', 'political life' or perhaps even 'the public square' or 'the polis'. For several decades now, much of the discussion of the stakes of Gadamer's philosophical hermeneutics for political life has been reduced to questions about the politics of Gadamer's thought. The frame of this discussion, in the first instance, turns on whether or not his philosophical hermeneutics is a form of 'conservatism', and whether other more recent figures associated with hermeneutics, such as Gianni Vattimo, Richard Rorty, John Caputo, Dennis Schmidt or James Risser are subject to the same critique.[1] In more recent years, this frame of discussion has been supplemented by, as it were, a 'frame within the frame' focused on the relation between the politics of Gadamer's thought and Gadamer's own politics. The *raison d'être* for this frame within the frame appears to be at least in part some sort of *iniquitatem patris*, centred on whether Gadamer's thought indicates Gadamer's complicity in National Socialism.[2]

In this chapter I wish to argue that these frames of debate, whatever they may have to teach, nevertheless miss some of the most important stakes of Gadamer's thought for the dimension of our lives lived in common. These stakes cannot be boiled down to questions about the politics of Gadamer's thought. Rather, Gadamer's thought aims at an elucidation of hermeneutical experience that, among other things, helps to clarify the character, and, with this, the limits and possibilities, of the political sphere as such. As we shall see, Gadamer recognises that his philosophical hermeneutics can contribute to the formation of political judgements and engagement in political agency. Yet, as I wish to show, Gadamer also brings into focus another, perhaps even more critical stake of his philosophical hermeneutics for political life. For Gadamer, philosophical hermeneutics is not only important for politics, but, more originally, for our efforts to make the political contexts of our lives and our place within them visible in the first place. To be sure, Gadamer elucidates this stake of philosophical hermeneutics along a number of lines. Still, in his later essays at least, one notion comes into greater focus than all others (or almost all others) to clarify the responsibility that attends our efforts to make the larger political context of our lives available to us and to contribute to its formation. This is the notion of 'solidarity'.

The stakes of Gadamer's philosophical hermeneutics for political life, then, are greater than questions about the politics of his thought or, for that matter, his person. Yet, even if these stakes are not yet a politics, they nevertheless bring into focus an important dimension of the political.

The Political as Not Yet Politics

We are familiar with Gadamer's alignment of his project of philosophical hermeneutics with practical philosophy. As we have already observed, Gadamer affirms the gesture (if not the metaphysical assumptions) of Aristotle's celebrated definition of human beings as *zoon politikon*. Building on Aristotle, he maintains that 'praxis, in short, is our "form of life"'.[3] As we have also seen, he argues that practical life is comprised of three distinctive if nevertheless interwoven dimensions: one with 'an "I and thou" character', another with 'an "I and we" character', and finally a third with 'a "we and we" character'.[4] The second and third dimensions in particular help clarify the stakes of philosophical hermeneutics for political life. As Gadamer's tripartite distinction of practical life suggests, the dimension of the 'I and we' is not yet concerned with political judgement, political agency or political matters of law and diplomacy. It is precisely these and related considerations that comprise the dimension of practical life signified by the 'we and we'. For Gadamer, the dimension of practical life signified by the 'I and we' concerns the opening of a context, in which we first come to see ourselves as belonging to a world of other persons that is larger than ourselves.

Gadamer's approach to the 'I and we' dimension may therefore be characterised as political, but not yet politics. The 'I and we' dimension is political in that it concerns the fact that to be human is to belong to a context that includes others. But, among these others are not only things, animals, friends and strangers; we also find a 'we', that is, a world oriented by commonly inherited, though of course often contested and conflicted, contexts of meaning – languages, artistic traditions, religious traditions, as well as legal traditions, government and customary practices. In other words, we find ourselves always already in a *world*, or, in what is originally signified by the Greek word, a *polis*. For Gadamer, the 'I and we' dimension of practical life concerns the fact *that*, as well as *how*, we make this larger political context available to ourselves and contribute to its formation. If this 'I and we' dimension is political, however, it is not yet politics, insofar as politics is a matter of deliberation and agency that is made possible by and takes place within the larger context that has thus first been made available. Our effort to make the larger political context available to ourselves is, as it were, upstream of our actual involvement in politics, in the determination of political judgements and engagement in political action.

To be sure, Gadamer's debts to Aristotle's practical philosophy already suggest his recognition that the three dimensions of practical life under consideration are intricately interwoven. A conversation with an intimate friend (or, we may add, an encounter with a feral cat in the neighbourhood) is at the same time an experience that helps to make the larger political context available to us and, indeed, can also call for responsible political action. In this, Gadamer may be contrasted with philosophers such as Emmanuel Levinas, who insists on a strict differentiation of the ethical stakes of relations of 'I and you' from those of our political relations.[5] Gadamer denies the possibility of such a strict differentiation, arguing instead that practical life is not only continuous, but, for this reason, always also complex and ambiguous.

Solidarity, as we shall see, allows the world to be made visible in a novel manner and, thus, helps us pose a challenge to received frames of debate in the sphere of politics.

Solidarity in the Age of Globalisation

Gadamer develops his notion of solidarity in a number of later essays. Although Gadamer's discourse is not one of 'globalisation' as we might recognise it today,[6] already in his lifetime he recognises that solidarity takes shape on a global stage. He maintains that we are called mutually to 'discover' our 'solidarities' not only with those in our own communities or nations but also with those from different traditions, and, thus also, different linguistic traditions.[7] Indeed, Gadamer's call for us to discover our solidarity derives, in part, from his concern that our potential to address the geopolitical challenges we face is currently in jeopardy. He begins from the observation that many at the present historical juncture have become aware that all of our prospects for the future are inviolably bound up with one another through a vast and complex nexus of political, economic and cultural relations. He argues that while this awareness leads us to understand ourselves within a global context, it thus also compels us to recognise the incredible challenges that take place on, and, moreover, can only be addressed on, a global scale. It is difficult to deny that our times are marked by a range of urgent global crises: of decolonisation, global economic justice, environmental justice, immigration and the threat of nuclear annihilation. It is, in any case, in the same interview we have cited before, that he describes the rising awareness of the global context and challenges in terms that are perhaps the plainest and most poignant:

I am convinced that our thinking today within the framework not only of the nation-state but also of Europe is proving to be outdated. Isolation from the rest of the world is no longer possible. Humanity today is sitting in a rowboat, as it were, and we must steer this boat in such a way that we do not all crash into the rocks.[8]

Today more than ever we face global challenges that require an equally global political response. Yet, decisive for Gadamer is that the scope and depth of these challenges means that they will not yield to ideologically driven political debate, quick scientific or technological fixes, or piecemeal policy changes. He suggests instead that such global challenges will require sustained commitment to the pursuit of political decisions whose effectiveness and legitimacy derive from inclusive deliberation, or dialogue, on a genuinely global scale. The idea behind Gadamer's call for us to discover our solidarities, then, is that these discoveries comprise the visibility of the political itself that will first make such a politics possible.

Gadamer's concern for the discovery of solidarities on the global stage therefore makes a distinctive contribution that cuts deeper than more widely discussed approaches to solidarity based on common identity. Here, we may take Richard Rorty's celebrated approach as an example of solidarity forged in common identity. Rorty, who describes his position as a form of 'postmodern' – because purportedly non-metaphysical or relativistic – 'liberalism', defines solidarity as the recognition of our 'common humanity'.[9] Although Rorty claims to reject notions of humanity based on a 'core self' or 'human essence', he nevertheless argues that our recognition of our humanity derives from our ability to perceive our purported identity with one another in our mutual susceptibility to pain and humiliation.[10] He writes that our recognition of our common humanity turns on 'the ability to see more and more traditional differences (of tribe, religion, race, customs, and the like) as unimportant when compared with similarities with respect to pain and humiliation – the ability to think of people wildly different from ourselves as included in the range of us'.[11] To be sure, we wonder whether Rorty's notion of humanity, despite his claims to the contrary, retains vestiges of metaphysical essentialism in his apparent assumption that pain and humiliation is uniform for all human beings. Yet, Gadamer's elucidation of solidarity contrasts with Rorty's whether or not Rorty's claims to reject essentialism hold up. It is true that Gadamer, too, maintains an interest in motifs of the humanist tradition. He does not, however, suppose that human solidarity requires the deflation of our differences that as it were clears the way for us to see our similarities. Quite to the contrary, his approach suggests that solidarity concerns our mutual interpretive openness that first allows a shared world to become visible and that thus first makes it possible for us to enter into political deliberation, judgement and action.

Gadamer thus holds that the call to discover solidarities is urgent. This, he argues, is because the visibility of our lives lived in common is threatened in modernity. As we shall see, his concern applies just as much our current moment of globalisation, whether this is grasped as an advanced iteration of modernity or as something else. For Gadamer, this threat takes shape as a form of alienation that he describes as an 'interrelated foreignness' that arises in modern life due to an increasing calculative management of human relations. Moreover, as he argues, this calculative management is sustained by what he calls 'the ideal of a society of experts'. In these claims, Gadamer's approach suggests not an interest in debate with current proponents of an Anglophone liberal tradition, such as Rorty, but rather his affinity with figures and themes in the tradition of critical theory. Here, we think in particular of the consanguinity between Gadamer's approach and Habermas's critical concerns about the place of experts in discursive practice.[12] We may also think of Hannah Arendt's concern for the 'ice cold reasoning' of totalitarianism, and be led, as Jennifer Gaffney recently has been, to recognise important comparisons between Gadamer's account of solidarity and Arendt's.[13] As Gaffney submits, differences notwithstanding, 'there are important parallels between their approaches to solidarity that may be discerned, first, in their respective efforts to understand the communal and political implications of human finitude and, second, in the dangers that both identify in the ascendance of calculative rationality in modern life'.[14] Gadamer's approach, in any case, coalesces around concerns for 'interrelated foreignness'.[15] By this, he suggests a form of alienation, in which we come to experience one another as empty of significance because our political, social, economic and even interpersonal relations are mediated by structures that are organised in numerical, scientific and technical terms. Increasingly, we experience one another as a number and not as a unique person: in hospitals, so goes his example, patients are represented by a code number in order to receive tests; their blood, once extracted, is labelled with this code; the tests are conducted through a pre-given procedure that is implemented by medical technicians who most likely never meet or know the name of the patient. It is not difficult to see analogies in any number of walks of life, including, as academics will agree, in the university setting.

Gadamer suggests that the reduction of the visibility of a shared world due to the calculative management of human relations not only leads to the experience of interrelated foreignness, but, with this, leaves us susceptible to misguided ideals that further rob us of our ability to become visible to one another in our respective exteriority. In the important 1974 essay, 'What is Practice? The Conditions of Societal Reason', he argues that the calculative management of human relations gives rise to belief in 'the ideal of a society of experts'.[16] Once we accept the terms of the calculative management of human relations, it becomes easy to overvalue the expert as the highest authority or final court of appeals to address whatever challenges we face. Under the spell of this ideal, 'one turns to the specialist [*Fachmann*] and seeks relief for the practical, political, economic decisions that one has to make'.[17] We relinquish our stake in dialogue concerned with decisions about how best to direct our lives in common, and, in this, any need to concern ourselves with the visibility of the other that first makes dialogue about such decisions possible. It is of note that Gadamer, already in the 1970s, recognised the rise of communication technologies as a heightened temptation. For, in our use of these technologies, we appear to be ready not only to allow specialists to dictate *what* is best for us but, moreover, even to dictate *how* we form our opinions in the first place by dictating the media and channels through which we first receive information and engage in public and even private discourse.[18] In short, in any case, Gadamer argues that our acceptance of the misguided ideal of expertise makes us complicit in our political, social and economic disenfranchisement. 'The society of experts', as he puts the point, 'is simultaneously a society of functionaries.'[19] In abdicating our fortunes to the experts, we reduce any stake we have in our lives in common to the function we perform or role we play in whatever 'apparatus' they devise and deploy.[20]

Gadamer concludes that the reduction in the visibility of the shared world due to the calculative management of human relations culminates in what he, in a term he adopts from Karl Jaspers, calls 'anonymous responsibility'.[21] As Gadamer interprets Jaspers' idea, our acceptance of such calculative management makes our experience of our responsibilities aimless, uniform and empty because such responsibilities are not directed toward the other in her exteriority but are instead mediated by the numerical, scientific and technical structures that organise our relations and define our functions. Under regimes of calculative management, our responsibilities are never really to a live person, but instead to the requirements of societal ordering; if our responsibilities involve us with one another at all, it is only in abstraction and by way of a detour through these requirements. In Gadamer's example of hospital operations, medical technicians' responsibilities are never to a live person, a patient, but, instead, to the performance of the procedures that constitute their conducting of the tests; to the extent the medical technicians encounter the patient at all, it is as a code number or in a vile that contains an extraction of blood, or other bodily fluid or material. Whenever we accept the calculative management of human relations, we reduce our responsibilities to a nameless 'third person': such responsibilities no longer concern a 'you' or a 'we', but rather always only 'it' or 'one'.

* * *

Gadamer does not yet invoke the notion of 'globalisation' as we might recognise it from discourses today. His concern for the alienation we experience in modernity is, however, just as relevant now, in the age of globalisation. That relevance may be drawn out, I believe, by means of a brief comparative interpretation of Jean-Luc Nancy's recent essay, 'Urbi et Obri'.[22] In this piece, Nancy offers a characterisation of globalisation that, I believe, suggests the relevance of Gadamer's concern for 'interrelated foreignness' in our globalised times.

The title of Nancy's piece, 'Urbi et Orbi', evokes a term used by the Papacy to refer to a formal address (typically at Easter and Christmas) to the entire world. The phrase means something like, 'as for the city', specifically Rome, 'thus also for the world'. But, as Nancy notes, it has now become an idiomatic phrase that simply means something like 'universally', 'ubiquitously' or 'anywhere and everywhere'.[23] Nancy suggests that this shift in meaning from 'as for the city, thus also for the world' to 'anywhere and everywhere' may not be inconsequential. Indeed, he proffers that it captures the experience of globalisation as it has unfolded from out of Western expansionism.[24] Here, Nancy observes, first, that the Papal term 'Urbi et Orbi' suggests the idea of a political, economic and cultural capital city – a centre of civilisation – whose civilisation was then in turn to be extended beyond the city, and ultimately across the entire globe. This idea can certainly be discerned in the Papal message that reflects the political, economic and cultural values of the capital Rome that were then to be extended to the entire church. But, of course, it is not difficult to hear echoes of the idea in the imperial and colonial period, so that we might exchange 'London' or 'the Metropol' for Rome, and think of the extension of the city to the world in terms of the global reach of empire.

Nancy maintains, however, that in the age of globalisation the West no longer has a specific (or constellation of specific) capital cities. For him, this is a sign that the expansion of Western political, economic and cultural values has passed a certain tipping-point – it has become so ubiquitous that one can no longer distinguish a centre, from which those values spread, and a periphery, to which they are spread. Rather, as the shift in meaning of the phrase 'Urbi et Orbi' suggests, Western values have simply expanded to point that they prevail 'anywhere and everywhere'. As Nancy puts it:

It is no longer possible to identify either a city that would be 'The City' – as Rome was for so long – or an orb that would provide the contour of a world extended around this city. Even worse, it is no longer possible to identify either the city or the orb of the world in general. The city spreads and extends all the way to the point where, while it tends to cover the entire orb of the planet, it loses its properties as a city, and, of course, with them, those properties that would allow it to be distinguished from a 'country'.[25]

What now remains, Nancy suggests, is 'megapolitical, metropolitan, or co-urbational, or else caught in a loose net of what is called the "urban network"'.[26] Distinctive of such an 'urban network', as he believes it is important to observe, is a redistribution of disparity. In Western civilisation, in the past, disparities in political, economic and cultural access were distributed between the centre, a capital city, and the periphery, the rest of the globe, whether in terms of provinces, colonies or otherwise. Now, by contrast, the redistribution of access has been decentred, and disparities continue to grow along increasingly inapparent avenues. He writes:

The result can only be understood in terms of what is called an *agglomeration*, with its senses of conglomeration, or piling up, with the sense of accumulation that, on the one hand, simply concentrates (in a few neighborhoods, in a few houses, sometimes in a few protected mini-cities) the well-being that used to be urban or civil, while on the other hand, proliferates what bears the quite simple and unmerciful name of misery.[27]

If globalisation sees the rise of a global 'network', this does not overcome the disparities left behind by European imperialism and colonialism, but, rather, redistributes them. In our globalised times, disparity is no longer distributed from capital to province, but along the nodes of a network; it can appear 'anywhere and everywhere', perhaps half-concealed just one block away from a node of wealth and power, perhaps likewise hidden in adjacent seats occupied by different students in the same classroom.

Nancy goes on to examine globalisation as the destruction of the world, in the sense of the foreclosure of possibilities of life in common that would circumvent the logics of global capital. In turn, he also considers the prospects for reorienting our political energies, resisting globalisation (in French, *globalisation*) through participation in world-creation (in French, *mondalisation*). For the purposes of the present enquiry, however, Nancy's characterisation of globalisation as 'anywhere and everywhere' helps clarify the global context of Gadamer's concerns about alienation. Gadamer, as we have seen, is concerned for the discovery of solidarities on a global scale, and argues that the pursuit of such solidarities is under threat due to the alienation of interrelated foreignness we experience in modernity. Nancy's considerations of globalisation suggest how we experience the global reach of such interrelated foreignness. As his approach makes clear, the global reach of interrelated foreignness extends not simply from centres of wealth and power to the margins of empire. Rather, interrelated foreignness is 'anywhere and everywhere', experienced in the nodes of a global network of disparity.

The Discovery of Solidarities

What is required if we are to discover our solidarities with one another, Gadamer argues, is an intervention against the destruction of our visibility in a shared world. His claim is that our experience of interrelated foreignness, our acquiescence to the logic of the expert, as well as the anonymity of responsibility that results, can be countervailed, resisted, by degrees even overcome, through our openness to the discovery of solidarities with one another. It is true that although this claim becomes a recurrent theme of his writings from the 1970s onwards, he never offers any comprehensive elucidation of his conception of solidarity itself. In a later essay, he suggests that the significance of the notion of solidarity may be discerned from connotations of other German words from the same etymological family. We learn about the notion of solidarity from the related German word for 'payment' (*der Sold*), which carries the connotation of 'sterling and reliable inseparability', the idea that our commitment will 'remain the same if, when in truth, differences in interests and life situations let . . . [us] be tempted to go . . . [our] own way and to set back the wellbeing of the other'.[28] This significance of the notion of solidarity also receives emphasis from the German word for 'soldier' (*der Soldat*), with the connotations of loyalty and sacrifice.[29]

Gadamer clarifies his approach to solidarity in no small part, however, in connection with ancient Greek conceptions of friendship. He suggests that our prospects for an intervention against the modern condition of calculative management turn on the recovery of an ancient notion. His considerations orbit around the idea not only that friendship is a relationship characterised by regard, affection and moral and emotional support, though it is this, but also that friendship is a virtue, or implies a virtue, which fosters our ability to flourish in ethical and political life.[30] In this context, and with reference to Aristotle's description of complete friendship in particular, Gadamer specifies that friendship can contribute to the virtue of *phronēsis*, the capacity to form good ethical and political judgements and thus to conduct ourselves well. This, as we have seen, is because friendship enhances our openness, first of all to see ourselves, and with this our limits, but also to see the other, as well as the context of our shared and respective factical situatedness. Gadamer, we recall, believes that the significance of friendship is not restricted to our private lives, but 'flows into the full stream of self-forming commonalities'.[31] For him, philosophers such as Aristotle give voice to the Greek belief that our prospects for living well, both individually and collectively, are enhanced by friendship because friends help open a space of visibility, in which we better recognise ourselves, the other and the world. Gadamer's call for us to discover our solidarities, then, may be grasped as a call to twist free from the reduction in visibility that attends the calculative management of human relations, through a recovery of the ancient virtue of, the capacity for, friendship.

What, precisely, is the character of the larger political context that becomes visible through the discovery of solidarities? For Gadamer, the answer to this question is not concerned with the discovery of a common identity. Rather, what becomes visible is, first of all, our relatedness in difference. This has been persuasively argued in a recent article by Georgia Warnke,[32] who notes that Gadamer's approach to solidarity focuses not on common identities (à la Rorty) but on the recognition of the common terms of our concrete existence and plurality. With this, she recognises that, for Gadamer, solidarity concerns our abilities to make ourselves visible to one another. She writes:

What is crucial here is not that we recognise others as like us but that we recognise them at all – that is, that we see them as distinct others with specific differences that pick them out from an undifferentiated homogeneity . . . Solidarity is thus a form of unconcealment, to use Heidegger's term, in which we are mutually revealed and opened up to one another as particular others.[33]

Warnke argues that Gadamer's later, explicit approach to solidarity is continuous with, but more reactive than, the notion of solidarity implicit in his overall notion of tradition. This, she thinks, is because his later approach conceives of the formation of solidarity as always a reaction to some external threat or crisis. In illustration, she cites Gadamer's examples of the solidarities that arose from the Persian invasion of Greece, the Allied aerial bombing of Germany in the Second World War, and the current environmental crisis that faces us all. Warnke's criticism is that it remains unclear how Gadamer's association of solidarity with the opening of possibilities for the future of our ethical and political relations can be addressed by such a reactive posture.

Warnke's claim that Gadamer's later, explicit approach to solidarity is continuous with the notion of solidarity implicit in his overall approach to tradition is insightful. But her claim that the later approach is more reactive than the earlier notion misses the sense of Gadamer's argument. Gadamer, in fact, distinguishes between solidarities that arise in response to danger or necessity (*Not*), and the free pursuit of what may thus be called 'elective' solidarities. Moreover, Warnke does not appear to glean the right lesson from Gadamer's elucidation of solidarities that arise in response to necessity. Here, we would do well to observe that his examples of solidarities that arise in response to necessity all concern the mutually imminent threat of death. The invasion by the Persians was experienced by the Greeks as an existential threat to their city-states; the Allied aerial bombing of German cities was experienced as a threat of death by the inhabitants (who included Gadamer himself, in Leipzig during the fire-bombings of the city); and the current environmental crisis is, or should be, experienced by us as a threat to human life as such. These examples highlight that in solidarities arising in response to emergencies we become visible to one another precisely in the fact that each of us, as finite, free beings, is an irreducible source of our own involvement with others and the world. As Gadamer no doubt learns from Heidegger, nothing reminds us of this fact more than our confrontation with our own mortality, the threat of our own death. Solidarities that arise in response to necessity, as Gadamer's examples suggest, concern our visibility to one another as beings marked by and for death; solidarity concerns the fealty that attends those with a shared sense of mortality.

But Gadamer believes, too, that our pursuit of solidarities extends beyond those that arise in response to necessity. The latter, he asserts, mark only the first phase of our discovery of the fuller depth of our global solidarities with one another. He writes:

We are still a far cry from a common awareness that this is a matter of the destiny of everyone on this earth and that the chances of anyone's survival are as small as if a senseless attack with atomic weapons of destruction were to occur if humanity in the course of one or perhaps many, many crises, and in virtue of a history of experience involving many, many sufferings, does not learn to rediscover out of need a new solidarity. . . . But I do not mean that this is all; it is but a beginning, an initial awareness of solidarity. Merely out of necessity, to be sure. But is that a real objection? Does it not rather say something for the availability of a *fundamentum in re*? Even a solidarity out of necessity can uncover other solidarities.[34]

If solidarities arise first from necessity, they are still a point of departure for us freely to pursue other solidarities. Gadamer, with this, maintains that we are called to seek our global solidarities in aspects of human experience that go – or, in any case, have gone – by the names of freedom and history, of spirit and love, of meaning and value. In the context of his discussion of the need to discover global solidarities, he writes: 'Solidarities are experienced in all of those things where, when many people have a share in them, they do not lose their value but on the contrary their value increases – which is also the case with what we call art and culture.'[35] If the call to discover global solidarities initially arises in reaction to necessity, then, this call also reaches beyond necessity toward an elective concern to make ourselves visible to one another. For Gadamer, this free pursuit of solidarities takes shape first and foremost through art and culture.

He suggests, however, that the discovery of global solidarities through art and culture is nevertheless more difficult. This has to do with the multiplicity of languages found across the earth. Global solidarities are, after all, distinguished from national, regional and local solidarities by the fact that they cut across traditions, including linguistic traditions. To be sure, the discovery of global solidarities of all kinds – whether by necessity or otherwise – is made difficult by the fact that they require us to cross traditions and mother tongues. But when it comes to the discovery of global solidarities through art and culture, that crossing is made all the more formidable as so many of the achievements of art and culture are dependent on and sustained by the linguistic heritages out of which they originate.

Gadamer, as we have seen, calls for us to discover solidarities in order to make visible the shared world that is increasingly being robbed from us by the calculative management of human relations. In a later public lecture, he compares those who simply accept or even advocate for such calculative management to the Biblical citizens of Babel.[36] To Gadamer's mind, today's proponents of calculative rationality, like their Biblical counterparts, turn in hubris toward an empty dream of omnipresent intelligibility that leads them to turn thanklessly away from the global wealth of meaning granted by the multiplicity of the traditions of the earth.[37]

Hermeneutics, the Political and Politics

Gadamer's elucidation of solidarity, then, concerns the political but is not yet a matter of politics. This, however, is not to conclude that his approach is inconsequential; on the contrary, it suggests that the discovery of solidarities, whenever and however they are made, always (as it were) precedes politics and in any case always gives politics a novel orientation. The discovery of solidarities, whenever and however they are made, provides new perspectives that require us to intercede in prevailing political deliberation, judgement and action, and this, accordingly, requires us seek out new directions in our political involvements. The discovery of a solidarity is political in that it calls on us to reframe political debates instead of all too quickly giving ourselves over to politics by taking a side in some well-worn debate. Gadamer's idea that solidarity is political but not yet a matter of politics may be grasped through a certain hermeneutical circularity involved in the discovery of solidarities. On the one hand, the discovery of solidarities always takes place factically, within a political context and amidst political deliberations, judgements and actions that are in media res. In this sense, it always arrives 'after', whether in consequence of some necessity or as a result of interpretive engagement with some cultural or artistic achievement. On the other hand, however, the discovery of solidarities always brings into relief a novel orientation that requires an equally fresh start for political deliberations, judgements and actions. Hence, even as the discovery of solidarities always arrives 'after', it likewise always stands 'before' politics.

Gadamer's call for the discovery of solidarities appears to respond first and foremost to challenges that threaten catastrophe on a global scale – as we have mentioned, challenges such as those of decolonisation, global economic justice, environmental justice, immigration and nuclear annihilation. It is thus no surprise that his overall approach is driven, initially at least, by a concern for solidarities that arise in response to necessity. Yet, his approach to the pursuit of elective solidarities through cultural and artistic achievements reminds us that one important vocation of the arts and humanities is to be political without yet engaging in politics – a vocation that seems increasingly to be overlooked in our times. For Gadamer, the discovery of solidarities through artworks is fostered by the possibility for art to make the world available to us in a novel manner that challenges the frames of debates that have become entrenched. His idea that solidarities can be discovered through art is thus consistent with his view, developed with emphasis before him by Heidegger, that art is world-disclosive. In Heidegger's analysis of the work of art with reference to the Greek temple, he argues that art can bring into relief a context of meaning that gives orientation to life. He writes, in an oft-cited passage:

It is the temple-work that first joins together and simultaneously gathers around itself the unity of those paths and relations in which birth and death, disaster and blessing, victory and disgrace, endurance and decline obtain the form of destiny for human being. . . . The temple first gives to things their look and to humanity their outlook on themselves.[38]

Gadamer's approach stresses novelty more than Heidegger's. For Gadamer, the pursuit of solidarity through the achievements of art allows things to appear always otherwise than before: when an artwork first gives things their look and human beings their outlook, this look and outlook are always something different, something new. But, for Gadamer as for Heidegger, what art makes visible are the contexts of meaning that first give sense to political deliberations, judgements and actions at all.

Gadamer, finally, may also offer us an intervention against the currents of political life today. As we have seen, he calls for us to, as it were, tarry on the political, to discover solidarities that will coun-teract the reduction of the shared world that has resulted from the rise of the calculative management of human relations. Tarrying on the political – and there seeking to discover solidarities – allows us to return to politics with a novel orientation and perspective, and, accordingly, a renewed capacity for political deliberation, judgement and action.

If there is a sign of our times, it may well be that we have lost our taste for tarrying on the political, with the result that we may already be standing on the precipice of a collapse of the political into politics. It seems, at least, that in many quarters, whether in the academy, the media, or even the arts, the concern to tarry on the political, to attempt to make things visible in a new way, is increas-ingly squelched in the name of frames of debate that already have accepted trappings and established channels of dissemination. It may seem, too, that, lacking an adequate concern to tarry on the political, our politics has become populated by frames of debate that are stale to the point of being kitsch. Indeed, with Milan Kundera, we may suggest that our politics embodies what happens when a 'kitsch attitude' takes over: much of it seems captured by 'the need to gaze into the mirror of . . . [a] beautifying lie and to be moved to tears of gratification at one's own reflection'.[39]

Whether the sign of the times really is our loss of taste for the political, and whether this leaves us on the brink of a collapse of the political into politics are, of course, matters in need of further con-sideration. In the meantime, though, Gadamer's approach suggests a path toward holding open, even expanding, the political through the discovery of solidarities – a path that, in turn, may allow us to return to politics with greater vitality. Given the challenges we are up against, this is a path we can perhaps ill afford to pass by.

7 Arts and Literature

Gadamer calls for an intervention against the calculative rationality that increasingly organises our experience on a global scale – with Nancy, a global 'network' – through the discovery of solidarities. As Gadamer's approach suggests, the calculative rationality of the global network fails to make good on promises to expand and enhance meaningful connection. Quite to the contrary, it results above all in the alienation of interrelated foreignness. In Gadamer's call for an intervention, he observes the significant role that the arts and humanities can play in our attempts to counter the calculative rationality of the global network through the discovery of solidarities. At a basic level, his point is simple. If the discovery of solidarities turns on making our lives in common visible, then the arts and humanities, which aim at nothing else than making things that matter to us visible, will be of invaluable help. Gadamer's approach thereby reminds us that the broken promises of the global network are no substitute for achievements in the arts and humanities that can and do arise from the world's multiple cultural and linguistic traditions.

Gadamer's call for us to intervene against the the calculative rationality of the global network surely calls for the discovery of solidarities with the help of all of the arts and humanities. In this chapter, though, I wish to focus on the contribution that can be made by the arts and literature in particular. Gadamer, as I wish to show, suggests that the arts and literature can help to make our lives in common visible because our experience of art as such aims at a distinctive experience of truth. For Gadamer, art discloses the truth as meaningful possibility. Accordingly, his account suggests that the arts and literature can make our lives in common visible as testimony to the possibilities of such a shared life.

Moreover, as I shall argue, Gadamer's approach suggests that this testimony unfolds in different, if no doubt always interrelated, spheres. First, as we shall see, Gadamer's discussion of art in *Truth and Method*, Part I, suggests that art is testimony to those possibilities of shared life that arise from our possibilities of belonging to tradition. Many scholars (and many of them critics) presume that Gadamer's association of art with such testimony of tradition is the long and short of his view. But his approach is more nuanced. Second, some of Gadamer's later essays concerned with modern art, such as 'Art as Mimesis', suggest that for him art is not restricted to a testimony of the possibilities of belonging to tradition, but also allows a testimony of possible ordering as such. In this, art has the potential to help us make the possibilities of shared life visible enough beyond the context of the traditions to which we belong. And, third, Gadamer's discussion of literature suggests a further testimony. As we shall see, he maintains that literature occupies a 'borderline' position among the arts because its reliance on the written word makes it maximally transmittable. Accordingly, literature is a testimony to the possibility of transmission as such, and, with this, to the possibility of our participating in attempts to make our lives in common visible across all times and places. Given this, special attention will be paid to the potential of 'world literature' (*Weltliteratur*) to foster global solidarity.

Art as Testimony to the Possibilities of Tradition

Gadamer's elucidation of the experience of truth at issue in the arts and literature follows from the consideration that the being of art is a matter of 'enactment (*Vollzug*)'.[1] For Gadamer, the character of artworks 'cannot be defined as object of aesthetic consciousness' that is to be experienced in full presence and actuality.[2] Rather, in our encounters with artworks, truth, if it is experienced at all, is always experienced as the culmination of an event; that is, at the culmination of a movement by which our interpretive involvement with the presentation of an artwork brings something into view in its essential truth. Given his emphasis on the enactment-character of art, Gadamer's approach finds an especially clear expression in performing arts such as drama. At the theatre, the insight of the drama on the evening's playbill never appears at first, in full presence and actuality, as it were, at the very moment of the opening curtain. Quite to the contrary, if we experience insight at all, then it is as a result of our interpretive involvement with the drama as it is performed. But, while Gadamer's view that the being of art is in enactment finds a clear expression in the performing arts, he nevertheless believes it defines all forms of art. Just as the experience of the truth in a drama takes shape in our interpretive involvement with its performance, so too does the experience of a painting or statue, for example, take shape through our interpretive involvement with its exhibition.

How, though – more precisely – are we to understand Gadamer's claim that the being of art is in enactment? While in *Truth and Method* his elucidation of the being of art as enactment is organised first of all in reference to the 'clue' provided by 'play', (*Spiel*), 'transformation' into what is only poorly translated as 'structure', (*Gebilde*) and 'contemporaneity',[3] his view also comes into focus through his consideration of the notion of *mimesis*. In *Truth and Method*, Gadamer's approach is keyed, in particular, to motifs in Aristotle, drawing on the latter's notion of *mimesis* to describe artworks as events of self-presentation that allow something to be recognised in its essence.

Gadamer identifies the being of art as enactment with Aristotle's notion of *mimesis* through a contrast he draws between our experience of 'the world in which we live', and what is 'real', and our experience of art.[4] In our experience of reality – or, as Gadamer might also have described it, factical life – we always find ourselves oriented by our cares. The context of factical life 'always stands in a horizon of desired or feared, or, at any rate, still undecided future possibilities'.[5] In view of the undecidedness of the future that characterises factical life, our experience remains always and again mired in ambiguity. Our desires and fears, both individually and in connection with one another, run in multiple directions at once, often at odds with one another, to the point that, as Gadamer puts it, 'mutually exclusive expectations are aroused', creating a 'superfluity'[6] that leaves factical experience always and again uncertain, conflicted and discordant.

Gadamer maintains that in our encounters with artworks, by contrast, experiences from factical life are transformed by being brought into sharper and more concentrated focus. He introduces the term *Gebilde*, only poorly translated as 'structure', to describe this concentrated focus achieved in art.[7] Despite the prevalence of the English translation of 'structure' for the German *Gebilde*, Gadamer's particular usage is perhaps better put into English with 'figure' or 'contour'. In our experience of artworks, aspects of factical life are given shape, figured, or contoured. Of course, with this idea Gadamer does not mean that our encounters with artworks purify factical life of ambiguities, or of its superfluity of mutually exclusive expectations, but, on the contrary, that artworks bring the ambiguities and contradictions of factical life into special focus.

For Gadamer, our encounters with art transform, that is to say, give the contour of truth to, our experience of the ambiguities and contradictions characteristic of factical life. He writes: 'From this viewpoint, "reality" is defined as what is untransformed, and art as the raising up (*Aufhebung*) of this reality into its truth.'[8] It is precisely in order to capture the character of this transformation that Gadamer introduces notion of *mimesis*. To be sure, his identification of this transformation into truth with *mimesis* will appear incongruous to anyone who upholds the received notion of *mimesis* as a facsimile of some original. While the notion of *mimesis* as facsimile appears to be prevalent in common parlance, its *locus classicus* is, whether justly or unjustly, typically taken to be Plato's *Republic*, Book X. There, we recall, Plato's Socrates decries the dangers of artistic *mimesis*. While he is also concerned that artistic imitations can excite excessive passions in the soul, his polemic comes to focus on the fact that artistic imitations are deceptive because they remain at a remove from reality. True being, Socrates argues, is found in the forms or ideas – in his example, the idea of the bed. True reality, Socrates argues, is produced by God, and this is the form or idea of the bed; once removed from this is the bed-maker's production based on this idea, a physical bed; and removed once more is the artist's imitation of the physical bed, whether in poetic or painted image.[9]

However we are to understand Plato's intentions in this discussion, the received definition of *mimesis* as facsimile derived from Socrates' discussion is clear. On Socrates' view, *mimesis* does not raise reality into truth, but, on the contrary, is untrue because at a remove from reality. Gadamer elucidates the being of art as enactment in reference not to this received notion of *mimesis*, but to the notion that he finds in Aristotle's *Poetics*.[10] His analysis focuses on what he calls the 'cognitive sense' or orientation (*Erkenntnissinn*) toward 'presentation' (*Darstellung*) that lies in Aristotle's notion of *mimesis*.[11] By this, Gadamer means that the purpose of *mimesis* is not at all to produce a deception, to pass off a facsimile for a genuine article, but, quite to the contrary, to allow something genuinely to be recognised. Thus, as he asserts, 'the cognitive sense (*Erkenntnis-sinn*) of *mimesis* is recognition (*Anerkennung*)'.[12] Gadamer finds support for his analysis in Aristotle's observation that *mimesis* is natural for human beings from a very young age:

> the joy that children take in dressing up, as Aristotle remarks, does not derive from a will to conceal themselves, to pretend to be something else in order to be guessed at and discovered behind the pretence; on the contrary, this joy derives from a will to present that wants only what is presented. The child wants at all costs to avoid being guessed at behind her costume. What she presents, is supposed to *be*, and if something is supposed to be guessed at, it is this. What is supposed to be recognized is what 'is' there.[13]

On Gadamer's analysis, then, there is a legitimate cognitive function that animates *mimesis*; its purpose is not to deceive but, rather, to allow something to be recognised.

Gadamer maintains, moreover, that this cognitive orientation of *mimesis* toward presentation also entails an 'ontological sense', because such presentation aims at 'knowledge of the essence' of something.[14] In *mimesis*, the orientation of presentation is to allow something to be recognised; but, ultimately, at least in the fuller development of mimetic practices achieved in the arts and literature, there is more at stake in recognition than merely to identify or pick out something in particular. With the description of this 'more' as an essence, Gadamer suggests that the purpose of mimetic presentation is ultimately to allow something to be recognised in its universality.

Yet, by this, he does not have in mind the universality of a concept, under which something presented in its particularity can be exhaustively subsumed and determined. Instead, I would submit, what is at stake is the universality of *meaningful possibilities*, which are elicited by something presented in its particularity but which cannot, however, be exhaustively determined.[15] The purpose of Aristophanes' *The Clouds*, for example, is neither to present something that will simply allow his audience to recognise the main character as the particular person Socrates, nor to allow his audience to recognise a conceptual definition of the human being such as 'man is a political animal' or 'rational animal'. Rather, to wit (quite roughly), the purpose is to allow the particular character, Socrates, to be recognised within the context of the broader possibilities of factical life: in the possibilities of the pursuit of wisdom; in the possibilities of conflict that arise within a decadent polis from such a pursuit; as well as the ambiguity of greatness, the folly, and perhaps even the inevitable hypocrisy that arise from such a pursuit in such a context.

In his discussion in *Truth and Method*, Gadamer stresses that the cognitive orientation of *mimesis* toward presentation is, more precisely, a matter of self-presentation. With this, he means to clarify that our experience of artistic presentations unfolds as a self-referential, unitary event. As self-referential, this event not only allows something to be recognised in its essence but also, thereby, allows those involved in the event to recognise something about themselves. He introduces this clarification in order to contrast what he interprets as our actual experience of art from the misinterpretations that result from the assumptions of modern aesthetics. He observes that it is characteristic of what he terms modern aesthetic consciousness to define encounters with artworks in terms of a spectator's or listener's subjective experience that is, in turn, strictly differentiated from the artwork taken as an aesthetic object.

It is against such aesthetic differentiation that Gadamer poses his elucidation of artworks as mimetic presentation. He argues that such presentations are self-presentations because, as they occur, all differentiations between spectator and performance, artwork and its subject matter, artwork and the occasion of its presentation, are 'superseded' through 'total mediation'.[16] What Gadamer means by these Hegelian formulations is that *mimesis*, as presentation, allows something to be recognised in its truth through the interpretive involvements of artists with their materials, as well as performers or exhibitors with the artworks that result from the artist's efforts, and also the spectators or listeners with the performance or exhibition. Such presentation is self-presentation first of all because, if it succeeds, all of these differences recede, creating an opening that allows something to be recognised in its essence. It is self-presentation, too, because as these differences recede, those involved in the event are able to recognise something about themselves in what the artistic presentation has made recognisable.

Gadamer argues that whenever an artwork succeeds as mimetic self-presentation, what comes to be presented is recognised in 'contemporaneity' (*Gleichzeitigkeit*). Originally developed by Kierkegaard

to characterise the relation that a modern Christian can have to the
Jesus of Biblical times, Gadamer uses the term to describe the relation
of an audience of a current artistic presentation to the history or tradition of that artwork's presentations. Because the being of artworks
depends on self-presentation, they do not persist in continual presence as do, say, a stone or a star – at least for a while. Rather, artworks
persist only through the repetition of such events. In this, Gadamer
argues, the being of artworks can be compared to that of festivals,
especially religious festivals, which exist through their periodic repetition alone. Now, for artworks as for festivals, each self-presentation
involves variation and difference. A performance of Aristophanes' *The
Clouds* today is no doubt dissimilar to a performance that took place in
ancient Athens in countless ways. Yet, Gadamer argues that if an artwork comes off successfully in a particular event of self-presentation,
then what is thus brought into recognition in its essence is the same
as what always is or can be brought into recognition in any of this
artwork's events of self-presentation. It is this sameness of recognition
through the difference of repeated self-presentations that Gadamer
terms 'contemporaneity'. He writes: '"contemporaneity". . . means
that in its presentation this particular thing that presents itself to us
achieves full presence, however remote its origin may be'.[17] Artworks,
in every unique event of self-presentation, remain as it were timeless,
because they allow something to be recognised in the same essence
each time.

Gadamer's elucidation of the being of artworks with reference to
Aristotle's notion of *mimesis* suggests, finally, that artistic presentation can be understood as a testimony to possibilities of tradition.
This is because artistic presentation, in the achievement of contemporaneity, attests not only to the fact that an artwork remains the
same over the span of different – indeed, indefinitely many – presentations. The achievement of contemporaneity also attests to the
continuity of the context of inherited meaning that makes such recognition possible in the first place. On Gadamer's view, our experience of truth in art results from our interpretive involvement with
a *mimesis* that allows the essence of something to be recognised in
its contemporaneity. But, this experience of truth is only possible
because in this *mimesis*, the tradition, or the inherited context of
meaning on which an artwork draws, remains effective. Indeed, for
Gadamer in *Truth and Method*, the experience of truth in art is always

a result of *mimesis* understood as *mimesis* of aspects of an inherited context of meaning. If it is possible for spectators of a performance of Aristophanes' *The Clouds* today to recognise something essential through their interpretive involvement, this is at least in part because its *mimesis* of the world of ancient Athens remains accessible, or, at least, accessible enough, to them. Here, our experience of truth in artistic *mimesis* thus also offers proof of the continuity of the tradition because this achievement is only possible thanks to that tradition's continued effectiveness. Every experience of truth in artistic *mimesis*, then, is testimony to the possibilities of the tradition that makes it possible.

Gadamer's *Truth and Method* account therefore sheds light on the role that art can play in the discovery of solidarities through the testimony of possibilities of tradition. The interrelated foreignness left by the calculative rationality of the global network severs us from even the contexts of meaning familiar from the traditions to which we belong. Indeed, this is precisely the focus of Gadamer's concern for the 'alienation' that results from 'historical consciousness' in his celebrated essay, 'The Universality of the Hermeneutical Problem'.[18] As his account in *Truth and Method* suggests, however, the arts can help to make visible aspects of our life in common from out of the inherited contexts of meaning familiar to us. Of course, these inherited contexts of meaning are themselves anything but monolithic, and part of what we inherit are contestations and forms of subjugation. But, thanks to the arts, these aspects of our life in common, as well as the conflicts, suffering and prospects for reconciliation that accompany them, are also able to be made visible. For Gadamer, the arts help us make our life in common, both as it is for better and as it is for worse, visible first of all through the testimony of the possibilities of tradition.

Art as Testimony to the Possibilities of Meaning-ordering

Our lives in common, however, are more expansive than the traditions to which we belong. Really, our lives in common are an intersection of meanings from multiple heritages, themselves just as much bound up in relations of contestation and various modes of subjugation as are the traditions to which we belong. In view of this, we may worry that Gadamer's *Truth and Method* account remains inadequate because it over-determines the dependence of our experience of artistic truth on tradition. After all, that account holds that artistic *mimesis*, when it succeeds, is nothing less than a testimony to the possibilities of tradition. The success of an artistic *mimesis* always already entails that the tradition to which it belongs and on which it draws remains effective.

Gadamer, however, offers a reconsideration of – or, perhaps better, a supplement to – his *Truth and Method* account. In 'Art as Imitation', he suggests that the experience of truth at issue in the arts and literature extends beyond the testimony of possibilities of a tradition to something much broader and more original: to the possibilities of meaningful ordering as such. Gadamer's concern in 'Art as Imitation' is that his account of *mimesis* in *Truth and Method* is not expansive enough to address the possibilities we have to experience truth, or something akin to truth, in avant-garde artworks, especially painting, that eschew or extend beyond a tradition, indeed, to the point of abstraction.[19] But, as we shall see, Gadamer's concern in 'Art and Imitation' may also have implications for our possibilities to experience not only artworks that extend beyond a tradition but also artworks that draw on traditions unfamiliar to us.

Strikingly, Gadamer's supplemental account in 'Art as Imitation' does not abandon the main lines of the notion of *mimesis* he developed in *Truth and Method*. Quite to the contrary, he instead argues that our experience of truth in artworks that extend beyond a tradition can be illuminated if we deepen his *Truth and Method* account through a further, more fundamental and encompassing consideration of *mimesis*. To this end, Gadamer proposes to supplement Aristotle's notion of *mimesis*, which relies on the testimony of tradition, with a Pythagorean sense of *mimesis*, understood as a testimony to what he describes in terms of the possibility of ordering as such.

In 'Art as Imitation' no less than in *Truth and Method*, Gadamer takes his point of departure from the consideration that artistic *mimesis* has a cognitive orientation that allows something to be recognised in its essence. Artistic *mimesis* thus allows those involved in the artistic presentation to recognise something about themselves in what is thus made recognisable. In the later essay, Gadamer once again finds support for this view in Aristotle's observation that *mimesis* is natural for human beings. He writes: '[Aristotle] initially draws attention to

the natural human tendency toward imitation and the natural plea-
sure we all take in such imitation. It is in this context that he claims
that the joy we take in imitation is really the joy of recognition.'[20]
Here, too, Gadamer once again maintains that this cognitive orientation of *mimesis* concerns the being of what it allows to be recognised.
He writes: 'It is part of the process of recognition that we see things
in terms of what is permanent and essential in them, unencumbered
by the contingent circumstances in which they were seen before and
are seen again . . . For what imitation reveals is precisely the real
essence of the thing.'[21] And, finally, Gadamer once again also maintains that *mimesis*, in allowing something to be recognised, thereby
also allows those involved in an artistic presentation to recognise
something about themselves: 'For it is also part of the process that
we recognise ourselves as well'; 'all art of whatever kind is a form of
recognition that serves to deepen our knowledge of ourselves and
thus our familiarity with the world as well'.[22]

Although Gadamer's 'Art and Imitation' begins from similar considerations about the cognitive orientation of *mimesis* as those in *Truth
and Method*, his concern in the later essay for artworks that extend
beyond a tradition lead him to suggest that his earlier account of this
cognitive orientation is inadequate. In both works, Gadamer turns to
Aristotle to argue that this cognitive orientation concerns the recognition of something in its essence and, with this, self-recognition. In
'Art and Imitation', however, his concern for art that extends beyond
a tradition brings into relief the limitations of his reliance on Aristotle
for his notion of recognition. Specifically, Gadamer suggests that the
notion of recognition found in Aristotle is unjustifiably limited in
scope precisely because it rests on the unquestioned assumption that
recognition depends on tradition. He writes:

> Recognition, as understood by Aristotle, presupposes the continuing exis-
> tence of a binding tradition that is intelligible to all and in which we can
> encounter ourselves. Myth played this role in Greek thought, providing
> common subject matter for artistic representation. And it was the recogni-
> tion of myth in pity and fear that deepened our familiarity both with the
> world and with ourselves.[23]

The notion of recognition found in Aristotle is not consanguine with
artworks that eschew tradition or extend beyond a tradition for the
very reason that his approach presupposes tradition, an inherited

context of meaning that remains effective. Gadamer upholds that even in artworks that eschew tradition, such as 'modern pictures built up out of meaningful elements that dissolve into something unrecognizable', we may nevertheless 'experience a fragmentary act of recognition' that draws on tradition.[24] But, he argues, even in view of the possibility of such fragmentary recognition, the notion of tradition found in Aristotle and that guides his *Truth and Method* elucidation remains too narrow to account for our experience of artworks that eschew tradition.

Gadamer's acknowledgement of the challenges introduced by modern artworks to his notion of the cognitive orientation of *mimesis* does not, however, lead him to disavow his earlier account, but rather to propose a deeper, more fundamental and encompassing elucidation of the cognitive function of *mimesis*. In pursuit of this supplement, however, he turns, not forward toward more purportedly up-to-date theories of imitation than Aristotle's, but further backward to motifs associated with Pythagoras. He writes: 'But perhaps it is possible to understand *mimesis* and the kind of knowledge that it brings in a more universal sense. In this attempt to find a key to modern art through a deeper understanding of the concept of imitation, I now wish to go even further back, before Aristotle, to Pythagoras.'[25] Gadamer's consideration of Pythagoras is rather focused; as he puts it, his aim is not to 'reconstruct or discover' all of Pythagoras' 'original doctrines', but, much more modestly, to focus on a 'couple of quite uncontroversial points that will lead us in the right direction'.[26]

The first point of Gadamer's turn to Pythagoras is that Pythagorean teaching, like that of Aristotle, maintains a cognitive orientation of *mimesis* toward the recognition of something in its essence.[27] For Pythagoras as for Aristotle, *mimesis* is no facsimile; rather, it contributes to knowledge of things in their essence. Gadamer's second Pythagorean point, however, is that whereas Aristotle identifies such recognition as the recognition of essential truths inherited from tradition, that is, from Greek myth and religion, Pythagoras, by contrast, identifies such recognition even more universally as the recognition of cosmic order as such, as reflected in 'numbers and the ratios between them'.[28] Gadamer, of course, has in mind here the Pythagorean idea that the visible ordering of the heavens, the audible ordering of music, and finally the proper ordering of the human soul, can all be recognised in ratios of number.[29] Central for Gadamer, however, is not foremost any purported affinities between Pythagorean number and the modern prejudice for the exactness of a mathematical description of things. Rather, what matters to Gadamer is that Pythagoras' alignment of *mimesis* with number introduces an approach to the cognitive orientation of *mimesis* that is completely liberated of dependence on tradition. As Gadamer believes, the Pythagorean view of what comes to be recognised in its essence through *mimesis* is a matter of order that is more universal than anything that can be derived from a given tradition or *mythos*.

Gadamer proposes a supplement to his *Truth and Method* account of *mimesis* based on precisely this possibility of the recognition of order that is more universal than that of tradition. In this, he suggests that our experience of artworks can provide not only testimony to tradition, but also, more widely, testimony to the possibility of ordering as such. Although Gadamer associates it with Pythagorean teaching, his supplementary proposal is not that this more universal possibility of recognition concerns number and ratio *per se*. It is not that the recognition of something in its essence means simply the recognition of the mathematical relationships that inform it (though, of course, our experience of artworks sometimes does involve the discernment of proportions or harmonies that can meaningfully be described mathematically). Rather, Gadamer's supplementary proposal about *mimesis* is perhaps better seen as taking Pythagorean teaching as an emblem.

Seen in this manner, the proposal is that Pythagoras' more universal conception of recognition concerns the recognition of the possibility of meaningful order, or ordering, as such. That is, Pythagoras' teaching is that the cognitive orientation of *mimesis* is not toward the recognition of some order or other – say, a particular ratio or other mathematical relation – but, more originarily, toward the recognition of the possibility of and the event through which order can appear at all – of the possibility, as it were, of an occurrence of the ordering of any order *überhaupt*. Of our experience of modern artworks in particular, he writes: 'of course, the order that we experience in modern art no longer bears any resemblance to the exemplary order formerly revealed by nature and the structure of the *cosmos*'.[30] Gadamer's proposal, then, is that in artistic *mimesis*, recognition – whatever else it involves – always also involves, at bottom, the recognition of the possibility of ordering at issue in the appearance of any order. Because of this, artistic *mimesis* may also be said always to testify to this possibility of recognising order as well.

In artistic *mimesis*, we may come to recognise something that can be derived from a tradition that remains effective and coherent, or we may come to recognise something that can be derived from fragments of a tradition that is losing its effectiveness, or, for that matter, we may come to recognise something that derives from an eschewal of tradition itself. In every case, Gadamer now proposes, whatever is recognised is recognised in terms of possibilities of ordering. Whether our experience is of the interplay of *stasima* and episodes in a Greek tragedy, of line and colour in a Dan Flavin installation, or of mountain, valley and water in a traditional Chinese landscape painting, our recognition of these interplays itself turns on and thus testifies to the possibility of orderings in general.

Gadamer's supplementary account of the arts speaks to the discovery of solidarities in a sphere that extends beyond that of the traditions familiar to us. The interrelated foreignness left by the calculative rationality of the global network alienates us from traditions foreign to us no less than from those that are familiar. Gadamer suggests, however, that the arts can make visible aspects of our lives even at the fringes and frontiers, and in the interstices, of familiar and foreign traditions. For the arts, as testimony to the possibility of meaningful ordering, allow us to discern orderings of life in common beyond any specific tradition. In this, they testify to the possibility not only of orderings that connect otherwise disparate meanings from diverse traditions, but perhaps also even to possibilities of ordering without dependence on traditions.

Literature as Testimony of Transmission

Gadamer maintains that literature is distinguished by what he calls the 'borderline position' it holds among the arts.[31] While he provides no cut and dried definition of literature, he has in mind above all the *belles lettres*, the fine arts of the written text, especially the novel, though also other forms of prose, and, indeed, in a later essay, he suggests that the genealogy of literature traces back to the lyric poem.[32] He also recognises the affinity between literature and other forms of the written text such as the scholarly or scientific treatise.[33]

Gadamer's claim is that literature stands at the borderline or limit position of the arts because, as written text, it involves a historical mode of being that allows it to be more readily historically transmitted than all other forms of art. Literature is, on the one hand, continuous with all of the other arts because its being, like that of all art, is enactment. Literature, Gadamer recognises, is not enacted in, say, a performance, as is a dramatic work of art, nor, for that matter, as an exhibition or installation, as a painting or other visual artwork may be. But, he argues, the being of literature may nevertheless be grasped as enactment insofar as it must be read. 'Literature', he states, 'has its original existence in being read, as . . . the epic has it in being declaimed by the rhapsodist or the picture in being looked at by the spectator. Thus the reading of a book would still remain an event in which the content comes to presentation.'[34] To be sure, it is possible to miss that the being of literature is enactment if we suppose that 'reading is a purely interior mental process'.[35] But, he argues, reading, even when it is conducted in silence, is no purely interior process. 'This is immediately obvious', he tells us, 'as long as reading means reading aloud. But there is obviously no sharp differentiation between reciting and silent reading. Reading with understanding is always a kind of reproduction, performance, and interpretation. Emphasis, rhythmic ordering, and the like are part of wholly silent reading, too.'[36] The being of literature, Gadamer upholds, no matter how inconspicuously reading seems to be undertaken, is no less a matter of enactment than it is in any art.

Yet, Gadamer maintains that even if the being of literature is thus continuous with the other arts, it is nevertheless distinguished by the maximal efficacy with which it may be transmitted. He does not elucidate his claim in detail, but his idea seems to be that literature is an achievement of civilisations in which customary practices prevail that sustain the writing and reading of texts. Here one must think of multiple and diverse practices, from the use of the alphabet, to societal structures that allow the written word to be produced and disseminated, to educational systems that enable people to learn to read. Gadamer argues that literature, in virtue of its written form and whenever the conditions that sustain this form prevail, is able to be passed down with less depreciation of its possibilities for enactment than any other form. As he explains: 'the existence of literature is not the dead survival of an alienated being . . . Literature is a function of being intellectually preserved and handed down, and therefore brings its hidden history into every age.'[37] Everything, including all art, is susceptible to the conflagration of history; everything, in the end, returns from memory into oblivion. Literature, however, because of the maximal efficacy of its historical being as something written, remains in force with a special intensity. We can read a work of literature passed down from ancient India, for example, in the full richness of its significance even once that time and place are long gone. By contrast, we can enact pieces of music from distant times and places with only a paucity of significance, if we can do so at all, as the conventions of period music come to be forgotten. Or, more remotely still, we can enact the cave paintings of our ancient ancestors with only an inkling of sense at all, as the presumably oral myths as well as the lifeways to which the paintings speak have sunk into oblivion.

Finite beings, whose understanding is conditioned by transmission, rely in their very being in myriad ways on messages passed down from the dead; within this context, artworks may be regarded as the most rich and complex messages that are thus passed down. Gadamer's point is that literature stands out because it allows the richness and complexity of the messages that characterise all artworks to be passed down with maximal efficacy. In a remarkable claim, he goes so far as to say that with literature, 'time and space seem to be superseded'.[38] He maintains, in fact, that literature, because of writing, contrasts not only with the other arts but also, and more than this, with all the artefacts of human history. He writes: 'The remnants of past life – what is left of buildings, tools, the contents of graves – are weather beaten by the storms of time that have swept over them, whereas a written tradition, once deciphered and read, is to such an extent pure mind that it speaks to us as if in the present.'[39] Literature, because it is written, may be enacted with less regard for context, for time and space, than any other human achievement.

Nota Bene. **World Literature**

Gadamer describes world literature as a development of literature itself. He suggests that awareness of and interest in the possibility of world literature first arises in the age of Goethe and foremost through Goethe's own introduction of the notion in the intellectual circles of the day. In a passage from Peter Eckermann's account of his conversations with Goethe, Goethe endorses the prospect of world literature in the context of his recent reading of a Chinese novel: 'national literature is now rather an unmeaning term; the epoch of world literature is at hand, and everyone must strive to hasten its approach'.[40] Gadamer's considerations, however, focus not on the actual historical appearance of interest in world literature or Goethe's reflections on the matter, but instead on the idea that world literature is an outgrowth of literature itself. For Gadamer, world literature is made possible at least in part by the historical mode of being that literature enjoys in virtue of its written form. Indeed, because of this, as Gadamer insists, 'it is by no means the case that world literature is an alienated form of what originally constituted a given work's mode of being'.[41] World literature, in virtue of the written form, can, without alienation, be taken up in a context larger than that from which it first arises.

Gadamer, as we have seen, holds that literature, as a written form, is more readily transmitted than any other kind of art. He argues that the appearance of and interest in world literature is possible in part because this same form allows literature to be so readily transmitted not only *historically* but also *geographically*. World literature is possible because literature can be enacted not only in any *time* where customary practices that sustain reading prevail, but also in any *place*. To be sure, the appearance of and interest in world literature requires the development of supplementary practices that sustain the ability to write and read texts. In addition to the practices we mentioned before, world literature requires practices such as translation, education in modern and classical languages, and perhaps even the adequate development of research in disciplines as diverse as philology, literary criticism and cultural studies. Given the perilously low share of the literature market held by works in translation in my own country, the US, it is difficult not to underscore the significance of this practice in particular. In this, we find a rapprochement between Gadamer and Edith Grossman, master translator of Spanish works into English (most recently her acclaimed translation of Cervantes' *Don Quixote*). As Grossman puts the point in her recent *Why Translation Matters*, 'the very concept of world literature . . . depends on the availability of translations . . . Translation is crucial to our sense of ourselves as serious readers, and as literate, educated men and women we would find the absence of translations to read and study inconceivable.'[42] World literature, because of the fact that the written text belongs to a global context even as it arises from a specific cultural milieu, must be protected and cultivated. As perilous as the situation in the US has become, Gadamer's idea is that world literature remains possible, in any case, as long as these practices are adequately in place, since a work of literature can be enacted with less dependence on the tradition from which it arises than any other kind of art.

Gadamer's characterisation of world literature as a body of literature that may be distinguished by the exceptional contribution it makes to our understanding of the human experience leads him to associate world literature with the 'classic' and, moreover, as providing 'examples to be followed'.[43] Gadamer describes world literature as a distinctive development of literature, which, therefore, does not supersede or replace other possibilities of literature. Because of this, his view of world literature is perhaps best grasped as an addendum to, and, crucially, not a substitute for, other possibilities, such as national literature, avant-garde literature, anti-colonial literature or feminist literature.

This being said, Gadamer's emphasis on the classic – in respect to world literature and the other arts – nevertheless relies on the possibility of canonicity and, with this, perhaps even an interest in what could be characterised as a global canon of 'great books'. Yet, he maintains a conception of canonicity concerned not with ideologically or dogmatically driven conservation but rather with hermeneutical evidence. He associates canonicity not with the conservation or protection of received opinions about which literature counts and which not. Rather, his approach suggests that canonicity first opens up possibilities of interpretation that allow us not only to learn from venerated texts, but also to test received opinions about literature, to discover new evidence of excellence in literature, and thereby to introduce, celebrate and consider heretofore undiscovered, neglected and excluded works. On Gadamer's view, we may say, we do not value works of world literature (or, for that matter, of any literature or art) because of the received opinion that they are classics; rather, it only makes sense to affirm that works are classics as they prove their exceptional significance through our hermeneutical experience of them.

Gadamer's conception of the canonicity of world literature, then, suggests the demands that are imposed on us whenever we engage with world literature, whether as scholars, teachers, students, readers or all of these. For, in the context of concern for world literature, it is never enough simply to accept received opinion about which books are 'great' and just what these books are supposed to teach. Quite to the contrary, Gadamer's approach suggests that world literature poses the project or task of involving ourselves in evidentiary contestation. This, to be sure, means being open to and attempting to understand the judgements of our predecessors. But it also means being open to the possibility that judgements inherited from the past require revision or even rejection, as well as being open to the possibility of novelty, whether that of heretofore undiscovered, neglected or excluded works, or that of new interpretations of familiar works. To involve ourselves in world literature, then, requires great ability and effort and, thus, may be described as one of the most difficult and elevated senses of the capacity to converse. For, when we involve ourselves in world literature, we find ourselves exposed to exteriority with a rare intensity, displacing us not only from the context of everyday experience of language to that of the sophisticated language of literature, but, moreover, from the context of our first language and the tradition that sustains it to a global context made possible by the written word.

Gadamer's considerations make clear, finally, that literature – and in a distinctive manner, world literature – can help us discover solidarities with one another. Gadamer, as we have seen, calls for us to discover solidarities in the name of an intervention against the anonymous responsibility that characterises the by now nearly ubiquitous reach of the calculative rationality of the global network. That calculative rationality threatens our ability to make visible our life in common and, with this, our ability to address the challenges we face, on a global no less than a local scale. As we have also seen, Gadamer suggests that the arts and literature can help us to discover solidarities in a number of spheres. Our experience of art testifies to possibilities that make our life in common visible, both in reference to the traditions we share as well as to originary orderings that extend beyond the limits of any specific tradition. As Gadamer's account of literature as a 'borderline' case of the arts suggests, literature, because of its reliance on the written word, testifies to the possibility of transmitting meaning through time and space, making our lives in common visible across any interval of history or geography. Indeed, as the experience of world literature suggests, literature harbours the potential to help make visible aspects of our lives in common on a genuinely global scale. Here, though, the life in common at stake is not merely the interrelated foreignness of a calculatively rational global network. Rather, with world literature, the globe can come into view not as an 'anywhere and everywhere', but, instead, in its visibility as a someplace, indeed, a someplace special – a genuine 'there', where we find the possibility of being in the world in common.

Finally, Gadamer's picture of the discovery of solidarities through the arts and literature sheds further light on his post-metaphysical affirmation of motifs from the tradition of humanism. As we have seen, Gadamer aligns the responsibility to understand with the post-metaphysical concern to elevate ourselves into our humanity through the enactment and cultivation of the capacity to converse. His account of the discovery of solidarities through the arts and literature identifies some of the most impressive heights to which this capacity can aspire. Here, the discovery of solidarities is not a question of the discovery of our common essence as human beings. Rather, it concerns the possibilities of our lives in common, possibilities that derive both from traditions familiar to us and in connection with traditions that are foreign, as well as from the transmission of meaning on a global scale. The discovery of solidarities through the arts and literature may therefore be said to concern our common humanity, as long as this refers not to some purported universal essence, but, instead, to our capacity to discern a life in common from out of every horizon of our possibilities for existence. In this, Gadamer's approach to world literature perhaps allows us to hear post-metaphysical echoes of the celebrated sentiment of Terrance: '*Homo sum, humani nihil a me alienum puto*' – 'I am a human being, I consider nothing that is human alien to me.'[44]

Not all philosophers, of course, agree that the pursuit of global solidarities is aided by our experience of world literature. Many have argued that the notion of world literature, far from contributing to global solidarities, is rather an ideology or mask for power. Already in 1848, only twenty years after Goethe introduced and popularised the idea, Marx and Engels criticised the notion of world literature as an ideology of capitalism. In the *Communist Manifesto*, they write that the rise of world literature is just one more tool by which the European bourgeoisie 'creates a world after its own image' as a result of its exploitation of world markets.[45] No doubt this criticism, and many more, can be directed toward all of the arts and literature.

Gadamer's approach, by contrast, is characterised by the hermeneutical trust that the shape of alienation of our times – the interrelated foreignness and anonymous responsibility that attend the calculative management of human relations – can be countervailed by art and culture generally and, as I have tried to argue, by the global bequest of literature in particular. He therefore not only clarifies one aspect of the political, social and economic significance of world literature, but reminds us, too, that our involvement with world literature poses the difficult challenge and infinite task of understanding the other.

This reminder is directed perhaps first and foremost to those engaged in the study of the humanities, whether in the capacity of scholars, teachers or students, or as serious thinkers and readers. In an age such as ours, in which the significance of the humanities is under ever more vitriolic attack, Gadamer's approach reminds us that the stakes are actually rather high:

The genuine task of the human future is the by now genuinely global range of tasks concerned with human coexistence on this earthly ball . . . [I]t is the tasks awakened in increasing measure in such a pluralistic interwovenness of humanity which pose tasks to the humanities; tasks of historical research, of research in the history of language, the history of art, the history of law, and the history of economics, that have an immediate effect in relation to reality.[46]

Given Gadamer's recognition of the global scale of the tasks posed to the humanities by our hopes for coexistence, it is no surprise that he believes we will need to enlist the whole range of humanistic research. In this, however, the study of the arts and literature on an equally global stage has an important and distinctive role to play.

8 Translation

This chapter considers the contribution that can be made to our discovery of solidarities through the experience of translation. Specifically, I shall focus on the responsibility that Gadamer suggests we have to foster a robust global culture of translation. Thus, again in this chapter, the concern is with a mainstay of hermeneutics – the idea that our experience of translation can displace our prejudices, this time, the very prejudices embedded in the language of one's speech or a text. In what follows, I will argue that the experience of translation contributes to the discovery of solidarities with those from linguistic traditions other than our own. As we shall see, such solidarities are not primarily of 'cross-cultural' or 'cross-linguistic' significance, in the sense of making a person's speech or a text from a foreign 'source' language accessible in a 'target' language with which we are familiar. Indeed, as we shall see, Gadamer's hermeneutics of translation suggests that such an approach misses the crucial issue: namely, that translation is itself always what he will call a 'betrayal' of its source. In view of this, translation contributes to the discovery of solidarities not primarily as a cross-cultural or cross-linguistic practice, but, as I shall argue, through the 'increase' of meaning that a translation can donate to its source text. In this sense, I shall suggest, translation, precisely as an experience of language at the limits of betrayal, underscores the ethical dimensions of Gadamer's attempt to advance Heidegger's ontological turn with a further turn to language. For here, in Gadamer's approach to one of our most extreme experiences of language, we find nothing less than an emblem of the responsibility that attends factical life.

This chapter's concern for the contribution that can be made by translation to our discovery of solidarities is timely. It speaks to what may be called a crisis in the culture of translation in the Anglophone world of publishing (the world through which the present enquiry has come to press). In her recent book already cited in the previous chapter, Edith Grossman lays out the evidence of this crisis in no uncertain terms: 'The sad statistics indicate that in the United States and the United Kingdom, for example, only two or three percent of books published each year are literary translations.' In Western European nations and Latin America, by contrast, 'the number is anywhere from twenty-five to forty percent'.[1] Grossman's observation reminds us of the indictment of US literary culture by Horace Engdahl, the former permanent secretary of the Nobel Prize jury. 'The US', Engdahl states, 'is too isolated, too insular. They don't translate enough and they don't really participate in the big dialogue of literature.'[2] Even if we suspect that Engdahl's assessment is tinged by hyperbole or even *ressentiment*, as some American literary critics have suggested, we nevertheless recognise the scope and depth of the political, social and humanistic crisis of translation in the Anglophone world. Again, Grossman:

Translation not only plays an important traditional role as the means that allows us access to literature originally written in one of the countless languages we cannot read, but it also represents a concrete literary presence with the crucial capacity to ease and make more meaningful our relationships to those with whom we may not have had a connection before. Translation always helps us to know, to see from a different angle, to attribute new value to what once may have been unfamiliar. As nations and individuals, we have a critical need for that kind of understanding and insight. The alternative is unthinkable.[3]

If we are called to understand ourselves in a global context, as Gadamer suggests that we are, then the need for a robust global culture of translation is not of marginal concern but of decisive significance.

The focus of the current chapter is to consider the contribution that Gadamer's philosophical hermeneutics makes to our concern to foster such a culture. Yet, in this, as we shall see, Gadamer confronts us with an apparent dilemma. On the one hand, he clarifies the stakes of, and makes a strong case for, the claim that we have a responsibility to translate. On the other hand, however, he maintains that the task of the translator itself results in continual resignation because every translation is like a betrayal of the original text, indeed to the point that in what he will call the 'borderline case' of lyric poetry, we are faced with the experience of untranslatability. In this chapter, I will propose that this dilemma can be resolved because Gadamer's second claim, his conclusion that the task of translation ends in renunciation, rests on a confusion. Building on a claim made by Derrida in a related context, I argue that Gadamer's conclusion relies on the questionable assumption that we experience our primary language with a privileged intimacy that is diminished in our experience of translated texts. In view of this criticism drawn from Derrida, I seek to rehabilitate Gadamer's approach, suggesting that the task of translation need not result in continual renunciation but can, on the contrary, lead to an 'increase' in our capacity to understand and interpret.

Gadamer on Translation

Gadamer, as we have seen, maintains that our potential to address the global political, social and economic challenges we face has increasingly been put into jeopardy by the ascendency of the calculative rationality of the global network. In resisting that calculative rationality Gadamer calls on us to recognise the factically given diversity of languages across the globe as a treasure trove of meaning with the potential to teach us about one another, and, thereby, about the multiple and varied perspectives on the human condition. In a public lecture from 1990, he says:

My concern is to show that it is our task not simply to want to organize away the diversity of languages through rationalization and bureaucratization but rather for each of us to learn to bridge and fill in the distances and oppositions between us, and this means: that we respect, care for and protect others and give one another a new hearing.[4]

If we are to address the global challenges we face, we will have to cut against the current of the calculative rationality of the global network and learn again to hear one another from out of the context of the planetary cacophony comprised by our respective languages.

It is true that Gadamer does not situate his philosophical hermeneutics within a global context of concerns until the final decades of his life. Yet, this fact need not be taken as evidence for the objection, still common among Gadamer's critics, that his earlier elucidations of philosophical hermeneutics in *Truth and Method* and elsewhere are examples of Eurocentrism or cultural conservatism. Gadamer's later concern for the global diversity of languages should, instead, be grasped as an attempt to complement, clarify and expand his previous considerations of the hermeneutical experience of language. In view of this, his concern for global diversity suggests that, as language, each language embodies a distinctive, ultimately irreducible arrangement of possibilities for understanding and interpreting, or, in other words, harbours a unique context of meaning. Moreover, as language, each language allows for the possibility of community, grasped as the filiation that is enabled, limited and sustained by tradition, grasped in its etymological sense as *tradere*, or the transmission, bequeathing, entrusting and giving over of meanings from the past, whether these are embodied in religion and myth (*muthos*), legal code and custom (*nomos*), characteristic attitudes or comportments (*ēthos*), or in the achievements of literature, poetry and the other arts (*poiēsis*). Gadamer's intervention against the calculative rationality of the global network comes to focus on the global diversity of languages because this diversity encompasses, safeguards and calls on us to recognise the bequests of meaning that will allow us to become visible to one another in connection with our respective linguistic and cultural heritages.

As we saw earlier, Gadamer compares the proponents of calculative rationality to the people of the Biblical city of Babel. He asserts that his intervention against the regime of calculative rationality calls for

precisely the opposite to what the story of Babel presents as the delusional ideal of the people there. The idea there was, 'Let us make for ourselves a name, otherwise we shall be scattered abroad upon the whole earth.' What kind of name is this, then, in which we want to stay together? It is the name that one has and that allows one, so to speak, no longer to listen to the other.[5]

The analogy that Gadamer draws is clear enough. For its proponents, the regime of calculative rationality promises a universal language, whose intelligibility transcends the diversity of factically given languages across the globe. This is a promise, as in the Biblical story, of a world in which 'the whole earth' would have 'one language and the same words'.[6] Whereas proponents of the regime of calculative rationality may advocate for the uniformity, regularity and efficiency that would result from the universal intelligibility afforded by such a situation, Gadamer, for his part, suggests that the calculative rationality of the global network is oriented by a flight from our responsibility to understand one another in our diversity and respective singularity. He argues, by contrast, that this responsibility to understand one another calls us to become open to, and develop our capacity for, the plurality of meaning that confronts us in the global diversity of languages and their religious, juridical and literary bequests.

Even as Gadamer calls on us to recognise the treasure trove of meaning that this global diversity represents, however, he nevertheless despairs of the finitude that it entails. For, as he acknowledges, it is not possible to become fluent in all or even a significant share of the numerous factically given languages that may be found across the globe. As such, it is not possible for us ever to access even a modest share of the world's rich heritage of religious, juridical and literary texts. What is worse, Gadamer argues, is that the possibility of translation, the very condition of our access to the vast majority of texts in diverse languages, is finite because it can never carry a text over from its original language without remainder – compared to the original text, the translated text remains always deficient, impoverished, lacking. In his 1989 essay, 'Reading is Like Translating', Gadamer asserts that this finitude of translation is so severe that translation should always be regarded in terms of 'betrayal'. He writes: 'a celebrated word of Benedetto Croce says, "Tradattore – traditore." Every translation is like a betrayal.'[7] Indeed, Gadamer will go so far as to argue that, in the 'borderline case' of lyric poems, we find ourselves confronted not merely with the betrayal of the original text, but with the very untranslatability of the original text as such.

What, however, does he mean by his claim that 'every translation is like a betrayal'? Gadamer's point may be elucidated in reference to a discussion of the limitations of translation found in *Truth and Method*. Here, his purpose is not foremost to elucidate the limitations of translation *per se*; rather, he brings those limitations into focus in order to shed light on the character of the hermeneutical experience of conversation. Gadamer, we recall, upholds such experience as the epitome not only of the event of hermeneutical understanding generally but also of the experience of text interpretation as well. In this, his turn to the limitations of translation may be grasped by analogy with what Karl Jaspers calls a 'limit situation'. By limit situation, Jaspers refers to a specific type of interruption in the course of ordinary experience that, in displacing us from the usual current of things, introduces a form of distance, or transcendence, that allows us to become conscious of the conditions of our experience as such.[8] Similarly, Gadamer focuses on the limitations of translation in order to shed light on the conditions of the hermeneutical experience of conversation. In his elucidation of that experience, he cites the need to rely on translations as a situation 'where coming to an understanding is disrupted and impeded', thereby allowing us to 'become conscious of the conditions of all understanding'.[9]

Gadamer's discussion of translation in relation to the experience of conversation, however, also clarifies his claim that translation is like betrayal. How? Gadamer maintains that every translation is guided by a purpose that no translation can achieve. On the one hand, the purpose of every translation is to conserve the meaning of the original text. On the other hand, no translation can achieve this purpose without remainder. With this latter claim that no translation does justice to its original, Gadamer is, of course, hardly saying anything novel. Yet, his elucidation of it is instructive. He maintains that no translation conserves the meaning of the original without remainder because every language comprises a unique context of meaning. Language, grasped as such, therefore shapes the meaning of every text comprised from it; indeed, not only every text, but even every word. In order for a translator to conserve the meaning of an original text, then, they must not only first interpret the manner in which the language, or context of meaning, of the original text shapes its meaning, they must also in turn attempt to recreate this shape within a language that comprises an irreducibly different context of meaning. Gadamer writes:

Here the translator must translate the meaning to be understood into the context in which the other speaker lives. This does not, of course, mean that he is at liberty to falsify the meaning of what the other person says. Rather, the meaning must be preserved, but since it must be understood within a new language world, it must establish its validity within it in a new way.[10]

Because the context that shapes the meaning of the original text is always irreducibly different from the context of the translated text, the translator's attempt to conserve the original meaning cannot turn on correspondence to the original, but must reconstitute the meaning of the text in a novel manner from out of the possibilities and limits of meaning that the language of the translated text provides. In consequence, Gadamer argues that translations are in fact the result, first, of a translator's interpretation of the text that, only second, is carried over into the language of the translated text. Although he maintains that translation, thus twice removed from the original, may conserve the meaning of the original to a greater or lesser degree, no translation can conserve the meaning of the original without remainder. Because the respective languages that shape the meaning of the two texts are irreducibly different, there remains always an irreducible difference in the meaning of original and translation. This irreducible difference, as Gadamer puts it, is 'a gap that can never be completely closed'.[11]

Gadamer's consideration of the limitations of translation clarifies why he believes every translation is like a betrayal. If no translation conserves the meaning of the original without remainder, Gadamer's approach suggests that this remainder itself must be grasped not as a depreciation or loss, but, rather, as a distortion of the original text. A translator, in first interpreting the original text and then carrying over this interpretation into another language, does not simply leave out, neglect or exclude some parts or aspects of the meaning of the original, but, instead, recreates the text in a novel context. This, however, involves an axial shift, in which the meaning of the text as a whole takes on another shape. This shift, no matter how great or small, comprises a mutation of the arrangement of meanings found in the original text. Thus, if no translation conserves the meaning of the original without remainder, this is not due to omissions but, rather, to mutations that render the translation, however slightly, an imposter.

Gadamer concludes that the finitude to which we are exposed in the experience of translation leads to 'renunciation'. As we have seen, he calls for us to combat the increasingly planetary reign of calculative rationality in no small part through the recognition of the treasure trove of meaning that is represented by the global diversity of languages and their religious, juridical and literary bequests. Yet, his considerations of the limitations of translation suggest that these riches remain always just beyond our reach. Of the translator, he writes, 'since he is always in the position of not really being able to express all the dimensions of the text, he must make a constant renunciation'.[12]

Gadamer, indeed, will maintain that in the 'borderline case' of lyric poetry, itself exemplified by *'poésie pure'*, we come to experience not only that every translation is like a betrayal, but, more than this, that some texts are untranslatable.[13] In his 1993 essay 'On the Truth of the Word', he suggests that there is a spectrum of kinds of texts that admit of higher and lower degrees of translatability, arguing that the maximum degree of translatability may be discerned in scientific and technical texts, 'whose wording', as he puts it somewhat polemically, is often 'randomly changeable, as occasionally holds in the case of artless scientific prose'.[14] In such texts, translation is possible almost 'without sacrifice' of the meaning of the original, because their principle function is simply to convey 'informational content'. To this end, such texts depend as little as possible on the unique context of meaning provided by the language in which they are originally presented, pushing instead toward what Gadamer calls the very 'threshold of non-language, using artificial symbols . . . [which have] the advantage (and disadvantage) of being unambiguous, in that the sign stands in a firmly established classification system for indicating what is designated'.[15] It is not difficult to recognise in Gadamer's description of scientific and technical texts the universal language of calculative rationality that comprises what he sees as the modern Tower of Babel. It is also difficult not to recognise, as Gadamer indeed does, that the English language is by now the ubiquitous receptacle for this universal language of calculative rationality. Today, as Gadamer observes, 'in the natural sciences', across the globe, 'the publication of results in English immediately follows'.[16] Of course, as we are all likewise aware, this trend to publish in English appears not only in the natural sciences but even in the humanities.

Gadamer maintains that, by contrast, the minimum degree of translatability, or rather what he calls the 'zero-point' of untranslatability, is reached in our experience of lyric poetry.[17] Whereas the 'artless' texts of the sciences depend as little as possible on the context of meaning provided by the language in which they are presented, the meaning of a text of lyric poetry is more inseparable from the context of meaning provided by its language than any other form of text. In this, Gadamer argues, the very arrangement of relations of meaning that comprise the text of the lyric poem depend even on the sound of the language, its distinctive musicality, patterns of speech and intonation, forms of pronunciation, and all of its overt and subterranean rhythms. Gadamer, building on the German poet Friedrich Hölderlin, refers to the fact that the lyric poem's dependence on the interplay of meaning and sound is a matter of the poem's rhythm.[18] Of this rhythm, he asserts, 'one can say that basically it has to do with a balance one can feel between two motions: the movement of the meaning and the movement of the sound. Both motions, which always blend into one motion . . . have their specific syntactical means . . . .'[19] In the text of a lyric poem, arrangements of meaning are not connected exclusively or even primarily by semantic or logical relations that typify the language in which it is presented. Rather, poetic arrangements of meaning also depend on the interpenetration of meaning and sound. Gadamer observes that the most 'blatant' examples of this poetic interpenetration are found in meter and rhyme.[20] Here, arrangements of meaning depend not only on the semantic and logical relations that typify the language, but also, and more importantly, on connections that are made precisely in virtue of the fact that words keep a certain beat or sound alike. Gadamer recognises, however, that the poetic interpenetration of meaning and sound may take shape in 'figurations of sound' so subtle or refined that they 'remain below the threshold of conscious notice and are drawn over via this more or less thick network, these more or less inexpressible logical links of meaning'.[21]

Gadamer argues that we experience the zero-point of untranslatability in the lyric poem, then, because its arrangements of meaning depend so thoroughly on the interdependence of meaning and sound that only the language in which the poem is originally presented can sustain it as the text that it is. If every translation is like a betrayal, then, in the borderline case of lyric poetry, we reach the limit at which such betrayal crosses over into untranslatability itself.

On Derrida's Example

Gadamer's approach, then, suggests the dilemma that we are both responsible to translate and that the task of translation is fraught, in some cases, to the point of being impossible. I believe it is possible to find in Gadamer a resolution of this dilemma. But, this possibility will come into view through a consideration of Derrida's approach to translation. Derrida, even more than Gadamer, elucidates his conception of translation with reference to the Biblical story of the Tower of Babel. For Derrida, too, the stakes of any consideration of translation are foremost political, social and ethical. Accordingly, in his 1985 writing, 'Of the Tower of Babel', Derrida observes, first of all, that the story of Babel offers a cautionary tale about the will to hegemony, perfection, finality and purity, whether this will is grasped, as in Gadamer, as a matter of calculative rationality or otherwise. Through God's punishment, Derrida suggests, the story of the Tower of Babel 'exhibits an incompletion, the impossibility of finishing, of totalising, of saturating, of completing something on the order of edification, architectural construction, system and architectonics'.[22] While Derrida's point here is thus comparable to Gadamer's approach to the story, Derrida furthermore stresses that the story cautions against the will to hegemony as this will guides imperial or colonial ambition in particular. Derrida argues that if God's punishment of the residents of Babel was certainly 'for wanting to accede to the highest, up to the Most High', the punishment was directed specifically at their hubris 'for having wanted to make a name for themselves'.[23] He interprets the desire of those in Babel to make a name for themselves as a will to assert their own identity as a nation or a people, not only through the establishment of the purity of their unique genealogy, but, moreover, through the assertion of the universality of the rationality embodied in their language. In this, God's punishment rails against the political violence that their desire for identity implies. Derrida writes:

In seeking to 'make a name for themselves', to found at the same time a universal tongue and a unique genealogy, the Semites want to bring the world to reason, and this reason can signify simultaneously a colonial violence (since they would thus universalize their idiom) and a peaceful transparency of the human community. Inversely, when God imposes and opposes his name, he ruptures the rational transparency but interrupts also the colonial violence or the linguistic imperialism.[24]

Here, as Derrida stresses, the will to assert a universal language, or, perhaps better, a language that makes a claim to universal rationality, leads to the desire to impose as universal something that is in truth always only one among others.

Derrida believes that the cautionary tale represented by the story of Babel is of utmost pertinence to our post-colonial era. In his 1996 writing, *Monolingualism of the Other; Or, the Prosthesis of the Origin*, he maintains that the European powers of the colonial period exhibited a will to impose their identity with no less imperial zeal than the Biblical residents of Babel. He elucidates the European powers' will to impose their identities on the world not through a general history of the colonial period, however, but with the example of his personal history as a colonial and post-colonial subject of France from the Maghrebian region, an area that today encompasses Morocco, Algeria, Tunisia and Libya. Parenthetically, it should be noted that Derrida's reflections on his personal experience of colonialism are no less poignant than they are illuminative. They stand not only as an indispensable contribution to the philosophical study of language but also as an irreplaceable testament to the oppression and violence suffered by the colonial subjects of the period, as well as their struggles and even the possibilities of human experience opened up their subjugation. Of the many ways that the French imposed their identity as a people on the Maghrebian region, Derrida focuses on what he refers to as the 'interdict' – not only legal but also cultural – by which the French imposed their language through their colonial educational apparatus to the exclusion of the local Arabic and Berber, as well as, in Derrida's case, Hebrew. He describes this 'interdict' as a 'monolingualism imposed by the other', which operated 'through a sovereignty whose essence is always colonial, which tends, repressively and irrepressibly, to reduce language to the One'.[25] In consequence of this French colonial interdict, Derrida found himself as a young pupil in a school that was part of the colonial educational apparatus, and that thus led him to acquire French as his primary language. Yet, he reports that he did at the time, and continues throughout his life, to experience the French language with an acute sense of alienation. He describes the terms of this alienation in what is surely the most celebrated turn of phrase from the essay: 'I have only one language; it is not mine.'[26]

Derrida suggests that general lessons about language, and, as we shall see, especially about translation, can be drawn from the example of his own experience of language as a colonial subject. In this, he characterises his own life experience as an 'exceptional situation', but one that is nevertheless 'exemplary of a universal structure' of our experience of language.[27] Specifically, he maintains that his experience of the French language exposes as a pretence what I shall refer to here as 'the myth of the mother tongue'. By this I mean the idea that our primary language is so much our own that, by the time we reach the age of maturity at least, we no longer need to acquire, adopt or appropriate it, experiencing it, instead, with the intimacy of something naturally given. On the basis of this myth, we take our relation to our primary language to be no less intimate or naturally given than the relationship of child to mother. Yet, if Derrida's experience of the French language exemplifies a universal structure, then our relation to our primary language – or, as he puts it, our only language, the only language we experience as our primary language – is never as intimate or naturally given as the myth of the mother tongue purports. Derrida writes: 'The language called maternal is never purely natural, not proper, nor inhabitable. *To inhabit*: this is a value that is quite *disconcerting* and equivocal; one never inhabits what one is in the habit of calling inhabiting. There is no possible habitat without the difference of this exile.'[28] Despite all pretence of familiarity, we are never fully at home within even our primary language. Our relation to our primary language never carries the intimacy of something naturally given, but, rather, remains always uncanny, at once seemingly familiar and yet at the same time also exterior, strange, other.

Derrida suggests that the European powers of the colonial period wanted to impose their languages on their colonial subjects as part of their effort to establish their national identities. A colonial power such as France, not unlike its Biblical predecessors in the city of Babel, seeks to assert its identity in no small part through the avowal of the ipseity of its language, its unity, integrity and purity, as well as the universality of its claim to rationality. In this, the attempt that a colonial power makes to assert its identity is bound up with the fantasy embodied in the myth of the mother tongue. Yet, as Derrida notes, this fantasy never fully holds up against the exteriority with which our experience of language always and again confronts us. In view of this, he argues, colonisers are led to avow the ipseity of their languages not only through a myth of intimacy, of natural givenness, but, moreover, through historical violence. He writes:

Because the [colonial] master does not possess exclusively, and *naturally*, what he calls his language, because, whatever he wants or does, he cannot maintain any relations of property or identity that are natural, national, congenital, or ontological . . . he can, thanks to that very fact, pretend historically, through the rape of a cultural usurpation, which means always essentially colonial, to appropriate it in order to impose it as 'his own'.[29]

The will of the coloniser – which is itself, for Derrida, derived from a will to assert the political identity of a people – leads to the avowal of the coloniser's language through violent imposition and exclusion.

Derrida's elucidation of the universal structure of language he takes to be exemplified in his experience of language as a colonial and post-colonial subject not only illuminates the logic of colonial violence but also sheds light on the experience of translation. He recognises that discussions of translation characteristically assume, whether overtly or tacitly, the myth of the mother tongue. Within such discussions translation is taken to concern the transfer of a text, or, in any case, a piece of writing or speech, from a language relatively unfamiliar to us into the intimacy of our naturally given language. Derrida's assertion that he has only one language that is nevertheless not his own suggests, by contrast, that we experience no such privilege of intimacy in our primary language. In view of this, we face the task of translation not only in our encounters with a piece of writing or speech in a language relatively unfamiliar to us, but even in our efforts to listen and read, speak and write, in our primary language. For, no more in our relation to another language than to our primary language, we find ourselves enjoined to an interminable struggle with the exteriority we experience in our efforts to engage in linguistic practice, to grasp something that has been addressed to us by the other, to search for just the right word in response. Derrida describes the challenge that thus confronts us, in our relation both to another language and to our primary language, as a task of 'absolute translation'. By this, he means that we find ourselves always abandoned to the task of translation without recourse to any firm linguistic ground that we could call our own. He writes that the task of absolute translation is 'without a pole of reference, without an originary language, and without a source language'. Faced with the challenge of absolute translation, 'there are only target languages, if you will'.[30]

Derrida does not conclude, however, that this task of absolute translation is cause for despair. Rather, he suggests that the need for absolute translation means that the desire for a relation of intimacy with a language, not only with other languages but even with our primary language, remains always something still to arrive, something that we orient ourselves toward as possible but that can never be fully realised or made actual. Although we find ourselves always already immersed in language, such language is never originally, and, indeed, can never completely be made, our own. Derrida writes: 'there is no given language, or rather, there is some language, a gift of language (*es gibt die Sprache*), but there is not a language. Not a given one. It does not exist . . . Like a charge [*enjoignante*], it remains to be given, it remains only on this condition: by still remaining to be given.'[31]

If the myth of the mother tongue purports that the intimacy of our primary language has always already been achieved, is always already behind us, then Derrida, by contrast, upholds that our primary language remains always to come, ahead of us. Immersed in language, this language is never yet our own. In Derrida's displacement of the myth of the mother tongue, we find ourselves rather always and again exposed, interminably, to the exteriority of the language we desire to acquire, adopt, create.

With and Against Gadamer

Derrida's reflections on translation provide a way for us to resolve the dilemma with which Gadamer's considerations leave us. As we have seen, Gadamer's approach on the one hand suggests our responsibility to foster a robust global culture of translation. His concern for the global context of political, social and economic challenges leads him to an intervention against our interrelated foreignness under the regime of calculative rationality. This intervention, in turn, calls for us to make ourselves visible to one another within the global context of the diversity of our respective linguistic traditions. Yet, on the other hand, Gadamer argues that the task of translation, itself our principal means of pursuing our responsibility to make one another visible within the context of this diversity, results always in renunciation. For, as he maintains, we experience every translation as a betrayal of the original, and, indeed, in the borderline case of lyric poetry, we are confronted with untranslatability itself. In consequence, his considerations appear to leave us suspended between responsibility and renunciation, between the call to make ourselves visible to one another through translation, and the disavowal to which this call inevitably leads. Derrida's reflections point us to a resolution of this apparent dilemma because they suggest that Gadamer's giving in to renunciation rests on a confusion. In view of this, we are able to return to Gadamer's philosophical hermeneutics to reconsider his conclusion. As we shall see, his recognition of the responsibility to translate need not result in renunciation, but may lead to an 'increase' in the being of the original and even of the possibilities to understand and interpret that belong to the language into which the translation of the original is introduced.

Gadamer's conclusion that translation results in renunciation appears to follow not simply from his claim that every translation is like a betrayal, even to the point of untranslatability. Rather, it appears to derive before all else from a comparison between the experience of the translation of a text from an unfamiliar language and the interpretation of texts within our primary language. If, for Gadamer, translation leads to renunciation, this seems to be not because translation is like a betrayal *per se*, but because our experience of such betrayal compares poorly to the fidelity he believes is possible in our interpretation of texts in our primary language. Derrida's reflections suggest that Gadamer's conclusion is invalid, however, because this comparison rests on the myth of the mother tongue. For, as Derrida believes his experience of language to exemplify, languages unfamiliar to us are, in essence, no less intimate, nor any less naturally given, than our primary language. In both instances, we experience language as something that remains to be appropriated, or, as Derrida also expresses this in the idiom of translation studies, we experience neither language as a source but rather both as a target language. Thus, while every translation is like a betrayal, this betrayal is, in essence, never any greater than in the interpretation of a text in our primary language, or, for that matter, in any of our attempts to listen or read, speak or write. To the extent that Gadamer's conclusion follows from his comparison of the experience of translation with that of the interpretation of a text in our primary language, then, he has no more reason to associate translation with renunciation than he does to do so with any other hermeneutical experience.

Derrida's reflections may therefore be understood to recommend that we pursue an alternative to the conclusion Gadamer asserts. One alternative, to be sure, is simply to adopt Derrida's conclusion that all translation, like all interpretation, requires us to engage in language as a language of the other that is always still to arrive. If we are convinced at all by Gadamer's concern that we make one another visible within the global context of the diversity of our respective linguistic traditions, however, we may worry that Derrida's approach will be of too little help. For, if all translation, and, indeed, all interpretation, remain always still to arrive, then the contribution that a translation can make to the visibility of another will remain always in deferral. Another alternative, in any case, is to look elsewhere within Gadamer's philosophical hermeneutics for resources with which to rehabilitate his conclusion that translation ends in renunciation. In pursuit of this alterative, I wish to take up Gadamer's claim, in a different but nevertheless related context, that artworks represent an *'increase in being'* of their original subject matter.[32] With this, we shall see that translation does not end in renunciation but rather to an increase both in the being of the original and in the possibilities for understanding and interpretation that belong to the language of the translated text.

Gadamer elucidates his claim that artworks comprise an increase in the being of their original subject matter in *Truth and Method*, in his discussion of the ontology of the artwork generally and of what he calls the ontological valence of the picture in particular, that is, of the painting or artistic image. He maintains that although the being of pictures remains 'essentially tied' to the originals they portray, pictures are not dependent in their being on their originals. The being of pictures is not that of a representation, reproduction or copy, which is characteristically taken to be derived from but also a 'diminution' of an original.[33] Instead, he argues that the being of the picture is 'autonomous' in that it comprises an *'increase'* in the *'being'* of the original.[34] By this he means that the picture presents us with meanings that characterise the original, or, as he puts the point without fanfare, the picture 'says something about the original'.[35] As such, the picture comprises an 'overflow' of the original because it makes explicit meanings that otherwise remain implicit within it. Gadamer maintains that there is no upper limit to this increase in being. No picture, or, for that matter, accumulation of pictures, can completely exhaust the meaning of the original. Rather, every picture of the original, as long as it succeeds, further draws out the meaning of the original. The being of the picture, far from being derivative of the original, is thus rather an overflow of meaning that allows the original to be ever more presented as 'fully what it is'.[36]

Gadamer's elucidation of the ontological valence of the picture suggests that the task of translation results not in renunciation but rather in an increase in being. Gadamer, as we have seen, maintains that every translation is like a betrayal, up to the zero-point of untranslatability. With this, he implies that every translation comprises a mutation of the meaning of the original and not merely a depreciation or loss. But why cannot this mutation itself be understood as an increase in being?[37] The mutation appears to involve an increase in being in at least two ways. First, a translation may be grasped as an increase in the being of the original text. By this, I mean that it can comprise an 'overflow' that makes explicit aspects of the meaning of the original that remain otherwise only implicit. In *Truth and Method*, Gadamer observes that every translation involves a 'highlighting' of features of the original text.[38] In 'Reading Is Like Translating', he complements this idea, arguing that a translation can represent a 'gain' for the interpretation of the text insofar as it 'increases' the 'clarity' and 'coherence' of the original, thus giving emphasis, contour or accent to aspects of the original.[39] Like the being of a picture, the being of a translation, too, comprises an overflow that makes explicit meaning that is otherwise only implicit in the original. Moreover, just as no picture or accumulation of pictures exhausts the meaning of the original, neither does any translation or accumulation of translations exhaust the original text. Rather, translation poses an infinite task of bringing out what the original says.

But there is also a second way in which translation represents an increase in being. Gadamer recognises that language, grasped as a context of meaning that grants possibilities of understanding and interpreting, shapes the texts composed from out of it. Yet, conversely, language, too, is shaped by the introduction of novel texts, or, for that matter, novel relations of meaning in any form. A language, too, undergoes an axial shift, however slight, whenever such texts or novel relations of meaning are introduced. If a translation comprises an overflow of the meaning of the original and is not simply a distortion or depreciation of it, then translations, too, can infuse the language into which they have carried over the original with novelty. In consequence, languages can undergo an increase in their possibilities of understanding and interpretation with the introduction of new translations. In short, translations represent the possibility of an increase not only in the being of the original text, but also, moreover, in the linguistic possibilities of understanding and interpretation.

Conclusion

In *Truth and Method*, but also in several of his later essays, Gadamer asserts that his project of philosophical hermeneutics takes both inspiration but also a critical distance from the Romantic hermeneutics of the nineteenth-century figure Friedrich Schleiermacher. The same may be said of our rehabilitation of Gadamer's conclusion about translation. For, on the one hand, the idea that translation can lead to an increase in being may be said to echo Schleiermacher's belief that a robust culture of translation can not only contribute to our interpretation of original texts, but also, especially, enrich the language into which those texts are translated. In a call Schleiermacher makes to foster such a culture in the context of his contemporary Germany, he writes:

Just as our soil itself has probably become richer and more fertile, and our climate more lovely and mild after much transplanting of foreign plants, so do we feel that our language, which we practice less because of our Nordic lethargy, can only flourish and develop its own perfect power through the most varied contacts with what is foreign.[40]

Notwithstanding Schleiermacher's perhaps now outdated knowledge of agricultural science and climatology, the point of his analogy is that a primary language expands through the infusion of other languages that translation provides. Yet, there is also a difference between our rehabilitation of Gadamer's conclusion and Schleiermacher's position. Whereas Schleiermacher's perspective appears to be animated by nationalism and even cultural imperialism, Gadamer's approach focuses on openness to the global context. For, as Schleiermacher asserts:

our nation seems to be destined, because of its respect for things foreign, and because of its disposition toward mediation, to carry all the treasures of foreign art and scholarship, together with its own, in its language, to unite them into a great historical whole, as it were, which would be kept safe in the center and heart of Europe.[41]

Gadamer's rehabilitated considerations indicate, by contrast, that our responsibility to foster a robust global culture of translation does not turn on the establishment of a 'centre', into which all the treasures of the global context of linguistic traditions may be gathered. Instead, this responsibility is really a call for us to decentre ourselves, to undergo a displacement that removes us from the possibilities of understanding and interpreting familiar to us from our primary language, so that we may, in turn, begin to place ourselves in the broader, global context of the diversity of linguistic traditions – in other words, in a context that will allow us to encounter one another in our respective otherness.

Gadamer's considerations suggest, then, that and how translation contributes to the discovery of solidarities. As we have seen in Chapter 6, for Gadamer, the interrelated foreignness of the calculative rationality of the global network calls for an intervention through the discovery of solidarities. In Chapter 7, we considered the contribution that can be made to the discovery of such solidarities by the arts and literature. The contribution made by the arts and literature, I argued, takes shape through testimonies to the possibilities of tradition, of meaningful ordering, and, in the 'borderline' case of literature, of transmission as such. Literature, and with it, the special prospect of world literature, was shown to concern the possibility for meaning-transmission not simply within the context of an individual tradition but globally – across any time and place. Translation, as we are now in a position to assert, is a comparable testimony. For it testifies to the possibility of transmission not simply within the context of an individual language, but also, rather, globally, from any language to any other. To be sure, this testimony of translation is fraught, in that it comes up against the limit of the multiplicity of factically given individual languages, so that any translation is also always at the same time a betrayal of its source. But, with translation, as we have seen, such a limit represents at the same time a new possibility: that of contributing to an increase of the being of its source. Accordingly, translation, to be sure, contributes to the discovery of solidarities by making visible aspects of our life in common in reference to its source. But, more than this, translation also involves the possibility of increasing the power of its source, expanding its potential to make such aspects of our life in common possible in the first place.

Gadamer's consideration of translation, finally, comprises something of a novel motto for his attempt to advance the ontological turn in hermeneutics through a 'concretisation' of Heidegger's hermeneutics of facticity. Gadamer, as we recall, sought to make Heidegger's hermeneutics of facticity more concrete through his considerations of tradition and language – and, as I have argued in the present enquiry, also through his considerations of originally ethical responsibility. Gadamer's consideration of translation may be seen as an emblem of his attempt to advance the ontological turn because, I would submit, the three folds of his concretisation reach an epitome in the experience of translation. In that experience we are confronted with the facticity of tradition and language in the extreme. For, although all understanding depends concretely on tradition and language, they are themselves fractured, appearing as a multiplicity of irreducible traditions and languages that we can never fully comprehend, let alone master. Thus also, in the experience of translation we are confronted with a responsibility in the extreme: we find ourselves intrinsically in a global context, one that brings into relief the limits of understanding on a grand scale precisely because we find ourselves in the 'between' of familiar and foreign traditions and languages. Once we rid ourselves of the empty promise of a Tower of Babel that would make the globe universally transparent through calculative rationality, we find ourselves simply there: on the earth but without ground, responsible for enacting and cultivating our capacity for just such a displaced life. The responsibility to translate, then, not only comprises a significant contour of our responsibility to understand in its own right, it also suggests a novel, supplementary terminology for the hermeneutical contours of ethical life as a whole. Building on Gadamer's celebrated emblematic description of hermeneutical experience in terms of 'conversation', I have aligned the responsibility to understand with the 'capacity to converse'. Now, at the limit we experience on the global stage, we see that this capacity reaches one of its highest summits in the capacity to translate.

Notes

Preface

1. Gadamer, *Truth and Method*, p. 277.
2. Heidegger, *Being and Time*, p. 11.
3. Ibid., pp. 45ff.
4. Kundera, *Art of the Novel*, p. 123.
5. Ibid.
6. Ibid.
7. Nietzsche discusses Christianity in this vein at several junctures. He evokes such a suspicion of science, for example, in his treatment of the 'Socratic tendency' in the *Birth of Tragedy*, p. 82.
8. Foucault, *Birth of Biopolitics*, p. 226.
9. Kundera, *Unbearable Lightness of Being*, p. 5.
10. Kundera, *Book of Laughter and Forgetting*, p. 259.
11. Kafka, *Briefe*, p. 27. Translation from Karl, *Kafka, Representative Man*, p. 98.

Introduction

1. Gadamer, *Gadamer in Conversation*, p. 79.
2. Ibid.
3. Gadamer, *Truth and Method*, p. xxiii.
4. Ibid.
5. Ibid., p. xxi.
6. Ibid., p. 259.
7. Ibid., p. 262.
8. See ibid., pp. 300 ff.

9. Ibid., p. 262.

10. Ibid.

11. Ibid., p. 264.

12. Ibid., p. 381, translation modified. Cf. Gadamer, *Wahrheit und Methode*, p. 385.

13. Gadamer, *Truth and Method*, p. 378.

14. Ibid., p. 389.

15. Gadamer notes that the central focus of his writings after *Truth and Method* seek to develop further his notion of language as 'conversation', in Gadamer, *Gadamer in Conversation*, p. 56. Gadamer's encounters with Jürgen Habermas and Jacques Derrida, for example, came to focus significantly on questions with language. Regarding Gadamer's encounter with Habermas, see, for example, Habermas, 'Hermeneutic Claim to Universality', in Ormiston and Schrift (eds), *The Hermeneutic Tradition*. See also Gadamer's response to Habermas, in 'Reply to My Critics' in the same volume. Regarding the initial phase of Gadamer's encounter with Derrida, see, for example, Michelfelder and Palmer (eds), *Dialogue and Deconstruction*. For a recent overview of these encounters, see Liakos and George, 'Hermeneutics in Post-war Philosophy', in Becker and Thompson (eds), *Cambridge History of Philosophy 1945–2015*.

16. Gadamer, *Truth and Method*, p. 458.

17. Ibid.

18. Ibid., p. 461.

19. Ibid., p. 474.

20. Ibid., p. 324.

21. Ibid., p. 312.

22. Ibid.

23. It should be noted, however, that Gadamer's interpretation of Aristotle's *Nicomachean Ethics* is itself heavily influenced by Heidegger's interpretation of Aristotle's text. Gadamer himself reports the influence of the 1923 lecture course he took from Heidegger on the *Nicomachean Ethics* in his 'Self Presentation'. See Gadamer, 'Selbstdarstellung', in *Gesammelte Werke*, vol. 2, p. 485. For context, see, for example, Grondin, *Philosophy of Gadamer*, pp. 6–9.

24. See, for example, Heidegger, 'Letter on Humanism', in McNeill (ed.), *Pathmarks*, pp. 286 ff.

25. See Heidegger, 'Letter on Humanism', in McNeill (ed.), *Pathmarks*.

26. For a brief overview of the reception of hermeneutics in the Anglo-American context, see, for example, Liakos and George, 'Hermeneutics in Post-war Philosophy', in Becker and Thompson (eds), *Cambridge History of Philosophy 1945–2015*.

27. Lyotard, *Postmodern Condition*, p. xxiii.

28. Ibid., pp. xxiii–xxiv.

29. Ibid.

30. Ibid., p. 5.

31. Ibid., pp. 60–7. Cf. Lyotard, 'Answering the Question', in *Postmodern Condition*.

32. Vattimo, *End of Modernity*, 11. See also Chiurazzi, 'Pareyson and Vattimo', in Malpas and Gander (eds), *Routledge Companion to Hermeneutics*, p. 184.

33. Ibid., p. 171.

34. I am appreciative for conversations with Alexander Crist about his approach to the translation of this word in the context of a lecture given by Gadamer.

35. Vattimo, *End of Modernity*, p. 171.

36. Ibid., p. 130.

37. Ibid., p. 132.

38. Ibid., p. 139.

39. Ibid., p. 142.

40. Figal has continued to develop his programmatic interest in more recent works, including Figal, *Aesthetics as Phenomenology* and *Unscheinbarkeit*.

41. Figal, *Objectivity*, p. 1.

42. Ibid.

43. Ibid.

44. Ibid.

45. Ibid.

46. Ibid., p. 2.

47. See, for example, Gadamer, *Truth and Method*, pp. 361–2.

48. Figal, *Objectivity*, p. 2.

49. See George, 'Translator's Introduction', in Figal, *Objectivity*, p. xii.

50. Ibid., p. 2.

51. See ibid., pp. 8–17.

52. Ibid., p. 15.

53. Ibid., p. 67.

54. Ibid., pp. 10–11.

55. Ibid., p. 12.
56. Ibid.
57. Ibid., p. 17.
58. See George, 'Translator's Introduction', in Figal, *Objectivity*. See also, George, 'Figal's New Direction'.
59. See George, 'Beyond Speculative Realism?', in Egel et al., *Gegenständlichkeit der Welt*.
60. Gadamer, *Gadamer in Conversation*, pp. 78–9.
61. Ibid., p. 79.
62. Dieter Misgeld provides an overview of questions related to the relation of 'we and we', in 'Poetry, Dialogue, and Negotiation', in Wright (ed.), *Festivals of Interpretation*.

Chapter 1

1. Gadamer, *Truth and Method*, p. 3.
2. Heidegger, 'Letter on Humanism', in McNeill (ed.), *Pathmarks*.
3. Gadamer, *Truth and Method*, pp. 9 ff.
4. Gadamer, 'Incapacity for Conversation', p. 358, p. 351, translation modified. Cf. Gadamer, 'Unfähigkeit zum Gespräch', in *Gesammelte Werke*, vol. 2, p. 214, p. 207, respectively.
5. Heidegger, 'Letter on Humanism', in McNeill (ed.), *Pathmarks*, p. 263.
6. Ibid., p. 241.
7. Ibid.
8. Ibid., p. 244.
9. Ibid., p. 245.
10. Ibid., pp. 244–5.
11. Ibid., p. 245.
12. In current debate, there are a range of critical perspectives on humanism. The devastating normative employment of the humanity/inhumanity dichotomy may, for example, be found in the period of European imperial and colonial expansion, in which it was used to justify practices of subjugation in the name of 'civilising' colonial subjects. For a recent, synoptic approach to this and other concerns, see Omar, 'Humanism Reconsidered'. Note that the author provides the synopsis in order to prepare the way for proposals of an alternative humanism for the postcolonial context. Note also that Heidegger observes the use of the dichotomy of humanity and barbarity in the

humanism of the Roman period. Heidegger, 'Letter on Humanism', in McNeill (ed.), *Pathmarks*, p. 244.

13. Ibid., p. 247.
14. Ibid.
15. Ibid., p. 252.
16. Ibid., p. 251. Cf. Ibid., p. 251, editor's note.
17. Ibid., p. 252. Cf. Ibid., p. 261.
18. Ibid., p. 253.
19. Ibid., p. 261.
20. Ibid., p. 260.
21. This phrase is often associated with the title *Oration on the Dignity of Man* given to the oration composed by Pico della Mirandola in the period of Renaissance humanism.
22. Heidegger, 'Letter on Humanism', in McNeill (ed.), *Pathmarks*, pp. 260–1.
23. Ibid., p. 263.
24. Ibid.
25. Ibid., p. 262.
26. Ibid.
27. Ibid., p. 263. For a definition of '*lucus a non lucendo*', see *Oxford English Dictionary Online*, s.v. 'lucus a non lucendo'.
28. Heidegger, 'Letter on Humanism', in McNeill (ed.), *Pathmarks*, p. 263.
29. Ibid.
30. Ibid.
31. Ibid.
32. Recent considerations of Levinas and Arendt in the context of humanism include Katz, *Levinas and the Crisis of Humanism* and McCarthy, *Political Humanism of Hannah Arendt*.
33. In recent scholarship, see, for example, Kögler, 'Ethics and Community'.
34. Schmidt, 'On the Sources of Ethical Life'. See also Schmidt, 'Hermeneutics as Original Ethics', in *Difficulties of Ethical Life*, ed. Sullivan and Schmidt; Schmidt, 'The Idiom of the Ethical', and Schmidt, 'Hermeneutics and Ethical Life', in Keane and Lawn (eds), *The Blackwell Companion to Hermeneutics*.
35. Heidegger, 'Letter on Humanism', in McNeill, ed., *Pathmarks*, p. 271, translation modified. Cf. Heidegger, 'Brief über den Humanismus', in *Wegmarken*.
36. Schmidt, 'On the Sources of Ethical Life', p. 38.

37. Schmidt, 'Hermeneutics as Original Ethics', p. 36.

38. Schmidt, 'On the Sources of Ethical Life', pp. 36–7.

39. Ibid., p. 37.

40. Heidegger discusses 'dwelling' throughout the 'Letter on Humanism'. He treats the topic of dwelling in the context of *ēthos* in McNeill (ed.), *Pathmarks*, p. 269.

41. Schmidt, 'On the Sources of Ethical Life', p. 37.

42. Ibid., p. 39.

43. Ibid., p. 41. Cf. Gadamer, *Truth and Method*, p. 307.

44. Schmidt, 'On the Sources of Ethical Life', p. 40.

45. Ibid.

46. Ibid., p. 41.

47. Ibid.

48. Ibid., p. 42.

49. Ibid.

50. Gadamer, 'On the Possibility of Philosophical Ethics', in *Hermeneutics, Religion, and Ethics*. See also Gadamer, 'Aristotle and Imperative Ethics', in *Hermeneutics, Religion, and Ethics*, and 'Selbstdarstellung', in *Gesammelte Werke*, vol. 2.

51. Gadamer, 'On the Possibility of Philosophical Ethics', in *Hermeneutics, Religion, and Ethics*, p. 21.

52. Ibid.

53. Ibid.

54. Gadamer, 'Aristotle and Imperative Ethics', p. 150.

55. Gadamer, 'On the Possibility of Philosophical Ethics', p. 23.

56. Ibid.

57. Ibid.

58. Ibid., p. 34.

59. Ibid., p. 30.

60. Gadamer, 'Incapacity for Conversation', p. 351.

61. Ibid.

62. Ibid.

63. Ibid., p. 358, translation modified. Cf. Gadamer, 'Unfähigkeit zum Gespräch', p. 214.

Chapter 2

1. This concern became, for example, a centrepiece of discussions about the relations and differences between Gadamer's hermeneutics and

Derrida's deconstruction. For an overview of these discussions, see Michelfelder and Palmer (eds), *Dialogue and Deconstruction*. See also Liakos and George, 'Hermeneutics in Post-war Philosophy', in *Cambridge History of Philosophy 1945–2015*. A significant formulation of the criticism that Gadamer gives too little credence to alterity, otherness or exteriority is Caputo, *Radical Hermeneutics*.

2. I introduce the phrase 'the whole of our factical lives' to suggest the possibility of a fruitful comparison to Heidegger's consideration of 'The Question of the Primordial Totality of the Structural Whole of Dasein', in *Being and Time*, § 39. While developing this comparison between Gadamer and Heidegger further is beyond the scope of the present enquiry, I would note here that in Gadamer's concern for the 'whole' of factical life, no less than in Heidegger's concern for the 'whole' of existence, 'wholeness' proves to be not a matter of completeness, but rather of ineluctable finitude.

3. Gadamer, *Truth and Method*, p. 295. That Gadamer's notion of belonging to tradition (and the closely related notion of historically effected consciousness) involves exteriority is treated with special insight in recent literature by Gander, 'Between Strangeness and Familiarity'.

4. Gadamer, *Truth and Method*, p. 254.

5. Gadamer, interestingly, believes that von Yorck anticipates Heidegger's contrast with Dilthey and Husserl. See Gadamer, *Truth and Method*, p. 251.

6. Ibid., p. 254.

7. Heidegger, *Being and Time*, p. 11.

8. Gadamer, 'Subjectivity and Intersubjectivity', p. 284, translation modified. Cf. Gadamer, 'Subjektivität und Intersubjektivität', in *Gesammelte Werke*, vol. 10, p. 97.

9. Gadamer, 'Subjectivity and Intersubjectivity', p. 285.

10. Gadamer, *Truth and Method*, p. 265.

11. Gadamer, 'Vom Zirkel des Verstehens', in *Gesammelte Werke*, vol. 2, p. 57, my translation.

12. Gadamer, *Truth and Method*, p. 266. Cf. Heidegger, *Being and Time*, pp. 145–6.

13. Gadamer, *Truth and Method*, p. 300, translation modified. Cf. Gadamer, *Wahrheit und Methode*, p. 305.

14. Ibid., translation modified. Cf. Gadamer, *Wahrheit und Methode*, pp. 305–6.

15. Ibid., p. 269.

16. Ibid., pp. 276–7.
17. Gadamer, 'Universality of the Hermeneutic Problem', in Richard Palmer (ed.), *Gadamer Reader*, p. 82.
18. Gadamer, *Truth and Method*, p. 255.
19. Gadamer's focus is on Hegel's *Phenomenology of Spirit*, and he mentions Heidegger's *Hegel's Concept of Experience* in *Truth and Method*, p. 354.
20. Gadamer, *Truth and Method*, p. 302.
21. Ibid., translation modified. Cf. Gadamer, *Wahrheit und Methode*, 307.
22. Ibid., p. 354.
23. Ibid., pp. 348 ff.
24. Ibid., p. 353.
25. Ibid., pp. 296–7.
26. James, 'World of Pure Experience', in *Essays in Radical Empiricism*, p. 87.
27. Gadamer, *Truth and Method*, p. 306.
28. Note, however, that Gadamer also returns to the notion of a fusion of horizons in his discussion of 'language as the medium of hermeneutical experience'. *Truth and Method*, p. 388.
29. Ibid., p. 302.
30. Ibid.
31. Ibid., pp. 306–7.
32. Nietzsche, *Gay Science*, p. 181.
33. Gadamer, *Truth and Method*, p. 304.
34. Ibid., p. 306.
35. Risser, *Life of Understanding*, p. 1.
36. Ibid.
37. Risser takes up the theme of convalescence in particular in *Life of Understanding*, pp. 8–26.
38. di Cesare, *Utopia of Understanding*.
39. Figal, *Objectivity*, p. 2.
40. Gadamer, *Truth and Method*, p. 355.
41. Ibid.
42. Ibid.
43. Ibid., p. 356.
44. Ibid., p. 357.

Chapter 3

1. Gadamer, *Truth and Method*, p. 245.
2. Ibid., p. 249.
3. Ibid.
4. This idea is, of course, ascribed to Protagoras, whom Plato counted as one of the sophists. Cf. Heidegger's discussion of Protagoras in 'Age of the World Picture', in *Question Concerning Technology*, pp. 143–7; cf. especially, however, Heidegger's reference to Hölderlin's treatment of the question of the measure in Heidegger, '. . . Poetically Man Dwells . . .', in *Poetry, Language, Thought*.
5. See, for example, Heidegger, 'Origin of the Work of Art', in *Poetry, Language, Thought*.
6. See, for example, Heidegger, 'The Thing', in *Poetry, Language, Thought*.
7. Biemel, 'Development of Heidegger's Concept of the Thing'.
8. Heidegger, 'Letter on Humanism', in McNeill (ed.), *Pathmarks*, p. 256.
9. Aristotle, *Parts of Animals*, 645a17 ff., cited in Heidegger, 'Letter on Humanism', in McNeill (ed.), *Pathmarks*, pp. 269–70. Cf. Aristotle, *Parts of Animals*, in Barnes (ed.), *Complete Works of Aristotle*, vol. 1, p. 1004.
10. Heidegger, 'Letter on Humanism', in McNeill (ed.), *Pathmarks*, p. 270.
11. Ibid.
12. Ibid.
13. Ibid.
14. Heidegger, as is well-known, discusses and criticises these three interpretations of the being of the thing in 'Origin of the Work of Art', in *Poetry, Language, Thought*, pp. 20–31.
15. Heidegger asserts that the 'thing things' in 'The Thing', in *Poetry, Language, Thought*, p. 172. He speaks of 'the worlding of the world' in same essay, p. 177. He states that 'the *world worlds*', in 'Origin of the Work of Art', in *Poetry, Language, Thought*, p. 43.
16. Heidegger, 'The Thing', in *Poetry, Language, Thought*, p. 172.
17. Ibid.
18. Ibid., pp. 175–8.
19. Mitchell, 'The Fourfold', in *Martin Heidegger: Key Concepts*, p. 208.
20. For a fuller account, see Mitchell, *The Fourfold: Reading the Late Heidegger*.

21. Heidegger, 'The Thing', in *Poetry, Language, Thought*, p. 175.
22. Ibid., p. 164.
23. Ibid., pp. 165 ff.
24. Ibid., p. 168.
25. For an excellent account of this, see Figal, 'Introduction', in *The Heidegger Reader*, pp. 22–5.
26. See Heidegger, 'Question Concerning Technology', in *Question Concerning Technology*.
27. See, for example, Heidegger, 'Science and Reflection', in *Question Concerning Technology*, pp. 162–3.
28. Heidegger's conception of modern technology actually builds on his notion of modern science. We are acquainted, for example, with his celebrated idea that the emergence of modern technology, while chronologically later than the appearance of modern science, is nevertheless historically earlier, as a decisive condition of the possibility of modern science. See Heidegger, 'Question Concerning Technology', in *Question Concerning Technology*, p. 21. We may be less familiar, however, with his equally important idea that the will-to-will, while its appearance in modern technology comes chronologically later than the birth of modern science, nevertheless simply gives fuller expression to what was already at stake in modern science as such. Heidegger suggests this, for example, in 'Science and Reflection', in *Question Concerning Technology*, p. 173.
29. Heidegger, 'Question Concerning Technology', in *Question Concerning Technology*, pp. 4–5, p. 12.
30. Ibid., p. 13.
31. Ibid., p. 14.
32. Ibid., p. 17.
33. Heidegger begins to develop this notion of 'setting-into-order', in ibid., pp. 14 ff.
34. Ibid., p. 17. Cf. Heidegger, *Country Path Conversations*, p. 128.
35. Heidegger uses this phrase in a related context, for example, in *Nietzsche*, vols 3–4. An excellent discussion of this idea is found in Ruin, 'Ge-stell: Enframing as the Essence of Technology', in *Heidegger: Key Concepts*, p. 168.
36. See Davis, 'Will and *Gelassenheit*', in *Heidegger: Key Concepts*. Cf. Davis, *Heidegger and the Will*.
37. See Heidegger, 'The Thing', in *Poetry, Language, Thought*, pp. 164 ff.

38. See Moore, 'Gelassenheit, the Middle Voice, and the Unity of Heidegger's Thought', in *Perspektiven mit Heidegger, Zugänge, Pfade, Anknüpfungen*.

39. Davis, 'Translator's Forward', in Heidegger, *Country Path Conversations*, p. xiv. See also Moore, *Eckhart, Heidegger, and the Imperative of Releasement*.

40. For a very good survey of these lines of Heidegger's thought, see Davis, *Heidegger and The Will*, pp. 216–18.

41. Figal, 'Universality of Technology and the Independence of Things', p. 367. Though this piece comes to centre on the aesthetic experience of things, it comprises an important supplement to Figal's treatment of things in *Objectivity*.

42. Heidegger's considerations of the thing have proved to be an important impetus not only for Figal, but for a number of contemporary considerations of things and our relations to them. Here, we might think especially of recent studies such as Charles Scott's *The Lives of Things*. Scott, moving beyond the context of Heidegger's own *Denkweg*, nevertheless builds on motifs of Heidegger's thought to examine how things have lives as it were all their own. In this, Scott focuses on the significance of the physicality of things for a number of themes, such as nature, memory, ethical life and nihilism. In addition to Scott's study, we might also think of other enquiries into life that take up questions of correlation, such as those by Michel Henry, for example, in 'Phenomenology of Life', as well as David Krell in his *Daimon Life*, and others. Few scholars, however, have sought to explore the notion of life from out of the constellation of Heidegger's concerns for issues surrounding thing and object with more emphasis than Günter Figal in his recent *Objectivity* and related essays.

43. In the final pages of *Objectivity*, Figal reminds us that our relation to things 'alone gives meaning to the enactment of desiring and willing' (p. 347).

44. Ibid., p. 2.

45. Ibid., p. 107.

46. Figal does not appear to employ this distinction systematically. Note, however, the title of a collection of essays on the question of the object in view of Figal's work: Espinet et al. (eds), *Gegenständlichkeit und Objektivität*.

47. Figal, *Objectivity*, p. 107.

48. Ibid., p. 108.
49. Ibid.
50. Ibid., pp. 108–14.
51. Figal, in his *Objectivity*, introduces this distinction in his elucidation of the role played by exterior relations for his notion of interpretation (pp. 66–7). He also uses this distinction to discuss conduct, however (p. 101). In light of these uses, I think it is reasonable to extend Figal's employment of the distinction to his view of our exposure to the independence of things.
52. Ibid., p. 172.
53. Ibid., p. 166.
54. Ibid.

Chapter 4

1. We have already treated this theme of belonging in some detail in the Introduction.
2. Beauclair, 'Speaking of Other Animals', p. 76.
3. Heidegger, *Fundamental Concepts of Metaphysics*, p. 177.
4. Jacques Derrida takes up Heidegger's *Fundamental Concepts of Metaphysics*, for example in *The Beast and the Sovereign*, vol. 2. Giorgio Agamben takes up Heidegger's same lecture course in *The Open*. For a significant scholarly treatment of Heidegger, Derrida and Agamben – as well as Levinas – on the topic of the animal, see Calarco, *Zoographies*.
5. Derrida discusses the experience of being naked in front of his cat in *The Animal That I Therefore Am*, pp. 3 ff. Kelly Oliver indicates that her *Animal Lessons* is 'inspired by, and dedicated to the memory' of her cat Kaos. See Oliver, *Animal Lessons*, dedication page.
6. Dillard, 'Living Like Weasels', in *Teaching the Stone to Talk*, p. 32.
7. See Nagel, 'What Is It Like to Be A Bat?'
8. Hegel, *The Difference Between Fichte's and Schelling's System of Philosophy*, p. 89, translation modified. Cf. Hegel, *Differenz des Fichteschen und Schellingschen Systems der Philosophie* in *Werke*, vol. 2, p. 20.
9. See Beiser, *Hegel*, p. 37.
10. Gadamer, 'Universality of the Hermeneutical Problem', in Palmer (ed.), *Gadamer Reader*, p. 78.
11. Ibid., p. 78, p. 80.
12. Ibid., p. 78.

13. See Gadamer, *Truth and Method*, pp. 477 ff.
14. Gadamer, 'Universality of the Hermeneutical Problem', in Palmer (ed.), *Gadamer Reader*, p. 78.
15. Ibid., p. 79.
16. Ibid., p. 78.
17. Ibid., p. 80.
18. Beauclair's 'Speaking of Other Animals' provides a rich and thorough hermeneutical consideration of purported claims about the 'abyss' between humans and animals. Beauclair focuses his account on the role that Heidegger and Gadamer take language to have with respect to the disclosedness of being. With this, he emphasises the distance between the worldliness of humans and the nature of animals. While Beauclair's essay ultimately returns us to a 'kinship' between humans and animals with respect to play, he does not, for this, take up the ethical sense of belonging that this kinship bespeaks, or think of the shared play as a continuity. Rather, his essay culminates in questioning whether or not animals may also grant a world.
19. Gadamer, 'Text and Interpretation', in *The Gadamer Reader*, pp. 169–71.
20. Ibid., p. 173.
21. See Gadamer's account of the 'eminent text' in 'Text and Interpretation', in Palmer (ed.), *Gadamer Reader*, p. 177. See also Schmidt, 'Text and Translation', in Malpas and Gander (eds), *Routledge Companion to Hermeneutics*.
22. Gadamer, 'Text and Interpretation', in Palmer (ed.), *Gadamer Reader*, p. 173.
23. Gadamer, 'On the Truth of the Word', in Palmer (ed.), *Gadamer Reader*, p. 137.
24. Ibid.
25. Gadamer, 'Text and Interpretation', in Palmer (ed.), *Gadamer Reader*', pp. 172–3.
26. Gadamer, 'On the Truth of the Word', in Palmer (ed.), *Gadamer Reader*, p. 137.
27. Ibid., p. 138.
28. Ibid., p. 139.
29. Ibid., p. 144.
30. Ibid., p. 139.
31. Ibid.
32. Ibid., p. 143.

33. Ibid., p. 139.
34. Ibid., p. 138.
35. Ibid., p. 144.
36. See, for example, Gadamer, *Truth and Method*, pp. 101–10; Gadamer, 'Relevance of the Beautiful', in Bernasconi (ed.), *Relevance of the Beautiful*; and 'Play of Art', in the same volume.
37. Gadamer, *Truth and Method*, p. 456.
38. Ibid., pp. 465–6.
39. Ibid., p. 466.
40. Ibid.
41. Gadamer treats this example at ibid.
42. I have Cynthia Nielsen to thank for the translation of '*Spielraum*' as 'leeway'.
43. Gadamer, *Truth and Method*, p. 468.
44. Ibid., p. 469.
45. Gadamer, 'Play of Art', in Bernasconi (ed.), *Relevance of the Beautiful*, p. 125.
46. Figal, 'Life as Understanding', p. 20.
47. See Aristotle, *On the Soul*, in Barnes (ed.), *Complete Works of Aristotle*, vol. 1.
48. Gadamer, 'Relevance of the Beautiful', in Bernasconi (ed.), *Relevance of the Beautiful*, p. 23, translation modified. Cf. Gadamer, 'Aktualität des Schönen', in *Gesammelte Werke*, vol. 8, p. 114.
49. Gadamer, 'Relevance of the Beautiful', in Bernasconi (ed.), *Relevance of the Beautiful*, p. 22.
50. Gadamer, *Truth and Method*, p. 103.
51. Eckermann, *Conversations of Goethe*, p. 169.
52. Ibid.
53. Ibid.

Chapter 5

1. Gadamer, *Truth and Method*, p. 358.
2. Ibid., p. 361.
3. Ibid.
4. For a more comprehensive consideration of this analogy in recent literature, see Lauren Swayne Barthold, 'Friendship and the Ethics of Understanding'. See also James Risser's comments on the matter in *Hermeneutics and the Voice of the Other*, p. 10.

5. Gadamer, *Truth and Method*, p. 358, translation modified (and perhaps somewhat freely). Cf. Gadamer, *Wahrheit und Methode*, p. 364.
6. Ibid., p. 358.
7. Ibid.
8. Ibid., p. 359.
9. Ibid.
10. Ibid. It is worthwhile to note that Gadamer, in this turn to Hegel, includes a note referring to Karl Löwith's approach to the 'reflective dialectic of I and thou'. *Truth and Method*, p. 359. While it will be beyond the scope of this chapter, it should perhaps further be noted that Axel Honneth also attends to this reference to Löwith with care in his analysis of Gadamer.
11. Unless I am mistaken, this term is omitted from the English translation (it would appear in Gadamer, *Truth and Method*, p. 361). See Gadamer, *Wahrheit und Methode*, p. 367.
12. Gadamer, *Truth and Method*, p. 361, translation modified. Cf. Gadamer, *Wahrheit und Methode*, p. 367.
13. Ibid.
14. Ibid.
15. Gadamer, 'Subjectivity and Intersubjectivity, Subject and Person', p. 276.
16. Ibid., p. 284. See also Vessey, 'Gadamer's Account of Friendship as an Alternative'.
17. Gadamer, 'Subjectivity and Intersubjectivity, Subject and Person', p. 284.
18. Heidegger, *Being and Time*, p. 241.
19. Camus, 'Myth of Sisyphus', in *Myth of Sisyphus*, p. 3.
20. Gadamer, 'Subjectivity and Intersubjectivity, Subject and Person', p. 284.
21. See, for example, Levinas, 'Ethics as First Philosophy', in *Levinas Reader*; Derrida, among many other writings, *Gift of Death*; and Caputo, *Against Ethics*.
22. Habermas's contributions to critical theory remain in many regards close to Gadamer. Habermas, in any case, lays out normative dimensions of communicative action, for example, in *Moral Consciousness and Communicative Action*. See also Honneth, *The Struggle for Recognition: The Moral Grammar of Social Conflicts*.
23. Honneth, 'Von der zerstörersichen Macht des Drittens', in Figal et al. (eds), *Hermeneutische Wege*.

24. Honneth, 'On the Destructive Power of the Third', p. 6.
25. Ibid.
26. Ibid., p. 18.
27. Ibid., p. 5.
28. Ibid., p. 6.
29. Ibid., p. 19.
30. Ibid., p. 20.
31. Ibid.
32. Ibid.
33. Ibid., p. 19.
34. David Vessey identifies Gadamer's main essays on friendship as 'Friendship and Self-Knowledge', in *Hermeneutics, Ethics and Religion*; 'Ethics of Value and Practical Philosophy', in the same volume; 'Friendship and Solidarity'; 'Logos and *Ergon* in Plato's *Lysis*', in *Dialogue and Dialectic*; and 'Subjectivity and Intersubjectivity, Subject and Person'. See Vessey, 'Gadamer's Account of Friendship', p. 66, footnote 8. Vessey examines Gadamer's views of the features of friendship relations in the same essay, p. 63.
35. Gadamer, 'Friendship and Solidarity', p. 7.
36. Ibid.
37. Ibid., pp. 7–8.
38. Ibid., p. 8.
39. Ibid.
40. Ibid., p. 9.
41. Gadamer, 'On the Possibility of a Philosophical Ethics', in *Hermeneutics, Religion, and Ethics*, p. 32.
42. Ibid.
43. For a helpful and nuanced account of this notion in Gadamer, and one which I have drawn upon in my discussion here, see Smith, *Hermeneutics and Human Finitude*, pp. 179–266.
44. See, for example, Gadamer, *Truth and Method*, Part II.
45. Gander, 'Between Strangeness and Familiarity', p. 126.
46. Gadamer, *Gadamer in Conversation*, p. 79. Cf. Smith, *Hermeneutics and Human Finitude*, pp. 216 ff.
47. See Risser, *Hermeneutics and the Voice of the Other*, pp. 105 ff., for one of the finest treatments of this issue.
48. Gadamer, *Gadamer in Conversation*, p. 79.
49. Michael Hofer suggests that 'definitive' for Gadamer's view of the relation of Kantian and Aristotelian ethics are his essays 'Ethos und Ethik (McIntyre u.a.)', in *Gesammelte Werke*, vol. 3; 'On the

Possibility of a Philosophical Ethics', in *Hermeneutics, Religion, and Ethics*; and 'Aristotle and Imperative Ethics', in *Hermeneutics, Religion, and Ethics*. See Hofer, 'Die "Abdämpfung" der Subjektivität', p. 606. I would add to the list Gadamer's 'Friendship and Self-knowledge', in *Hermeneutics, Religion, and Ethics*.

50. Risser, *Hermeneutics and the Voice of the Other*, p. 105.
51. Ibid.
52. Ibid., p. 107.
53. Ibid.
54. Gadamer uses this turn of phrase in his discussion of Aristotle's notion of the application of natural law in particular. As Risser points out, however, Aristotle's approach to natural law is exemplary of the problem of application in general. See ibid., p. 107.
55. Gadamer, *Truth and Method*, pp. 333–4.
56. Gadamer, 'Friendship and Self-Knowledge', in *Hermeneutics, Religion, and Ethics*, p. 140.
57. Ibid., p. 136.
58. Ibid., p. 137.
59. Ibid., p. 128.
60. Gadamer, 'On the Possibility of a Philosophical Ethics', in *Hermeneutics, Religion, and Ethics*, p. 32.
61. Gadamer, 'Friendship and Self-Knowledge', in *Hermeneutics, Religion, and Ethics*, p. 139. Cf. Dieter Misgeld, who explains that in friendship, 'dialogue and conversation, in their various forms, are constitutive of what the world is for people. And nothing is more important than having a world in common. Having a world in common means living in solidarity.' Misgeld, 'Poetry, Dialogue, and Negotiation', in *Festivals of Interpretation*, p. 166.
62. Gadamer, 'Culture and Media', in Honneth et al. (eds), *Cultural-Political Interventions*, p. 183.
63. Ibid., p. 184.
64. Ibid., p. 174.
65. Ibid., pp. 175–6.
66. It is worth noting, as Walter Brogan does, that for Gadamer this isolation is not foremost a matter of irreparable alienation, but rather a loneliness that entails a desire to recover our sense of connection. See Brogan, 'Gadamer's Praise of Theory', p. 151.
67. Gadamer, 'Culture and Media', in Honneth et al. (eds), *Cultural-Political Interventions*, p. 176.
68. Ibid., p. 186.

69. Ibid., p. 185.
70. Ibid., p. 176.
71. Ibid., p. 184.
72. Ibid., p. 174.
73. Ibid., p. 187.

Chapter 6

1. One of the decisive frames of this debate originates with Caputo's *Radical Hermeneutics*. Risser's *Hermeneutics and the Voice of the Other* stands as an original interpretation of Gadamer's hermeneutics that also provides an influential counterpoint to Caputo. A recent contribution to the debate – really, an effort to change the subject of debate – is George, 'Are We a Conversation?' The debate is also reiterated by Krajeweski, 'Hermeneutics and Politics', in Keane and Lawn (eds), *Blackwell Companion to Hermeneutics*.
2. The terms of this 'frame within the frame' have been introduced in no small part by Orozco, 'Art of Allusion'. A strong defence of Gadamer against Orozco's charges appears in Grondin, *Hans-Georg Gadamer: A Biography*, pp. 165–9.
3. Gadamer, *Gadamer in Conversation*, pp. 78–9.
4. Ibid., p. 79.
5. See Levinas, *Totality and Infinity*.
6. While concerns about the global reach of capital and instrumental rationality have been around for some time, contemporary discussions have coalesced around the term 'globalisation' only more recently. In illustration, see, for example, Derrida, 'Enlightenment Past and to Come', excerpt printed in *Le Monde* diplomatique, November 2014.
7. Gadamer, 'Friendship and Solidarity'.
8. Gadamer, *Gadamer in Conversation*, p. 81.
9. Rorty, *Contingency, Irony, and Solidarity*, p. 192.
10. Ibid.
11. Ibid.
12. Habermas provides a succinct account of his concern for experts in 'Philosophy as Stand-In and Interpreter', in *Moral Consciousness and Communicative Action*.
13. Arendt famously evokes such 'ice cold reasoning', in *Origins of Totalitarianism*, p. 471, p. 477.

14. Gaffney, 'Solidarity in Dark Times'. Gaffney's article provides an important comparative consideration of Gadamer and Arendt.
15. Gadamer, 'Friendship and Solidarity', p. 4.
16. Gadamer, 'What is Practice?', in *Reason in the Age of Science*, p. 72, translation modified. Cf. Gadamer, 'Was ist Praxis?', in *Gesammelte Werke*, vol. 4, p. 218.
17. Ibid., translation modified.
18. Gadamer, 'What is Practice?', p. 72.
19. Ibid., p. 74.
20. Ibid.
21. Gadamer, 'Friendship and Solidarity', p. 4.
22. Nancy's 'Urbi et Orbi' is from a collection of related essays that has been titled *Creation of the World, or, Globalization*, published in English in 2007. 'Urbi et Orbi' concerns the trend toward globalisation and was originally written for a lecture that Nancy delivered in 2001 in Bordeaux.
23. Nancy, 'Urbi et Orbi', in *Creation of the World, or, Globalization*, p. 33.
24. Nancy recognises that Western expansionism reached a first fever pitch in the imperial and colonial periods of European nation-states, but he suggests that this tendency toward expansion is endemic to the West as he understands it.
25. Ibid.
26. Ibid.
27. Ibid.
28. Gadamer, 'Friendship and Solidarity', p. 11, translation modified. Cf. Gadamer, 'Freundschaft und Solidarität', in *Hermeneutische Entwurfe*, p. 64.
29. Ibid.
30. Aristotle introduces friendship as a 'virtue' or 'something that implies virtue', in the *Nicomachean Ethics*. See Aristotle, *Nicomachean Ethics*, in Barnes (ed.), *Complete Works of Aristotle*, vol. 2, 11545a/p. 1825.
31. Gadamer, 'Friendship and Self-Knowledge', p. 139.
32. Warnke, 'Solidarity and Tradition in Gadamer's Hermeneutics', p. 10.
33. Ibid., p. 11.
34. Gadamer, 'What is Practice?', pp. 85–6.
35. Gadamer, *Gadamer in Conversation*, p. 81.
36. Gadamer, 'Vielfalt der Sprachen', in *Gesammelte Werke*, vol. 8, pp. 340–1.

37. Ibid., pp. 346–7.
38. Heidegger, 'Origin of the Work of Art', in *Poetry, Language, and Thought*, pp. 42–3.
39. Kundera, *Art of the Novel*, p. 135.

Chapter 7

1. Gadamer, 'The Artwork in Word and Image: "So True, So Full of Being!"', in Palmer (ed.), *Gadamer Reader*, p. 215, translation modified. Cf. Gadamer, 'Wort und Bild – "so wahr, so seind"', in *Gesammelte Werke*, vol. 8, p. 391.
2. Ibid., p. 116.
3. Ibid., pp. 101–69.
4. Ibid., p. 112.
5. Ibid.
6. Ibid.
7. Ibid., p. 110.
8. Ibid., p. 113.
9. Plato, *Republic*, 595c–599a/pp. 277–82.
10. In fact, Gadamer associates the lessons of Aristotle's notion of *mimesis* with another aspect of Plato's doctrine – not his polemic against artistic imitation but rather his notion of *anamnesis*.
11. Gadamer, *Truth and Method*, p. 113.
12. Ibid., translation modified. Cf. Gadamer, *Wahrheit und Methode*, p. 119.
13. Ibid., translation modified, somewhat freely. Cf. Gadamer, *Wahrheit und Methode*, p. 119.
14. Gadamer, *Truth and Method*, p. 114.
15. Aristotle, it is well known, makes a comparable point in the *Poetics* when he asserts that poetry is more like philosophy than history. He writes, 'The distinction between historian and poet is not in the one writing prose and the other verse . . . it consists really in this, that the one describes the thing that has been, and the other the kind of thing that might be. Hence poetry is something more philosophic and of graver import than history, since its statements are of the nature rather of universals, whereas those of history are singulars.' Aristotle, *Poetics*, in Barnes (ed.), *Complete Works of Aristotle*, vol. 2, 1451b5–7/p. 2323.
16. Gadamer, *Truth and Method*, p. 120.

17. Ibid., p. 127.
18. See Gadamer, 'Universality of the Hermeneutical Problem', in Palmer (ed.), *Gadamer Reader*, p. 78.
19. Gadamer, 'Art and Imitation', in Bernasconi (ed.), *Relevance of the Beautiful*, p. 93.
20. Ibid., p. 98.
21. Ibid., p. 99.
22. Ibid., p. 100.
23. Ibid.
24. Ibid.
25. Ibid., p. 101.
26. Ibid.
27. Here, Gadamer builds on his earlier observation of the relation between Aristotle's notion of *mimesis* and Plato's notion of *anamnesis*, suggesting that both have their common origin in Pythagoras' notion of *mimesis*.
28. Gadamer, 'Art as Imitation', in Bernasconi (ed.), *Relevance of the Beautiful*, p. 101.
29. Ibid., p. 102.
30. Ibid.
31. Gadamer, *Truth and Method*, p. 159.
32. Ibid., p. 161.
33. Ibid., p. 163.
34. Ibid., p. 160.
35. Ibid.
36. Ibid.
37. Ibid., p. 161, translation modified.
38. Ibid., pp. 163–4.
39. Ibid., p. 163.
40. Eckermann, *Conversations of Goethe*, pp. 165–6.
41. Gadamer, *Truth and Method*, p. 162.
42. Grossman, *Why Translation Matters*, p. 13.
43. Gadamer is discussing Western practices of preserving classics in particular here. Gadamer, *Truth and Method*, p. 161.
44. Terrance, *Self-Tormentor*.
45. Marx and Engels, 'Manifesto of the Communist Party', in Tucker (ed.), *Marx-Engels Reader*, p. 477.
46. Gadamer, 'Zukunft der europäischen Geisteswissenschaften', in *Hermeneutische Entwürfe*, p. 127, my translation.

Chapter 8

1. Grossman, *Why Translation Matters*, pp. 28–9.
2. McGrath, 'Lost in Translation?', *New York Times*, 4 October 2008.
3. Grossman, *Why Translation Matters*, pp. x–xi.
4. Gadamer, 'Vielfalt der Sprachen', in *Gesammelte Werke*, vol. 8, p. 347, my translation.
5. Ibid., my translation.
6. Genesis 11:1.
7. Gadamer, 'Lesen ist wie Übersetzen', in *Gesammelte Werke*, vol. 8, p. 279, my translation.
8. Jaspers discusses the notion of limit situation in *Philosophy*, vol. 2. Grondin observes that Gadamer saw affinities between Jaspers' thought and his own. *Hans-Georg Gadamer: A Biography*, p. 301.
9. Gadamer, *Truth and Method*, p. 384.
10. Ibid.
11. Ibid.
12. Ibid., p. 386.
13. Gadamer, 'On the Truth of the Word', in Palmer (ed.), *Gadamer Reader*, p. 149.
14. Ibid.
15. Ibid.
16. Ibid.
17. Ibid.
18. Ibid.
19. Ibid.
20. Ibid., p. 150.
21. Ibid.
22. Derrida, 'Des Tours de Babels', in Schulte and Biguenet (eds), *Theories of Translation*, p. 218.
23. Ibid., p. 221.
24. Ibid., p. 226.
25. Derrida, *Monolingualism of the Other*, pp. 39–40.
26. Ibid., p. 1.
27. Ibid., p. 63.
28. Ibid., p. 58.
29. Ibid., p. 23.
30. Ibid., p. 61.
31. Ibid., p. 67.

32. Gadamer, *Truth and Method*, p. 140.
33. Ibid.
34. Ibid.
35. Ibid.
36. Ibid., p. 143.
37. Cf. Sallis, *On Translation*, pp. 71–3, pp. 103–5.
38. Gadamer, *Truth and Method*, p. 386.
39. Gadamer, 'Lesen ist wie Übersetzen', in *Gesammelte Werke*, vol. 8, p. 279, my translation.
40. Schleiermacher, 'On the Different Methods of Translating', in Schulte and Biguenet (eds), *Theories of Translation*, p. 53.
41. Ibid., pp. 53–4.

Bibliography

Agamben, Giorgio, *The Open: Man and Animal*, trans. Kevin Attell (Stanford: Stanford University Press, 2002).

Arendt, Hannah, *The Origins of Totalitarianism* (New York: Harcourt, Inc., 1973).

Aristotle, *Nicomachean Ethics*, in Jonathan Barnes (ed.), *The Complete Works of Aristotle: The Revised Oxford Translation*, vol. 2 (Princeton: Princeton University Press, 1984, fourth printing 1991), pp. 1729–867.

Aristotle, *On the Soul*, in Jonathan Barnes (ed.), *The Complete Works of Aristotle: The Revised Oxford Translation*, vol. 1 (Princeton: Princeton University Press: 1984, fourth printing 1991), pp. 641–92.

Aristotle, *Parts of Animals*, in Jonathan Barnes (ed.), *The Complete Works of Aristotle: The Revised Oxford Translation*, vol. 1 (Princeton: Princeton University Press, 1984, fourth printing 1991), pp. 994–1086.

Aristotle, *Poetics*, in Jonathan Barnes (ed.), *The Complete Works of Aristotle: The Revised Oxford Translation*, vol. 2 (Princeton: Princeton University Press, 1984, fourth printing 1991), pp. 2316–40.

Barthold, Lauren Swayne, 'Friendship and the Ethics of Understanding', *Epoché: A Journal for the History of Philosophy*, vol. 14, no. 2, Spring 2010, pp. 417–29.

Beauclair, Alain, 'Speaking of Other Animals', *Research in Phenomenology*, vol. 44, 2014, pp. 76–106.

Beiser, Frederick, *Hegel* (New York and London: Routledge, 2005).

Biemel, Walter, 'The Development of Heidegger's Concept of the Thing', *Southwestern Journal of Philosophy*, vol. 11, no. 3, Fall 1980, pp. 47–66.

Brogan, Walter, 'Gadamer's Praise of Theory: Aristotle's Friend and the Reciprocity Between Theory and Practice', *Research in Phenomenology*, vol. 32, 2002, pp. 141–55.

Calarco, Matthew, *Zoographies: The Question of the Animal from Heidegger to Derrida* (New York: Columbia University Press, 2008).

Camus, Albert, 'The Myth of Sisyphus', in *The Myth of Sisyphus and Other Essays*, trans. Justin O'Brien (New York: Vintage International, 1991), pp. 1–138.

Caputo, John D., *Against Ethics: Contributions to a Poetics of Obligation with Constant Reference to Deconstruction* (Bloomington and Indianapolis: Indiana University Press, 1993).

Caputo, John D., *Radical Hermeneutics: Repetition, Deconstruction, and the Hermeneutic Project* (Bloomington and Indianapolis: Indiana University Press, reprint edition, 1998).

Cesare, Donatella di, *The Utopia of Understanding: Between Babel and Auschwitz*, trans. Naill Keane (Albany: State University of New York Press, 2012).

Chiurazzi, Gaetano, 'Pareyson and Vattimo: From Truth to Nihilism', in Jeff Malpas and Hans-Helmut Gander (eds), *The Routledge Companion to Hermeneutics* (New York: Routledge, 2015), pp. 179–90.

Davis, Bret W., *Heidegger and the Will: On the Way to Gelassenheit* (Evanston: Northwestern University Press, 2007).

Davis, Bret W., 'Translator's Foreword', in Martin Heidegger, *Country Path Conversations* (Bloomington and Indianapolis: Indiana University Press, 2010), pp. vii–xxii.

Davis, Bret W., 'Will and *Gelassenheit*', in *Heidegger: Key Concepts*, ed. Bret Davis (Durham: Acumen Publishing Limited, 2010), pp. 168–82.

Derrida Jacques, *The Animal That I Therefore Am*, ed. Mary Louise Mallett, trans. David Wills (New York: Fordham University Press, 2008).

Derrida, Jacques, *The Beast and the Sovereign*, vol. 2 (The Seminars of Jacques Derrida), trans. Geoffrey Bennington (Chicago: University of Chicago Press, 2011).

Derrida, Jacques, 'Des Tours de Babels', excerpt in Rainer Schulte and John Biguenet (eds), *Theories of Translation* (Chicago and London: University of Chicago Press, 1992), pp. 218–27.

Derrida, Jacques, 'Enlightenment Past and to Come', excerpt printed in *Le Monde diplomatique*, November 2014.

Derrida, Jacques, *The Gift of Death*, trans. David Wills (Chicago: University of Chicago Press, second edition, 2017).

Derrida, Jacques, *Monolingualism of the Other, or the Prosthesis of Origin*, trans. Patrick Mensah (Stanford: Stanford University Press, 1998).

Dillard, Annie, 'Living Like Weasels', in *Teaching the Stone to Talk: Expeditions and Encounters* (New York: Harper Collins, 1983).

Eckermann, Johann Peter, *Conversations of Goethe*, ed. J. K. Moorhead, trans. John Oxenford (Boston, MA: Da Capo Press, 1998).

Espinet, David, Friederike Rese and Michael Steinmann (eds), *Gegenständlichkeit und Objektivität* (Tübingen: Mohr Siebeck, 2011).

Figal, Günter, *Aesthetics as Phenomenology: The Appearance of Things*, trans. Jerome Veith (Bloomington and Indianapolis: Indiana University Press, 2015).

Figal, Günter, 'Introduction', *The Heidegger Reader*, trans. Jerome Veith (Bloomington and Indianapolis: Indiana University Press, 2009), pp. 1–32.

Figal, Günter, 'Life as Understanding', trans. Elizabeth Sikes, *Research in Phenomenology*, vol. 34, 2004, pp. 20–30.

Figal, Günter, *Objectivity: The Hermeneutical and Philosophy*, trans. Theodore George (Albany: State University of New York Press, 2010).

Figal, Günter, 'The Universality of Technology and the Independence of Things: Heidegger's *Bremen Lectures* Once More', trans. Margot Wielgus, *Research in Phenomenology*, vol. 45, 2015, pp. 358–68.

Figal, Günter, *Unscheinbarkeit: Der Raum der Phänomenologie* (Tübingen: Mohr Siebeck, 2015).

Foucault, Michel, *The Birth of Biopolitics: Lectures at the Collége de France 1978–1979*, trans. Graham Burchell (Houndmills: Palgrave Macmillan, 2008).

Gadamer, Hans-Georg, 'Aktualität des Schönen. Kunst als Spiel, Symbol, und Fest', in *Gesammelte Werke*, vol. 8 (Tübingen: Mohr Siebeck, 1993, unaltered paperback edition, 1999), pp. 94–142.

Gadamer, Hans-Georg, 'Aristotle and Imperative Ethics', in *Hermeneutics, Religion, and Ethics*, trans. Joel Weinsheimer (New Haven: Yale University Press, 1999), pp. 142–61.

Gadamer, Hans-Georg, 'Aristotles und die imperitivische Ethik', in *Gesammelte Werke*, vol. 7 (Tübingen: Mohr Siebeck, 1991, unaltered paperback edition, 1999), pp. 381–95.

Gadamer, Hans-Georg, 'Art and Imitation', in *The Relevance of the Beautiful and Other Essays*, ed. Robert Bernasconi, trans. Nicholas Walker (Cambridge: Cambridge University Press, 1986), pp. 92–105.

Gadamer, Hans-Georg, 'The Artwork in Word and Image: "So True, So Full of Being!"', trans. Richard Palmer, in *The Gadamer Reader: A Bouquet of Later Writings*, ed. Richard Palmer (Evanston: Northwestern University Press, 2007).

Gadamer, Hans-Georg, 'Culture and Media', in Axel Honneth, Thomas McCarthy, Claus Offe and Albrecht Wellmer (eds), *Cultural-Political Interventions in the Unfinished Project of Enlightenment*, trans. Barbara Fultner (Cambridge, MA: MIT Press, 1992), pp. 171–88.

Gadamer, Hans-Georg, 'The Ethics of Value and Practical Philosophy', in *Hermeneutics, Ethics, and Religion*, trans. Joel Weinsheimer (New Haven: Yale University Press, 1999), pp. 103–18.

Gadamer, Hans-Georg, 'Ethos und Ethik (MacIntyre u.a.)', in *Gesammelte Werke*, vol. 3 (Tübingen: Mohr Siebeck, 1987, unaltered paperback edition, 1999), pp. 350–74.

Gadamer, Hans-Georg, 'Freundschaft und Selbsterkenntnis. Zur Rolle der Freundshaft in der griechischen Ethik', in *Gesammelte Werke* vol. 7 (Tübingen: Mohr Siebeck, 1991, unaltered paperback edition, 1999), pp. 396–406.

Gadamer, Hans-Georg, 'Freundschaft und Solidarität' in *Hermeneutische Entwurfe: Vorträge und Aufsätze* (Tübingen: Mohr Siebeck, 2000), pp. 56–65.

Gadamer, Hans-Georg, 'Friendship and Self-knowledge: Reflections on the Role of Friendship in Greek Ethics', in *Hermeneutics, Religion, and Ethics*, trans. Joel Weinsheimer (New Haven: Yale University Press, 1999), pp. 128–41.

Gadamer, Hans-Georg, 'Friendship and Solidarity', trans. David Vessey and Chris Blauwkamp, *Research in Phenomenology*, vol. 39, no. 1, 2009, pp. 3–12.

Gadamer, Hans-Georg, *Gadamer in Conversation: Reflections and Commentary*, ed. Richard Palmer, with Carsten Dutt, Glenn M. Most, Alfons Griender and Dörte von Westernhagen, trans. Richard Palmer (New Haven: Yale University Press, 2001).

Gadamer, Hans-Georg, 'The Incapacity for Conversation', trans. David Vessey and Chris Blauwkamp, *Continental Philosophy Review*, vol. 39, 2006, pp. 351–9.

Gadamer, Hans-Georg, 'Lesen ist wie Übersetzen', in *Gesammelte Werke*, vol. 8 (Tübingen: Mohr Siebeck, 1993, unaltered paperback edition, 1999), pp. 279–85.

Gadamer, Hans-Georg, '*Logos* and *Ergon* in Plato's *Lysis*', in *Dialogue and Dialectic: Eight Hermeneutical Studies on Plato*, trans. P. Christopher Smith (New Haven and London: Yale University Press, 1980), pp. 1–20.

Gadamer, Hans-Georg, 'On the Possibility of Philosophical Ethics', in *Hermeneutics, Religion, and Ethics*, trans. Joel Weinsheimer (New Haven: Yale University Press, 1999), pp. 18–36.

Gadamer, Hans-Georg, 'On the Truth of the Word', trans. Richard Palmer, in Richard Palmer (ed.), *The Gadamer Reader: A Bouquet of Later Writings* (Evanston: Northwestern University Press, 2007), pp. 132–55.

Gadamer, Hans-Georg, 'The Play of Art', in *The Relevance of the Beautiful and Other Essays*, ed. Robert Bernasconi, trans. Nicholas Walker (Cambridge: Cambridge University Press: 1986), pp. 123–30.

Gadamer, Hans-Georg, 'The Relevance of the Beautiful, Art as Play, Symbol and Festival', in *The Relevance of the Beautiful and Other Essays*, ed. Robert Bernasconi, trans. Nicholas Walker (Cambridge: Cambridge University Press: 1986), pp. 1–53.

Gadamer, Hans-Georg, 'Reply to My Critics', trans. George H. Leiner, in Gayle L. Ormiston and Alan D. Schrift (eds), *The Hermeneutic Tradition from Ast to Ricoeur* (Albany: State University of New York Press, 1990), pp. 273–97.

Gadamer, Hans-Georg, 'Selbstdarstellung Hans-Georg Gadamer', in *Gesammelte Werke*, vol. 2 (Tübingen: Mohr Siebeck, 1986, corrected [*durchgesehen*] edition 1993, unaltered paperback edition, 1999), pp. 479–508.

Gadamer, Hans-Georg, 'Subjectivity and Intersubjectivity, Subject and Person', trans. Peter Adamson and David Vessey, *Continental Philosophy Review*, vol. 33, no. 3, July 2000, pp. 275–87.

Gadamer, Hans-Georg, 'Subjektivität und Intersubjektivität, Subjekt und Person', in *Gesammelte Werke*, vol. 10 (Tübingen: Mohr Siebeck, 1995, unaltered paperback edition, 1999), pp. 87–99.

Gadamer, Hans-Georg, 'Text and Interpretation', trans. Richard Palmer, in Richard Palmer (ed.), *The Gadamer Reader: A Bouquet of Later Writings* (Evanston: Northwestern University Press, 2007), pp. 156–91.

Gadamer, Hans-Georg, *Truth and Method*, Second, Revised Edition, trans. rvsd. Joel Weinsheimer and Donald G. Marshall (New York: Continuum, 1995).

Gadamer, Hans-Georg, 'Über die Möglichkeit einer philosophischen Ethik', in *Gesammelte Werke*, vol. 4 (Tübingen: Mohr Siebeck, 1987, unaltered paperback edition, 1999), pp. 175–88.

Gadamer, Hans-Georg, 'Die Unfähigkeit zum Gespräch', in *Gesammelte Werke*, vol. 2, (Tübingen: Mohr Siebeck, 1986, corrected [*durchgesehen*] edition 1993, unaltered paperback edition, 1999), pp. 207–15.

Gadamer, Hans-Georg, 'The Universality of the Hermeneutical Problem', trans. David E. Linge, in Richard Palmer (ed.), *The Gadamer Reader: A Bouquet of Later Writings* (Evanston: Northwestern University Press, 2007).

Gadamer, Hans-Georg, 'Die Vielfalt der Sprachen und das Verstehen der Welt', in *Gesammelte Werke*, vol. 8 (Tübingen: Mohr Siebeck, 1993, unaltered paperback edition, 1999), pp. 339–49.

Gadamer, Hans-Georg, 'Vom Zirkel des Verstehens', in *Gesammelte Werke*, vol. 2 (Tübingen: Mohr Siebeck, 1986, corrected [*durchgesehen*] edition 1993, unaltered paperback edition, 1999), pp. 57–65.

Gadamer, Hans-Georg, *Wahrheit und Methode* in *Gesammelte Werke*, vol. 1 (Tübingen: Mohr Siebeck, 1986, corrected [*durchgesehen*] edition 1990, unaltered paperback edition, 1999).

Gadamer, Hans-Georg, 'Was ist Praxis? Die Bedingungen gesellschaftlicher Vernunft', in *Gesammelte Werke*, vol. 4 (Tübingen: Mohr Siebeck, 1987, unaltered paperback edition, 1999), pp. 216–28.

Gadamer, Hans-Georg, 'What is Practice? The Conditions of Social Reason', in *Reason in the Age of Science*, trans. Fredrick G. Lawrence (Cambridge, MA: MIT Press, 1981), pp. 69–87.

Gadamer, Hans-Georg, 'Wort und Bild – "so wahr, so seind"', in *Gesammelte Werke*, vol. 8 (Tübingen: Mohr Siebeck, 1993, unaltered paperback edition, 1999), pp. 373–99.

Gadamer, Hans-Georg, 'Die Zukunft der europäischen Geisteswissenschaften', in *Hermeneutische Entwürfe: Vorträge und Aufsätze* (Tübingen: Mohr Siebeck, 2000), pp. 112–28.

Gaffney, Jennifer, 'Solidarity in Dark Times: Arendt and Gadamer on the Politics of Appearance', *Philosophy Compass*, 4 October 2018, DOI: 10.1111/phc3.12554.

Gander, Hans-Helmut, 'Between Strangeness and Familiarity: Toward Gadamer's Conception of Effective History', *Research in Phenomenology*, vol. 34, 2004, pp. 121–36

George, Theodore, 'Are We a Conversation? Hermeneutics, Exteriority, and Transmittability', *Research in Phenomenology*, vol. 47, no. 1, 2017, pp. 331–50.

George, Theodore, 'Beyond Speculative Realism? Günter Figal's Phenomenological Realism and the Exteriority of Correlation', in Antonia Egel, David Espinet, Tobias Keiling and Bernhard Zimmerman (eds), *Die Gegenständlichkeit der Welt: Festschrift für Günter Figal zum 70. Geburtstag* (Tübingen: Mohr Siebeck, 2019), pp. 57–73.

George, Theodore, 'Günter Figal's New Direction in Hermeneutics', *Philosophy Compass*, vol. 4, no. 6, 2009, pp. 904–12.

George, Theodore, 'Translator's Introduction: Objectivity and Finite Transcendence in Günter Figal's Hermeneutical Philosophy', in Günter Figal, *Objectivity: The Hermeneutical and Philosophy*, trans.

Theodore George (Albany: State University of New York Press, 2010), pp. xi–xvi.

Grondin, Jean, *Hans-Georg Gadamer: A Biography*, trans. Joel Weinsheimer (New Haven: Yale University Press, 2003).

Grondin, Jean, *The Philosophy of Gadamer*, trans. Kathryn Plant (Montreal and Kingston, Ithaca: McGill-Queen's University Press, 2003).

Grossman, Edith, *Why Translation Matters* (New Haven: Yale University Press, 2010).

Habermas, Jürgen, 'The Hermeneutic Claim to Universality', trans. George H. Leiner, in Gayle L. Ormiston and Alan Schrift (eds), *The Hermeneutic Tradition from Ast to Ricoeur* (Albany: State University of New York Press, 1990), pp. 245–72.

Habermas, Jürgen, *Moral Consciousness and Communicative Action*, trans. Christian Lenhardt and Shierry Weber Nicholsen (Cambridge, MA: MIT Press, 1999).

Habermas, Jürgen, 'Philosophy as Stand-In and Interpreter', in *Moral Consciousness and Communicative Action*, trans. C. Lenhardt and S. Weber Nicholsen (Cambridge, MA: MIT Press, 1990).

Hegel, G. W. F., *The Difference Between Fichte's and Schelling's System of Philosophy*, trans. H. S. Harris and Walter Cerf (Albany: State University of New York Press, 1977).

Hegel, G. F. W., *Differenz des Fichteschen und Schellingschen Systems der Philosophie* in *Werke*, vol. 2 (Frankfurt am Main: Suhrkamp, 3rd printing 1996), pp. 8–138.

Hegel, G. W. F., *The Phenomenology of Spirit*, trans. A. V. Miller (Oxford: Oxford University Press, 1977).

Heidegger, Martin, 'The Age of the World Picture', trans. William Lovitt, in *The Question Concerning Technology and Other Essays* (New York: Harper and Row, 1977), pp. 115–54.

Heidegger, Martin, *Being and Time*, trans. Joan Stambaugh with revisions by Dennis J. Schmidt (Albany: State University of New York Press, 2010).

Heidegger, Martin, 'Brief über den Humanismus', in *Wegmarken* (Frankfurt am Main: Vittorio Klostermann, 2013).

Heidegger, Martin, *Country Path Conversations*, trans. Bret W. Davis (Bloomington and Indianapolis: Indiana University Press, 2010).

Heidegger, Martin, *Fundamental Concepts of Metaphysics: World, Finitude, and Solitude*, trans. William McNeill and Nicholas Walker (Bloomington and Indianapolis: Indiana University Press, 1995).

Heidegger, Martin, *Hegel's Concept of Experience: With a Section from Hegel's* Phenomenology of Spirit *in the Kenley Royce Dove Translation*, English and German Edition (New York: Harper and Row, first paperback edition, 1989).

Heidegger, Martin, 'Letter on Humanism', trans. Frank A. Capuzzi, in William McNeill (ed.), *Pathmarks* (Cambridge: Cambridge University Press, 1998), pp. 239–76.

Heidegger, Martin, *Nietzsche*, vols 3–4, trans. Joan Stambaugh, David Farrell Krell and Frank C. Capuzzi (San Francisco: Harper, 1987).

Heidegger, Martin, 'The Origin of the Work of Art', trans. Albert Hofstadter, in *Poetry, Language, Thought* (New York: Harper and Row, 1971, reissued in Harper Perennial Modern Thought in 2013), pp. 15–86.

Heidegger, Martin, '. . . Poetically Man Dwells . . .', trans. Albert Hofstadter, in *Poetry, Language, Thought* (New York: Harper and Row, 1971, reissued in Harper Perennial Modern Thought in 2013), pp. 209–27.

Heidegger, Martin, 'The Question Concerning Technology', trans. William Lovitt, in *The Question Concerning Technology and Other Essays* (New York: Harper and Row, 1977), pp. 3–35.

Heidegger, Martin, 'Science and Reflection', trans. William Lovitt, in *The Question Concerning Technology and Other Essays* (New York: Harper and Row, 1977), pp. 155–82.

Heidegger, Martin, 'The Thing', trans. Albert Hofstadter, in *Poetry, Language, Thought* (New York: Harper and Row, 1971, reissued in Harper Perennial Modern Thought in 2013), pp. 161–84.

Henry, Michel, 'Phenomenology of Life', trans. Nick Hanlon, *Angelaki*, vol. 8, no. 2, 2003, pp. 97–110.

Hofer, Michael, 'Die "Abdämpfung" der Subjectivität, Drei Beispiele aus der amerikanischen bzw. französischen Gadamer-Rezeption', *Zeitschrift für philosophische Forschung*, vol. 54, 2002, pp. 593–611.

Honneth, Axel, 'On the Destructive Power of the Third: Gadamer and Heidegger's Doctrine of Intersubjectivity', *Philosophy and Social Criticism*, vol. 29, no. 1, 2003, pp. 5–21.

Honneth, Axel, *The Struggle for Recognition: The Moral Grammar of Social Conflicts*, trans. Joel Anderson (London: Polity Press, 1995).

Honneth, Axel, 'Von der zerstörersichen Macht des Drittens, Gadamer und die Intersubjektivitätslehre Heideggers', in Günter Figal, Jean Grondin and Dennis J. Schmidt (eds), *Hermeneutische Wege, Hans-Georg Gadamer zum Hundertsten* (Tübingen: Mohr Siebeck, 2000), pp. 307–24.

James, William, 'A World of Pure Experience', in *Essays in Radical Empiricism* (London: Longman, Greens, and Co., 2012).

Jaspers, Karl, *Philosophy*, vol. 2, trans. E. B. Ashton (Chicago: University of Chicago Press, 1969).

Kafka, Franz, Letter to Oskar Pollak, 8 November 1903, in Max Brod (ed.), *Briefe, 1902–1924* (New York: Schocken, 1958).

Karl, Frederick R., *Franz Kafka, Representative Man* (New York: Ticknor & Fields, 1991).

Katz, Claire Elise, *Levinas and the Crisis of Humanism* (Bloomington and Indianapolis: Indiana University Press, 2013).

Kögler, Hans-Herbert, 'Ethics and Community', in Jeff Malpas and Hans-Helmut Gander (eds), *The Routledge Companion to Hermeneutics* (New York: Routledge, 2015), pp. 310–23.

Krajeweski, Bruce, 'Hermeneutics and Politics', in Niall Keane and Chris Lawn (eds), *The Blackwell Companion to Hermeneutics* (Chichester: John Wiley & Sons, 2016), pp. 72–7.

Krell, David, *Daimon Life: Heidegger and Life-Philosophy* (Bloomington and Indianapolis: Indiana University Press, 2002).

Kundera, Milan, *The Art of the Novel*, trans. Linda Asher (New York: Harper Perennial, 1988).

Kundera, Milan, *The Book of Laughter and Forgetting*, trans. Aaron Asher (Perennial Classics, 1999).

Kundera, Milan, 'Sixty-three Words', trans. Linda Asher, in *The Art of the Novel* (New York: Harper Perennial, 1988), pp. 121–53.

Kundera, Milan, *The Unbearable Lightness of Being*, trans. Michael Henry Heim (New York: Harper Colophon, 1985).

Levinas, Emmanuel, 'Ethics as First Philosophy', in Seán Hand (ed.), *The Levinas Reader* (Oxford: Blackwell Publishing, 1989), pp. 75–87.

Levinas, Immanuel, *Totality and Infinity: An Essay on Exteriority*, trans. Alphonso Lingis (Pittsburgh: Duquesne University Press, 1961).

Liakos, David and Theodore George, 'Hermeneutics in Post-war Philosophy', in Kelly Becker and Iain D. Thompson (eds), *Cambridge History of Philosophy 1945–2015* (Cambridge: Cambridge University Press), pp. 399–415.

Lyotard, Jean-François, 'Answering the Question: What Is Postmodernism?', trans. Régis Durand, in *The Postmodern Condition: A Report on Knowledge*, trans. Geoff Bennington and Brian Massumi (Minneapolis: Minnesota University Press, 1984, ninth printing, 1993), pp. 71–82.

McCarthy, Michael H., *The Political Humanism of Hannah Arendt* (Lanham, MD: Lexington Books, 2014).

McGrath, Charles, 'Lost in Translation? A Swede's Snub of US Lit', *New York Times*, 4 October 2008.

Marx, Karl and Friedrich Engels, 'The Manifesto of the Communist Party', in Robert C. Tucker (ed.), *The Marx-Engels Reader*, second edition (New York: W. W. Norton, 1978), pp. 469–500.

Michelfelder, Diane P. and Richard E. Palmer (eds), *Dialogue and Deconstruction: The Gadamer-Derrida Encounter* (Albany: State University of New York Press, 1989).

Mirandola, Pico della, *Oration on the Dignity of Man*, trans. Charles Glenn Wallis, Paul J. W. Miller and Douglas Carmichael (Indianapolis: Hackett Publishing Co., 1998).

Misgeld, Dieter, 'Poetry, Dialogue, and Negotiation: Liberal Culture and Conservative Politics in Hans-Georg Gadamer's Thought', in Kathleen Wright (ed.), *Festivals of Interpretation: Essays on Gadamer's Work* (Albany: State University of New York Press, 1990), pp. 161–81.

Mitchell, Andrew, 'The Fourfold', in Bret W. Davis (ed.), *Martin Heidegger: Key Concepts*, (Durham: Acumen Publishing Limited, 2010), pp. 208–18.

Mitchell, Andrew, *The Fourfold: Reading the Late Heidegger* (Evanston: Northwestern University Press, 2015).

Moore, Ian, *Eckhart, Heidegger, and the Imperative of Releasement* (Albany: State University of New York Press, 2019).

Moore, Ian, '*Gelassenheit*, the Middle Voice, and the Unity of Heidegger's Thought', in Gerhard Thonhauser (ed.), *Perspektiven mit Heidegger, Zugänge, Pfade, Anknüpfungen* (Freiburg and Munich: Karl Alber Verlag, 2017), pp. 25–39.

Nagel, Thomas, 'What Is It Like To Be A Bat?', *The Philosophical Review*, vol. 83, no. 4, October 1974, pp. 435–50.

Nancy, Jean-Luc, 'Urbi et Orbi', in *Creation of the World, or, Globalization*, trans. François Raffoul and David Pettigew (Albany: State University of New York Press, 2007).

The New Oxford Annotated Bible, New Revised Standard Version, Fully Revised Fourth Edition (Oxford and New York: Oxford University Press, 2010).

Nietzsche, Friedrich, *The Birth of Tragedy*, in *The Birth of Tragedy and the Case of Wagner*, trans. Walter Kaufmann (New York: Vintage Books, 1967).

Nietzsche, Friedrich, *The Gay Science*, ed. and trans. Walter Kaufmann (New York: Vintage Books, 1974).

Oliver, Kelly, *Animal Lessons: How They Teach Us To Be Human* (New York: Columbia University Press, 2009).

Omar, Sidi M., 'Humanism Reconsidered: Post-Colonial Humanistic Proposals', *Recerca: Revista de Pensament i Analisi*, vol. 12, 2012, pp. 143–61.

Orozco, Teresa, 'The Art of Allusion: Hans-Georg Gadamer's Philosophical Interventions under National Socialism', *Radical Philosophy*, vol. 78, July/August 1996, pp. 17–26.

Plato, *The Republic*, second edition, trans. Allan Bloom (New York: Basic Books, 1968).

Risser, James, *Hermeneutics and the Voice of the Other* (Albany: State University of New York Press, 1997).

Risser, James, *The Life of Understanding: A Contemporary Hermeneutics* (Bloomington and Indianapolis: Indiana University Press, 2012).

Rorty, Richard, *Contingency, Irony, and Solidarity* (Cambridge: Cambridge University Press, 1989).

Ruin, Hans, 'Ge-stell: Enframing as the Essence of Technology', in Bret W. Davis (ed.), *Martin Heidegger: Key Concepts* (Durham: Acumen Publishing Limited, 2010), pp. 183–94.

Sallis, John, *On Translation* (Bloomington and Indianapolis: Indiana University Press, 2002).

Schleiermacher, Friedrich, 'On the Different Methods of Translating', in Rainer Schulte and John Biguenet (eds), *Theories of Translation* (Chicago and London: University of Chicago Press, 1992), pp. 36–54.

Schmidt, Dennis J., 'Hermeneutics and Ethical Life: On the Return of Factical Life', in Niall Keane and Chris Lawn (eds), *The Blackwell Companion to Hermeneutics* (Chichester: John Wiley & Sons, 2016), pp. 65–71.

Schmidt, Dennis J., 'Hermeneutics as Original Ethics', in Shannon Sullivan and Dennis J. Schmidt (eds), *Difficulties of Ethical Life* (New York: Fordham University Press, 2008), pp. 35–47.

Schmidt, Dennis J., 'The Idiom of the Ethical', *Epoché: A Journal for the History of Philosophy*, vol. 17, no. 1, 2012, pp. 15–24.

Schmidt, Dennis J., 'On the Sources of Ethical Life', *Research in Phenomenology*, vol. 41, no. 1, 2012, pp. 35–48.

Schmidt, Dennis J., 'Text and Translation', in Jeff Malpas and Hans-Helmuth Gander (eds), *The Routledge Companion to Hermeneutics* (New York: Routledge, 2015), pp. 345–53.

Scott, Charles E., *The Lives of Things* (Bloomington and Indianapolis: Indiana University Press, 2002).

Smith, Christopher P., *Hermeneutics and Human Finitude* (New York: Fordham University Press, 1991).

Terrance, *The Self-Tormentor*, in *Volume I. The Woman of Andros. The Self-Tormentor. The Eunuch (Loeb Classical Library No. 22)*, trans. John Barsby (Cambridge, MA: Harvard University Press, revised edition, 2001).

Vattimo, Gianni, *The End of Modernity: Nihilism and Hermeneutics in Postmodern Culture*, trans. Jon R. Snyder (Baltimore: Johns Hopkins University Press, 1988).

Vessey, David, 'Gadamer's Account of Friendship as an Alternative to an Account of Intersubjectivity', *Philosophy Today*, SPEP Supplement, 2005, pp. 61–7.

Warnke, Georgia, 'Solidarity and Tradition in Gadamer's Hermeneutics', *History and Theory*, vol. 51, 2012, pp. 6–22.

Index